REVOLUTIONISM

REVOLUTIONISM

Abdul A. Said

Daniel M. Collier

Allyn and Bacon, Inc.   Boston

•••••••• CONTENTS

•••••••• PREFACE

The exploration of the philosophical implications of revolution has not been exhausted. With overemphasis on methodology and detail, authors have pursued the many theoretical and situational variables. The questions "Revolution—why?" and "Revolution for what?" continue to prove intractable to the best efforts of analysts. Symptomatic of contemporary emphasis on specific events and indifference to a total perspective on man, many writers have provided a more insightful knowledge of various revolutions and revolutionary situations. The necessity for a perspective within which to order the data must be reinforced.

Revolution is not exclusively the result of a situation. While a particular situation may serve as a revolutionary spark, the essence of revolution is found in man's quest for relevance.

Revolution is a highly subjective phenomenon whose manifestations have often obscured its essential nature. The overromanticized view of revolution prevalent in our age has distorted the reality of revolution; we tend to be captured by the romantic mystique. If one rejects the concept of revolution as the beginning of something new, then a rather simple but pertinent truth is being ignored. Whether violent or nonviolent (Mao Tse-tung or Gandhi), the goal of revolution is rebirth and the affirmation of life. The quest for faith is one which all beliefs share from the secular (communism and nationalism) to the theological (Buddhism, Judaism, Islam, and Christianity). On this ground, mankind shares an affinity.

We consciously avoid the terminological clichés found in many works of political scientists; many are but traps couching partial evidence. We submit a number of concepts and generalizations—more than ever we need perceptive simplifications to gather more relevant matter. The authors are deeply indebted to the empirical studies of social and political scientists. Without their illustrious labors we would have a still cruder understanding of our world. But in the realm of interpretation and basic meaning, they deserve more elaboration. We maintain that without a meaningful perspective the important questions of existence, which are the real problems of modern man, would go unnoticed in a barrage of fragmented detail. Now, more than ever, we must seek commonalities among those things that have been arbitrarily regarded as diverse.

We must confess that we do not fight shy of normative judgments in our discussion of man and politics. It is only when the minds of students of politics are turned to the problems that divide men that the task of building a better world may begin. To approach these problems with human compassion, the tools of the laboratory and the problems induced by one's own system of inquiry must be put into proper perspective. The cause of scientific truth is no more advanced than that of human freedom if "frontier thinking" implies a suspension of moral judgment on the objects of inquiry.

By a philosophical approach to the phenomenon of revolution, we hope to illustrate the blending of the past and present and to demonstrate that modern man suffers equally from philosophical dislocation and tangible changes in the environment.

Our theme will concentrate on revolutionary activity in the non-West. The United States is used as a point of reference and comparison. We dismiss as arbitrary and artificial the usual topical subdivision into chapters focusing on different regions—as if each had completely exclusive problems.

Our labor is part of a larger effort that can be classified only as an intangible "attitude." We feel that man must be put back into politics and that alienation is partially a result of the isolation of man from a meaningful environment. Man cannot yield his creativity to the impersonality of society and sustain his individuality. Revolution results when society loses the delicate equilibrium that enables man to develop and maintain his individuality with a fulfilling social identity. Hopefully, as long as man survives, revolution will always remain a threatening and promising phenomenon.

A. A. S.
D. M. C.

Daniel Collier has coauthored this book, not in his capacity as an officer in the Armed Forces or as a member of the faculty of the United States Military Academy, but as an individual concerned with the contemporary nature of revolution. His views are his own and do not necessarily reflect his official affiliations.

•••••••• ACKNOWLEDGMENTS

Edward Feinberg, Richard Eurich, David Frame, Keith Rosenberg, Luiz Simmons, Sidney Lindenberg, Mack Shelley, Petra Kelly, Robert Scuka, and Ralph Curtis, student assistants, added inspiration to the creation of this work and helped maintain an atmosphere of constant enthusiasm and intellectual excitement. Col. Amos A. Jordan, Jr., Major Howard M. Potter, Capt. Frank D. McCann, Major Claude L. Clark, and Major Alfred K. Richeson of the United States Military Academy provided incisive insights and offered valuable criticism. Mohammed Mughisuddin, Hari Zandler, and Raja Helou, graduate Fellows, contributed great efforts. Professor Brady Tyson and Marta San Martin helped refine our thoughts on the Latin American study. Mrs. Susanne MacVaugh typed the manuscript with good cheer and finesse. Finally, our families tolerated our pursuits with an understanding that exceeds human expectations.

REVOLUTIONISM

1
•••••••• REVOLUTIONISM: AN IDEOLOGY

Revolutionism has become institutionalized. It is no longer a transient phenomenon characterized by massive political upheaval that acts as an interlude between the disparities of one age and those of the next.

Revolution is not simply a political or military action. It is a state of mind that sees man and the state in a process of constant change. As such, it assumes a permanence that cannot be captured within the traditional political order. The credo of revolution has become divorced from the execution of revolution; the intangible and seductive concept of change has succumbed to the idiosyncrasies of the political system.

A world characterized by accelerating change dramatically illustrates the shortcomings and inherent inadequacies of the accepted political order. Revolution is an attempt to attack the vestiges of past ages and to inaugurate a philosophy that meets the challenges of the present and the projected possibilities of the future. The fallacy of most revolutionists is that in their commitment to political change they seldom achieve an authentic departure from the old institutions. Revolution is often a synthetic masquerade that outwardly hides the frustrations internally experienced by a state. It usually effects only a temporary institutional departure. In its attempt to formulate a philosophy that will convincingly resolve the dichotomy between tradition and innovation, it assumes the stature of an ideology. This systematic attempt to solve the complexities of the world provides an ideational framework to an essentially value-free political milieu. The ideology of revolutionism is a political offspring of an age floundering between the luxury of a self-assured past and the immensity of an uncertain future.

Revolutionism—the ideology of constant and total political change —seeks to incorporate the perplexities of an era that is largely reflective of political events, cultural upheavals, and technological advances in the West, into a political philosophy that will have relevance and appeal in the non-West. It is also heralded by the disaffected and disenchanted in the West who are dissatisfied with the by-products of an age of maximum transition. When discussing the non-West, we can only use the West as a point of reference. For the tone and character of Western revolutionism originates in a vastly different environment from the non-West. Westerners are therefore concerned with posing an alternative to conspicuous consumption and the unforeseen problems of technological affluence amid still-existent poverty. Atomization, automation, and alienation are the watchwords of a philosophy that has little relation to a revolutionism that still views technology as a socio-political panacea and cannot yet foresee its devastating by-products.

Revolutionism is not simply an outgrowth of the turmoils of the twentieth century. It originates in man's search for rebirth and is intensified by his reservoir of faith. With the breakdown of the Church as a primary ordering principle, man views life with confusion and the knowledge that the only certainty in life is death. His quest for rebirth, contrasted to his impulse to adhere to an eschatological vision or a charismatic leader, illustrates the precarious dichotomy between individual liberation and enslavement to the state. Revolution still enables man to fulfill his yearnings for the "ought" and to commit himself to the achievement of an earthly paradise. Revolution appeals to the hidden essence of man that rebels against order and is captivated by abstract assurances of achievement and satisfaction in the present life.

Many men who once considered their existences fixed refuse to accept the philosophy of things as they are, things as they were, and things as they are destined to be. Man is ever more determined to become master of his own destiny. In this endeavor he is limited only by his intellect and imagination. The belief in change has been conditioned by the primary circumstances of our era. The human condition can be altered.

The nature of revolutionary phenomena is bound to the nature of man and his never-ending quest for relevance during the finite period allotted to him on this planet. Born with an irrevocable death sentence, man is engaged in a search for faith that will endow his short-term lease with a deeper, more satisfying meaning. Whether the wellspring has its source in Judaeic-Christian, Buddhist, Hindu, Muslim, or animist origins, man's quest for faith has common features: it is situational, dynamic, and subjective.

Man's quest for faith is situational in that its interpretations, its manifestations, and the degree of its conscious pursuit are variables dependent upon the operational environment. It is the quest and striving which is universally evident. The spark of faith which man pursues may be manifest or elusive. The faith which he seeks may be founded in the past or the present; its exploration may be facile or arduous. Paramount, however, is man's search for human strategy in his attempt to intervene in the human condition.

This is essentially a political search for a political strategy and, as a result, the quest for man's faith is a dynamic experience. Man refuses to abandon his human project, his search for an explanation, and his quest for environmental supremacy. This is the projection of man's faith; this is what endows it with unique flavor. Whether one refers to a man in Africa or a man in Asia, the dynamics of his exploration and his insistence on mastery are unending. When man confronts man, this meeting is an extension of the dynamic feature of his existence and of the attempt to impose his will over others.

Finally, the quest for faith is subjective, since it exists in its totality and cannot be viewed as the sum of many components. It is this subjectivity which permeates man's institutions and structures for, in essence, man is a myth-maker. Man lives by the things he cannot prove; and we lose much if, in our search for human understanding, we forget that the truth about man is not as important as the miracle that he exists at all.

Man intrinsically abhors utter rationality, and scientific politics cannot satisfy his intangible valuational needs. In an age when so many people mirror Prufrock's life "measured out with coffee spoons" and so many more live on the edge of economic despair and the threshold of an age that is alien and frightening, the politics of chaos have startling appeal. Revolution is thus pacifying and electrifying to the human spirit. Life becomes simplified. The world becomes understandable. And the expectations of rebirth and utopia lose their abstractness and become tangible goals worth fighting for.

The abstract myths that man has created become the foundations of his economic, political, and social structures. When man begins to doubt these myths, his confidence in the structures undergoes a commensurate decline. Man never ceases his quest for faith although changes of direction and emphasis of manifestation may occur.

Man relates himself to the facts of life by creating myths which shield him from, and make comprehensible to him, the realities of social life. Political society is invariably sanctioned by myth. Even such theorists as Hobbes and Locke, who appeal to reason for a basis of political society, posit such notions as "rational man" and "natural right."

The widening of the gap between the environment and the institutions supported by myth provides a revolutionist situation. The revolutionist process becomes heightened when the old beliefs become distorted and their once self-evident meaning clouded with uncertainties. When man can no longer share the beliefs of his ancestors, a break with the past usually translates to disruption of the present. Man's quest for faith then leads him to abrupt processes of change. Revolutionist changes may be recognized by the demands for a new beginning and the affirmation of rebirth. Most of the time the result is violence, but there have been nonviolent revolutions. In man's quest for faith and his desire for rebirth, the passion of the human spirit knows no limits in its exuberance. As the gulf between the environment and structures deepens, the search for tomorrow becomes more compelling. When man can no longer believe in the old, the search for faith becomes a condition in seeking something new to fit his altered or transformed circumstances. It is from this symbolic stance that we speak of rebirth.

From Christ, to Luther, to Lenin, to Mao, the motivation for revolution has been inspired by the irrelevance of the present and the assurance of a brighter future. This forms the basis of the new myth which will in turn support new structures. Man thus assumes a new perception of the environment which is colored with bright images and re-enforced with a messianic testament to the future.

Though revolutionism is not as elaborately defined as socialism or capitalism, it still warrants delineation as a distinct ideology. For not only does it explain the fears and expectations held by much of the world, it also posits assumptions about man and society that question the Western Enlightenment tradition and its troubled offshoot, Marxism.

Contemporary revolutionism differs from past revolutionary ideology in that it no longer seeks to affirm the power of the West. Though non-Western revolutionists have not as yet formulated an alternative doctrine to the tradition that originated in the Enlightenment, they are philosophically opposed to the supremacy of the West. Both the French and Russian revolutions were peculiarly Western movements that sought to return to, or inaugurate, a form of government and outlook toward man that was rooted in the fabric of Western society. The secularized French trinity, *"liberté, égalité, fraternité,"* was not a rejection but a glorification of a progressive and virile Western *Weltanschauung*—a celebration of individualism and nationalism. The French Revolution liberated man from the hierarchy of Church and Empire and permitted him to express his new individualism within the political doctrine of nationalism. The Russian Revolution liberated man from economic enslavement by transforming this individualism into a class identification that sought to make synonymous the notions of class emancipation and individual freedom.

Contemporary revolutionism is a mixture of this Western thought with an instinctual philosophical disdain for Western culture. While verbally celebrating an alternative to Western civilization, few comprehensive doctrines have been put forward that have widespread appeal and that marshal indigenous cultural resources to be considered authentic non-Western philosophies. Thus, revolutionism is at best a type of revisionism, an attempt at a new blending of Western philosophy to the needs of non-Western culture. Yet the non-Western revolutionists persist in their dream of creating a completely novel political philosophy that will have relevance to their nations, inspire technological achievements, and demonstrate to the West that mere emulation of the one-time colonial powers is not the exclusive ambition of the new elites.

Revolutionism is antisupremacist, socialist, and nationalist. It seeks to assert a romantic vision of the past which is both idealized and irrelevant to the contemporary international milieu. It condemns ideology yet adheres to dogma. It doctrinally lauds the collective power of the people but is reflective of the elites. It at once emulates and rejects the West. It aspires to a nationalism that can only artificially arouse the populace. Revolutionism is partially premised on strict political order and partially on an unstructured nihilism. Most importantly, it has features that cannot be generalized. For revolutionism is dependent upon specific political circumstances operating within a particular political environment.

Revolutionists are those few who are most sensitive to the needs of the times. The recurrent, much-maligned terms of the "revolution of rising expectations," "the revolution of the masses," and "mass revolution" postulate misleading assumptions about contemporary revolutionist phenomena. These terms proceed from at least three erroneous assumptions: first, that the increase in means and techniques of communication has generated a concomitant rise in the awareness of the masses to change; second, that this new awareness can be translated into revolutionary actions with mass support; and third, that the propelling factor of the above propositions will be energized by values and goals which are unique to the particular milieu.

These propositions fail to distinguish between the concept of revolution and the operational techniques involved. The increase in communication has meant that some, but not all, elements of society have been able to glimpse at something beyond their individual or corporate experience. While communication might well increase mass awareness, we must assess its meaning and impact. The quantum increase in communications has facilitated control over the masses, but it has also posed many difficulties in manipulating them during the revolutionary process. For example, Nkrumah and Ben Bella failed to establish a meaningful power base to manipulate the masses. For the most part, revolutionists proceed in the name of, but not actually with, the masses. This is particularly evident in the initial phases of action.

The examples of Castro and Mao illustrate that revolutions may be conducted in the name of the masses, although they are not active participants. The illusion of mass support that contemporary revolutionists have managed to convey is in fact one of their most significant operational achievements. It has become a theoretical *sine qua non* to consider the revolutions of this era as being constructed on a mass base, when in reality they are elitist-oriented.

The conclusion that the values and goals of revolutionism are situationally unique has thus prevailed. While we cannot deny that the operational milieu adds a particular flavor to revolutionist activity, and that the inherent rationale of revolutions vary, the fundamental values and goals of revolution still appear to have an enduring quality. Whether we speak of nineteenth-century Europe or of twentieth-century Russia, China, or Algeria, it has been perceived that change was needed because the structure and institutions of government were no longer relevant to changing conditions.

The linkages between individual revolutionist situations are an aspect of the totality of their comprehensive experience. In order to examine this factor, the United States will serve as a point of reference.

The United States has had a reaction to every revolution in this century; it has also experienced revolutionist problems of its own.

In the twentieth century the United States has tended to view revolution abroad as essentially an unsettling experience, both from its own standpoint and from that of the international system. It did, however, dichotomize revolutions into those that could be attributed to the communist camp and those that could not. From the first intervention in a communist-oriented revolution (Archangel, 1918) to Vietnam, the United States has tended to view revolution as a kind of *sub rosa* back door utilized by communists to gain illegitimate power. However, little thought has been given to the local basis for revolution in those countries in which it occurred. Were the prerevolution institutions of Russia and China relevant to the then-prevailing conditions of those two societies? The same question might also be raised regarding Vietnam, the United Arab Republic, Algeria, and Indonesia. The United States has applied a rigid international legal doctrine to many contemporary revolutions, frequently neglecting an examination of possible internal justifications.

The antecedents of this attitude have their roots in the abrupt manner in which the United States was expelled from the international paradise of the pre-Wilsonian era. The British Navy could no longer protect the sea lanes; the United States could not remain aloof from European wars. It was the Wilson doctrine which assumed a moralistic stance on the recognition of regimes where it was perceived that power was wrongly acquired. This was also the era of international law and organization which hopefully could be utilized to order the system. The United States subscribed to this aspiration, but remained outside the League of Nations in the belief that it could once again return to a Jamesian state of innocence. When the United States realized that expulsion from paradise precluded any eventual return, its foreign policy became more rigid, first regarding the unconditional surrender of the Axis powers, then in its response to communism, and presently in its attitude toward all revolutions whatever their justification.

Very little has changed from the days of Woodrow Wilson in the American projections onto the international system. The totally corrupt Batista regime was considered preferable to that of Castro when it became known that the latter identified itself as communist. Stability has become a paramount goal of American diplomatic strategy. While any evaluation of United States foreign policy is obviously beyond the purpose of this discussion, it should be noted that the American people appear to have endorsed these attitudes. If there exists a validity test for foreign policy in a democracy, it must be that the electorate perceive it to be in the national interest.

It also appears that the linkage between worldwide domestic unrest and the Vietnam conflict is of more than sequential significance. It is too simplistic to dismiss this phenomenon as a passing phase of frustration of world youth or mere agitation of misguided groups located especially within, but not limited to, the United States. The fact remains that basic political assumptions are being questioned, particularly those that hinge on systemic change and its perception.

Proceeding from the international to the domestic scene, the existence of communications has contributed to the bestowal of more positive emphasis on individuals and ideals rather than on more narrow national symbols; one has only to remember the global tide of emotion after the death of John F. Kennedy. Ideals of peace, egalitarianism, and human rights enjoy an articulate universality. Consequently, national leaders of largely literate countries have found it more difficult to rally their people around national issues that demand and involve sacrifice.

The myths supporting the state are less credible to a progressively more informed and more skeptical citizenry. Even in an extensively reward-oriented bureaucracy, the Soviet Union finds it difficult to sell the myth of the proletariat. British and French youth certainly do not believe that the state is worth much sacrifice. In the United States, the liberal ethos is being trampled underfoot by those who believe it to be irrelevant, while in China the Red Guards helped destroy the Communist party myths in favor of a personified one centered on Mao.

While not so much a trend of the past, the generation gap appears to be a significant factor in gauging the degree of present revolutionist temper. No country is exempted from youth in ferment today. Taken individually, much of this activity is not revolutionist yet. When viewed collectively, it forms a mosaic which is change-oriented in a revolutionist mold of profound value conflict. At its core lies the issue of management; youth seems to be resisting the efforts of an older, alien generation to manage its existence.

Experiences, truths, and institutions of one generation seem to be inadequate for others. Thus, revolution can be partial in the sense that its focus or foci can be oriented in certain directions for specific purposes, for example, against universities. Ultimately, however, it is the system, its institutions, and its myths which lack relevance for most revolutionist youth at present.

Considered as manifestations of a generational conflict, revolutionist themes are directed against institutions in the system. The antisupremacist and antiestablishment themes prevail the world over, yet the forms differ. In China, during the Cultural Revolution, it manifested itself against the self-satisfied party bureaucracy; in France, against DeGaulle. In the United States, the target is the "Military-Industrial" ruling complex. The so-called "devil-theories" of youth have given rise to much of their own quest for relevance. Adequate responses to this phenomenon have not as yet been formulated.

Although there are linkages between specific revolutionist experiences, each has had its own particular quality which has been both dynamic and situational. While the theme of revolution and its manifestations vary within fairly well-defined parameters, it has been the loci of time and milieu which impart to revolution its unique and varied flavor. In recent years, this has not been fully appreciated by either theorist or practitioner. For example, Regis Debray had acknowledged that the Cuban Revolution was not likely to be repeated, but Ché Guevara nevertheless made the attempt in Bolivia and failed. Disciples of Mao have tried to apply his theories in various environments only to discover that they could not be successfully transplanted to alien soils.

This does not mean that social theories, revolutionist or otherwise, cannot become cross-cultural. As guides to action programs, however, revolutionist theories have not been transferable. Another reason that suggests itself is that the specific circumstances of revolution are also unique. While history in kind may repeat itself, history in specific never does. There is, in this sense, no historical lesson or rule which is obvious and demands adherence. Those who have attempted to draw circumstantial parallels to revolutionary experience fail to remember that a historical condition of the past is unique and that each age's perception and evaluation of it will differ.

Contemporary primary revolutionists (Mao, Lenin, Ho Chi Minh, Castro) have realized that successful revolution is distinctively adapted to a total milieu, one with which the revolutionist is best acquainted. Each of these actors capitalized on circumstances present in his society at a given and opportune time. Although it is doubtful that these circumstances can be repeated elsewhere in an identical manner, the revolutionist theme and its various manifestations will. The primary revolutionist of the future will cast his revolution into the general cultural patterns that underlie his environment even though he will be actively seeking the destruction of an existing social order which is no longer relevant.

Like history, revolutions do not repeat themselves in their specifics. As the Soviet Revolution occurred at one time in one place, so it may be expected that others such as the Chinese and the Cuban are similarly locked in a cultural vise. This uniqueness elucidates another aspect of the contemporary dimension of revolution. Though revolutionists proclaim the universality of their own revolutionary experience, they have, in fact, been relatively culture-bound. The disparate environments in which they operate mold the form and determine the content of their respective revolutions.

Although individual revolutions, large and small, are not likely to be repeated, the cry for revolution will be heard with increasing frequency in the next third of the century. Environments will become more fragmented, as the consensual basis of domestic and international institutions will continue to narrow. In such an environment, the trend toward authoritarianism, even in democratic societies, will acquire greater momentum. Contemporary revolutionist experience has opened a floodgate which cannot easily be closed; the ideology of revolution has become too strongly embedded in this permissive and paradoxically egalitarian era.

In the near future, revolutionist temper is likely to increase in intensity throughout the world. The principal causal factor will probably turn on large societies becoming progressively less capable of ordering and governing their own domestic concerns. Larger segments of populations will experience increasing alienation. The reaffirmation of man's faith in his own spirit and dignity will lead him to question the relevance of the large state.

As previously stated, the altered conditions of the post-World War II world have not been accommodated in a like manner by sociopolitical structural changes. Perhaps, in this particular area, it is man's perception that has lagged behind the altered conditions. While many people recognize a number of these changes, the perception of *our own image* in their midst has not kept pace. There are few common perceptions of state images, either domestically or internationally. This again is an area where consensus formerly in evidence can no longer be found.

This is not to suggest that consensus has a value in and by itself; it is merely to point up the trend toward divergence. Part of this divergence may be accounted for by the vast disparities that exist in distribution—economic, demographic, and political. These are in evidence both in the domestic as well as in the international environment. As these disparities increase across ever larger patterns, perception of the relevancy of structures will decrease.

This is what is already occurring in the international system. The impact of the revolutionist mood has caused a fundamental fragmentation. Other than survival, there are few values shared in common. Distribution is so uneven that the image of the system has no common basis among its members. The great-powers' level of satisfaction with the status quo is higher than that of revolutionist members, yet the latter have found maneuvering easier. The precise expression of their objectives, however, has been relatively absent. Revolutionists reject the present system but have few ideas as to what might constitute an effective replacement. In this respect, the trend will be toward increased frustration, accompanied by a corresponding lack of faith in the relevancy of the old order.

Revolutionism is thus a logical political phenomenon in an environment of instability and unknown constants. Its dream of unlimited and undefined change has attracted those who in other times would have followed other systems that demanded total belief and unswerving faith.

In posing this thesis of revolutionism, we have merely formulated several related questions which must be considered within the context of contemporary revolutionist experience. Present phenomena of style and environment, types of revolutionists, patterns of revolutionist thought, revolutionist visions and models, and the revolutionist perception of politics will be identified. This skeletal structure establishes the setting and constitutes the frame of reference for the examination of revolutionism in the chapters that follow.

2
•••••••• STYLE
AND
ENVIRONMENT

Post-World War II changes in the international system, technology, and communications have resulted in a new revolutionary temper that transcends geographical boundaries. These factors have conditioned, and in turn have been conditioned by, the quest for new and relevant socio-political and economic structures that would give them meaning.

Current institutional structures are deeply imbedded in the nine-teenth century. These structures are seriously out of tune with the new conditions in the human environment. The issue is not merely one of antiquated institutions and rapidly changing conditions, but rather of the altered nature of their relationship. As this has changed, political cultures have become fragmented and cleavages have set in. Disparities are accentuated as entire societies are gripped by inhibitions and frus-trations that nullify efforts of governments. This glaring disproportion between effort and result is best illustrated by the changing relationship between power and influence. Influence is no more the handmaid of power. The dissolution of this traditional generic relationship, both on the domestic and international levels, is causing traditional ordering concepts to become irrelevant.

On the international level, super and lesser states alike have been left with ill-defined goals. The superstates no longer govern the dy-namics of the international system; as a corollary, the lesser ones enjoy a wider spectrum of political alternatives. The superstates lack the situational capability to control the course of events outside their frontiers. The very fact that they possess thermonuclear weapons compels them to deploy conventional force cautiously; the threat of escalation to the nuclear threshold is a constant restraint.

The lesser states do not possess a nuclear delivery capability; the restraints imposed by the bipolar strategic balance do not exist for them. Much of the power of the United States and the Soviet Union has not proven politically useful except in their dealings with each other. Lesser actors, particularly revolutionist states, are encouraged to ignore the power of these two giants in their international behavior. When confronting an undisputedly more powerful United States, North Vietnam and North Korea have successfully sensed a certain impotence which accrues to those possessing advanced weapons. It is considerably more difficult to conduct international relations in a climate where a disparity exists between one's traditional perception of power and the actual influence he is able to wield.

The near impotence of the superstates to translate power into influence has caused value conflict to become sharper in the international system. Power standards below the nuclear level have become irrelevant, especially to revolutionist states. Power has little meaning in gross terms, and power inventories defy quantification.

On the domestic level, the erosion of authority is spreading rapidly in many societies. In such situations, power becomes an end rather than a means. Competing factions share influence unevenly while contending for usable power. This is always accomplished in the name of defending the relevant or attacking the irrelevant. The United States today is a model of this phenomenon.

The set of historically validated political ideas and patterns has come in abrupt conjunction with contemporary realities. A large part of tensions in domestic politics comes from the inevitably frustrating efforts of governments to fit the contemporary environment into traditional political categories. Inherent in this particular disparity is the whole process of communication, which also has been subjected to radical alteration. That which we learn one day can, and does, change the next. Truths that were self-evident are no longer believable.

If the world has become smaller or, in the McLuhan sense, "a global village," its heterogeneous nature has become more evident. Although technology has forced all of us to live under the same sword of Damocles, it has not distributed its benefits in a similarly impartial manner, and more people are aware of this inequality than in any previous time. The revolution in communications has magnified these formerly unnoticed nuances of change. There is a new visibility and a new perspective inherent in the contemporary political milieu. It should be noted again, however, that this new visibility and new perspective can be discerned primarily in the elite of a particular country. The effect of the revolution in communications has not been as extensive as some would affirm.

In many areas of the world, the hopes of the post-World War II revolutionists are fast being smothered, and defenders of the status quo hold the reins of power. And though it often falters and yearns for placid security, the soul of man is not finally satisfied with dependence and mass poverty. "The Revolution is dead! Long live the Revolution!" The pendulum now swings toward reaction against extravagant dreams and minimal performance. But the pendulum always swings back, the revolution will rise again, this time from the cold ashes of the sterility of reaction-as-a-program. Hope does not stay in its tomb. And men are destined to push the stone of hope up the mountain, only to see it roll back, and begin again, until such time as men learn to institutionalize a permanent, total revolution. Such is the imperative of the modern world.

A Comparative Stylistic Overview

Generally speaking, revolutionists relate immediate choices to long-range purpose—hence they lack resilience and adaptability. Their style dictates casting issues in moral terms and viewing politics as a series of crises. But this is not to suggest that revolutionists share many stylistic traits.

Revolutionists perform activities in a way uniquely appropriate to the environment in which they operate. They are materially affected by the prevailing traditions of their respective societies. Style and environment are important in shaping revolutions because of their effect in setting the analytical pattern of the revolutionist himself.

In the United States, militant groups have found an urban context most effective for their increasingly violent actions, while Mao Tse-tung and his fellow Asian revolutionists achieved their successes through ideological alignment with the rural masses. In Latin America, the Arab world, and Africa—areas where the perceptions of the national environment are in flux—the emphasis of revolutionists has been on establishing a unified national identity, separate from the shadow of colonialism.

In the United States, the fundamental relevance of certain elements in the political culture has recently been subjected to challenges never before experienced. While quantification of this phenomenon is difficult, perceptible examples of it exist that substantiate its extent and influence. Extreme civil disobedience, lack of faith in the government and its decision-making and judicial processes, together with a profound divergence not only on means but ends as well, are all manifestations of this crisis of belief.

In the past decade the style of revolution in the United States was expressed in an essentially nonviolent manner. More recently, the pendulum is swinging to violent solutions for problems. While there is no open rebellion in the United States, acts of militancy are on the increase, being less limited to specific times and places.

Revolution is both group- and issue-oriented in the United States. Different groups crystallize on different issues and are split over ideological points. The New Left, the women's liberation movement, students, and blacks focus on different problems with little in common other than the belief that systemic change should take place and that institutions have become irrelevant to contemporary needs.

The urban areas of an increasingly complex urbanized society provide the staging ground of revolution. These areas, plagued by overextended scale, contain the most vulnerable institutions, where the temper of revolution runs highest and is the most articulated. It is difficult indeed to separate riot from insurrection, and disobedience from rebellion.

As with many other activities in the United States, revolution is a young man's game. It is youth-oriented and youth-controlled. On the balance, American revolutionists have known the world only since the end of World War II. Normalcy to them is the cold war, nuclear weapons, Korea, and Vietnam. Their political cognizance has moved from crisis to crisis. They hear and read about equality, yet they observe the condition of blacks and other poor. Each succeeding age group perceives the world differently with a rapidity of change that is unprecedented.

Revolutionists in the United States today are aware of their increased influence and power. While the extent of this influence is difficult to measure, it has been a factor in accelerating the tempo of revolution. Forces of conservatism have added fuel to an already volatile situation. If revolutionary methods are successful for some elements in the population, then others may be expected to follow suit with increasing frequency.

Methodological styles have varied, but this is to be expected in a pluralistic nation whose citizens have different objectives, goals, and interests, all of which must be constantly balanced. In this sense, the revolutionist may be viewed as the representative of yet another interest group. This view fails to appreciate the fact that it is the balancing of interests to the detriment of the masses that American revolutionists object to the most.

Though revolutionist activity is just beginning to manifest itself in the United States, it has become a way of life in a large part of the Asian continent. The diversity of the Asian political and cultural landscapes is reflected in the variety of revolutionary styles. Every revolution in Asia has served only as a model for itself, and all have proven unexportable, primarily because their indigenous roots are too deeply embedded in their respective native soils. Their diverse manifestations have varied significantly, in degree more than in kind, however. It was one thing to conduct revolutionary warfare in Indochina, quite another to move large armies as Mao did during the third revolutionary civil war in China, and yet still another to conduct terrorist operations that characterized the communists in Malaya.

Yet there was one feature that all shared, and this trait presents the distinctive element in Asian revolution. In the United States, potential revolutions are confined to urban areas; revolution in Asia has principally emanated from the rural regions. This has been no accident, but rather a carefully planned stratagem. When the early Chinese communist movement initiated the revolutionary civil wars, the first efforts were directed at and concentrated on urban areas. The Soviet Revolution had originated in such areas; adopting this experience as a guide, the communists were convinced that the urban masses would ally with them.

However, Mao Tse-tung did not favor resorting to urban insurrection. In the early development of Chinese communism, he opted for revolution in the countryside, using the peasant rather than the urban masses as his vehicle. There were two basic factors that account for this significant development. First, Mao was of peasant, although relatively well-to-do, origins. He knew the Chinese peasant mentality with an intimacy that could not be expected of those from the essentially foreign-dominated urban areas. In other words, he was convinced that the soul as well as the salvation of China was in the countryside, which had been affected but essentially uncorrupted (from Mao's viewpoint) by foreign influences. The second factor was the failure of both the early Comintern and Chinese communists to grasp the inherent difficulties of urban revolution in China.

Graphically recorded by André Malraux, the urban insurrections in 1925–1927, in which Mao did not participate, failed in Shanghai and Canton. In spite of this, the party, as it existed at the time, remained enthusiastic about the possibilities inherent in the cities following the Soviet model. When added to the perfidy of Chiang Kai-shek and his Kuomintang during the period, it is obvious in retrospect that the urban intellectuals failed to grasp the reality of their revolutionary possibilities.

During this formative period for Mao, his methods went unnoticed by the party when he organized peasants as early as 1925. This state of affairs continued in essence, and in 1930 he broke with his comrade Li Li-san over the latter's concepts of using the Red Army and fomenting urban insurrections. The Li Li-san line and the communists were defeated in Changsha, which was the capital of Mao's home province.

After Changsha, Mao became more committed to the peasant army concept which forms a linkage with the contemporary People's Liberation Army. While the efforts of the army met with defeat in battle, Mao triumphed after his "Long March" and established complete control over the remnants who would fight the Japanese, wage revolutionary war from 1945 to 1949, and become the leadership of the People's Republic of China.

Rural revolution has thus been common to most revolutionary movements in Asia since 1945. While not all have been successful, these movements have nevertheless awakened the formerly politically docile and widely disparate rural populations. Emphasizing programs of social and economic reform, revolutionists have been able to communicate an image of something truly new to those whose horizons had been confined to the local environment for centuries. These programs were first presented in a pragmatic rather than an ideological fashion. However— and especially in the case of China—once power over the territory had been consolidated, the ideological approach was employed.

So far, the socio-political overtones of the revolutionary temper in Asia have been more pronounced than the economic aspects. It is natural, perhaps, for revolutionists to emphasize political and social change. Since the establishment of a new socio-political foundation must of necessity precede economic change, Asian revolutionists have shaped their revolutionist thrust in that direction. In addition, the factors on which economic change is contingent have been difficult for Asians to cope with. Economic transformation has been more prevalent in nonrevolutionist states such as Japan, South Korea, and Formosa, all of which benefit from close ties to United States military and economic assistance.

In Asia, political change was initially directed against either colonial- or United States-supported regimes. Since the end of World War II, the primary impetus has been the desire for national independence and, in the case of China, the desire to establish a state based on Mao's interpretation of Marx. Independence has not been achieved at a low price in Asia, and there have been several genres of conflict. Although essentially nonviolent in India, active conflict and violence erupted in both Indonesia and Indochina, while the Philippines, Malaya, and Burma exhibited conflicts of a predominantly guerrilla nature. The civil war waged by Mao Tse-tung sought to achieve a new China which eventually would be restored to its historic position of dominance in Asia.

Despite the fact that Asia has experienced more revolutionist activity, Latin America maintains a reputation as one of the most "revolutionary" areas of the world. Perhaps this label has been earned because violence seems so endemic and perpetual throughout the area, perhaps because regimes experience the cycle of accession to power, challenge, and overthrow so rapidly. In any event, it has become the basic assumption of United States policy for Latin America that political stability is the most important prerequisite for development, and that the lack of this stability has made significant political, social, and economic development all but impossible for the past several decades.

Nevertheless, Latin America is a strange study, like the other areas of the so-called "underdeveloped," or "third world," of seeming instability on the one hand, and basic social, economic, and political stability (or stagnation) on the other. For all of the apparent political changes every year in Latin America, it can still be argued that basic changes have been few and far between, and the notable exceptions (Mexico, Peru, Cuba, and perhaps Bolivia) prove the rule by being limited solely to those countries.

It has become fashionable in many intellectual circles of both Latin and North America to speak about the imminence of the revolution in Latin America as if such a prediction were based on obvious realities. Yet, despite the "Castro complex" of many North and Latin Americans, the probabilities or even possibilities of significant social, economic, and political revolutions must be seen as very limited within the three-to-five year scope within which it is fairly safe to project present trends. However desirable revolution might be, or appear to be, there are certain fundamental conditions that must exist before a revolution can take root and achieve the potential to overthrow the dominant social, economic, and political order.

Latin America has contributed very little to world politics, but rather has been the passive recipient of pressures, influences, and ideas that have come especially from Western Europe and North America. Latin American intellectuals themselves speak of Latin America as being "peripheral" to the arena of world politics. If Latin America is that area where "the West stopped" in its eighteenth- and nineteenth-century tide of expansion, colonization, and conquest, and if the process of Westernization of Latin America has been successful and complete only in the official and top levels of society, it becomes easier to understand why Latin America, so apparently Western at first glance, is really so difficult to understand when using only Western concepts. Indeed, one of the problems may be that Latin Americans themselves are sometimes unaware of the extent to which their societies differ radically from Western society in general. Another problem could be that their Western thought forms do not permit them to grasp adequately all the significant phenomena of their own nations.

One expects Africa, the Middle East, and Asia to be differentiated. It is understood that national and cultural characteristics, as well as political styles, will demand appropriate conceptual systems. What many a Western observer neglects is the fact that Latin America, because it appears to be so Western when in reality it is only half Western, demands special conceptual tools and special care also. This "other Latin America," the docile, ignored, and often despised folk-peasantry—many but not all of its members still clinging to the remnants of an Indian culture—seems resolutely to resist attempts at "Westernization" or "Latinization," as the conquerors called their mission.

It can be imagined that at some time in the future, Latin America will make its peace with its heritage and develop its own personality, integrating into a new identity elements of both its Iberian and indigenous cultures, as the United States is still struggling to do in its "melting pot" process of national identity building. Perhaps Mexico, in the experience of its revolution and the residual thrust of it, has come closer than even the United States to achieving its own identity. Perhaps the "American man" is yet to appear—if indeed he will appear in a world increasingly denationalized and ahistoricized by mass, intercontinental communications.

Latin America has not been without its revolutionist dreamers and martyrs, even though it has had more frustrated revolutionists than successful revolutions. The paucity of successful revolutions has not resulted from any lack of the need for revolution, or of potential revolutionist situations, but in part because of the lack of a better understanding of the revolutionist process by Latin American revolutionists. The stifling influence of external forces on Latin America at various critical times has also inhibited, to a great extent, successful attempts at revolution.

Many of the same "third world" identity problems that plague Latin America are also obstructions to revolutionist action in the Arab world. Wedged between vast deserts and deep seas, Arab expectations have mirrored the solace and enigma of their environment. Clustered in isolated settlements, the Arab peoples have a geographical heritage of barriers to community and communication. Modern Arabs, unwilling to wander in the desert, but resentful of the intrusions from the West, have constructed their own geographical prisons.

As in the United States, most Arab revolutionists have confined themselves to urban concentration and operations. In part, this can be attributed to the vagaries of their environment, to the deserts surrounding them that defy cultivation and life, to the seas that preclude expansion to more inhabitable areas. Most important, however, is the fact that the isolated Arab settlements present the most propitious opportunities for success. A settlement community cannot escape revolutionist harangues as can a nomadic tribe. The revolutionist is also abetted by the distance separating Arab cities. Such a situation can perhaps be compared to a medical quarantine: the infectious bacillus cannot escape the city, but, then, neither can an effective antidote (in this case, an armed force dispatched by the legitimate government) speedily enter it.

Contemporary Arab revolutionary style is very similar to the Arab environment, leaving the Arabs with a frustrated search for faith and counterfeit promissory notes of rebirth. Concern centers around the notion of revolution rather than its content. The trimmings of revolution are exhibited to mask the essence of a nonrevolutionary situation. Substance is subordinated to form.

Armed with a prepolitical mind that lacks the requisite filter to convert sentiment into action, the Arab wages his revolution on the battlefield of rhetoric. Revolution becomes the favorite topic of discourse in a region where traditionally there have always been appreciative audiences and garrulous orators. The gulf between image and reality widens, and the Arab flounders in waves of frustration.

Generated by endless and, in most instances, fruitless debate, the Arabs' frustrations inexorably mount until they explode in sporadic cataclysms of violence. In this respect, Arab revolutionary style is similar to that exhibited in both Latin America and in the United States. It deviates from the latter country in that Arab recourse to violence appeared much sooner and is resorted to more frequently than in the United States.

Arab revolutionists have been unable to forge a potent force among themselves. Though they frequently align themselves into various groups, these amalgamations very seldom unite in concerted action. The various Arab nationalist groups, stationed around the boundaries of Israel, present a clear display of this tendency. Though all are committed to the reacquisition of Arab lands lost in the War of 1967, and although most are dedicated to the ultimate "liberation" of Palestine, still it has been virtually impossible for them to coordinate their actions in the past. Rivalry, pride, and the exuberance of youth—as elsewhere, modern Arab revolutionists are predominantly young and youth-oriented—no doubt contribute greatly to this noncooperation, yet more important is the seemingly innate inability of the Arab revolutionists to formulate clear and concise plans for a viable future.

Armed with vaguely defined programs, they can only turn to the Army, the only cohesive force capable of decisive action. The revolutionist-Army coalition provides a combination of force and intellectual-theoretical framework, the prerequisites for raising a regime to a revolutionist level.

The Arab revolutionist maintains a set of social goals, a collection of those promissory notes he considers long overdue, to proselytize to the masses—but above all to the Army, which is the main source of support—the necessity of power and sacrifices. Although such revolutionary goals as land reform, industrialization, or nationalization of foreign interests are presented in the guise of a formal ideology, such programs hold little promise of galvanizing the population. Nevertheless, they become a vehicle for the consolidation of power and perpetuation of the *raison d'être* of the revolutionist. The realization of these goals is secondary; revolution becomes an end in itself.

After the revolution by coup, claims to leadership are based upon the past glories of those revolutionists who survive the consolidation of the ruling elite. Revolution becomes a substitute for history; it assumes the posture of a national myth that ensures the demonization of the former regime.

As are the Arabs, African revolutionists are straining to find some reconciliation between the past and the present; at the heart of the African revolutionist temper lies the problem of direction in African history and the concept of a uniquely African personality. The present African dialogue expresses the troubled psychological ambivalence of the new Africa: a pattern of attraction to and repulsion from modernization. It connects the rational with the irrational and joins objective circumstances with the consciousness of new Africans. It searches for ideal and spiritual elements and beliefs of African character and origin.

The juxtaposition of so many apparent dichotomies is the result not only of the contemporary African situation but also of the curious mix that characterizes modern African revolutionists. Though presently not as youth-oriented as those in the United States and in the Arab world, African revolutionists were themselves relatively young when they commenced their revolutionary activities. As youth they confronted the dilemma raised by the conflicting values of their early tribal experience contrasted with their later student adventures in the West. It should be emphasized that it is primarily these foreign-educated Africans who emerge as the revolutionists in their societies. Yet their education sets them irrevocably apart from the majority of their countrymen. African revolutionists thus constitute something of an elite, a status that effectively isolates them from the people they seek to represent.

European colonialism produced cultural misfits, men without roots or genuine values. It succeeded only in divorcing the revolutionists-to-be from contact with their compatriots; as a result, African revolutionists could find identity either in the traditional culture that the colonialists had disparaged and repressed, or in total acceptance of foreign values.

Colonialism has left behind a complex legacy of inadequacy; to generate a new and genuine sense of identity, African revolutionists must struggle to transform a negative revolt into a positive affirmation of the self. Many of the revolutionists are victims of an upbringing which makes them only superficially modern and only superficially African. The West has implanted within them the notion of utilitarianism, but not the essential conditions and values which have made utilitarianism successful. As a result, they tend to confuse means and ends and to see their culture in its uncreative, ossified, passive side which allowed Africa to be dominated for so long.

The African reaction to this inheritance of inadequacy and weakness often is a resort to violence. Violence not only will destroy the decadent influences of colonialism and enable a new beginning untainted by colonial contamination, but will also make possible a nascent determination to present a strong and invulnerable front to foreign transgressions. As in the United States, Latin America, and the Arab world, African revolutionists find it necessary, and sometimes expedient, to wield the weapon of violence in their struggle against the existing order.

Comparative Environmental Conditions

Revolutionary activity is a dynamic, cyclic process of destruction and rebirth, and the political and socio-economic environments of the five areas we are considering are all in various stages of this cycle. America is just now beginning to articulate and act upon the gap that is perceived to exist between American myth and American reality. In China the process has completed one full turn, in that revolutionists have successfully abolished an old order, created a new myth, and implemented it institutionally. Latin America, the Arab world, and Africa have all been freed from an external domination, but they are striving to find some new and relevant ethos upon which to base their development programs.

The United States of America

The factors which have precipitated present revolutionary pressures are hardly unique to this era. The diminished belief in the prevailing political system is a function of a new perception of, and emphasis upon, previously existing phenomena. In the past, national beliefs were determined by national norms. The relevance of the latter to the individual or various social groups in no way inhibited their acceptance by the vast majority of people. These norms were considered to represent the mainstream of the American environment, and thus effectively obscured any objective assessments that would have negated their effect.

This wide acceptance of, and belief in, national norms or myths was in part responsible for the continued maintenance of societal equilibrium. There was very little questioning of the liberal ethos; its inherent contradictions were not readily perceptible. The society was not shaken or disrupted by disbelief in fundamental points. In spite of its heterogeneous character, the American society was in agreement as to the existence and relevance of the myth.

There was also a corresponding acceptance of those institutions which were supported by the myth. This acceptance of myths and institutions led to the belief that there was some sort of a divine relationship between them, a relationship which would preserve the system against any and all onslaughts. This belief, in itself, constituted yet another myth.

The American revolutionist's image of his contemporary environment, however, differs from that of the past. Initially, it has been characterized by less certainty than in previous periods. The virtually absolute acceptance of the American myth, and to a lesser extent of the institutions it supports, has evaporated. While the factors that generated this situation are not necessarily new, the degree to which they influence the environment and have altered their former relationship to it comprise a relatively novel experience for the United States.

One such factor is the perception of the gap between social groups, which the "liberal ethos" had successfully obscured in the past. This change has been effected because the belief in the myth and its relevance has decreased in the contemporary environment. Less-favored groups have, relatively recently, voiced their dissatisfaction with the system's values and outputs. As a result of their acquiring a new perception of their situation, they have moved from a position of political docility to one of political activism on behalf of their own interest.

The puritan ethic has long enjoyed a dominant position in the American political culture, affirming the necessity for absolutist standards in the conduct of human behavior. Today, puritanism has been supplanted by permissive attitudes which pervade both culture and environment. The new relativism, which has resulted from this situation, defines the extent of this permissiveness.

When societal standards become elastic, there are no norms for behavior. The absence of previously held behavioral norms in the American environment has affected its political culture as well, thus causing the socio-political turbulence which has occurred with increasing degrees of frequency. Socially permissive attitudes have been transfused into the political realm; the societal standards of the past have been replaced by the more individualistic ones of the present. This can be partially explained by reference to the confusion surrounding the nature of public versus individual ethics and prerogatives.

Another factor that has been altered in the environment is related to the type of democracy most relevant to contemporary demands. As government at every level increases in complexity, the risk that the decision maker as well as the bureaucrat will become separated from the electorate is ever-present. In the major urban areas, this factor, or the perception of it, is already in evidence as greater percentages of people have become politically cognizant. There exists a greater desire to participate in the decision-making process, which was formerly reserved for those solely in positions of authority. This phenomenon has not been directed against the government alone, but also at political parties, universities, high schools, labor unions, and other hierarchical organizations.

The question of who should participate—and when, where, and how—is a very real one in the American culture. How much participation can a representative democracy endure without changing its basic character? The exact determination of this question is difficult, but mass participation eventually results in a chaotic situation which impairs a system's effectiveness. In any event, this is a changed factor and one which, developed to its logical conclusion, could fundamentally alter the system.

In connection with this, the confidence of the populace has declined not only in the decision makers and their decisions, but in the system as well. An obvious manifestation of this is seen in the various "credibility gaps" which have developed regarding communication between decision makers and their population; the former are questioned not only on the correctness of their decisions, but also on the truthfulness of their reports to the latter. The educational level of the populace has risen, and acceptance of the system and of the decision makers has correspondingly decreased. This can be partially ascribed to the awareness of objective factors which confute statements made by decision makers. If one of these statements is proved false, might not all be so proven? And if not false, how can one tell? These are questions that by their very nature defy categorical and absolute answers, yet there is an increasing imperative at least to pose them.

If pronouncements by decision makers appear less credible, then the system supported and continued by their decisions is thus perceived to be less legitimate. Greater numbers of people judge state actions on the basis of individual ethics and conscience. If the acts of a state do not conform to these, they are viewed, *ipso facto*, as illegitimate. By the same line of reasoning, the legitimacy of a system which permits those in authority to act contrary to these maxims must be questioned. The ramifications and cross-currents of this type of rationale in the environment are numerous. It is a relatively new phenomenon and has been in part responsible for some of the turbulence pervading the contemporary American scene.

When a system is perceived to be lacking in legitimacy, the occurrence of violence is justified by various rationalizations. Initially, it is argued that violence presents the only viable method that can be utilized to redress the wrongs that permeate society. Secondly, it is contended that the use of violence, in reality, is no different from the methods used by the system to implement its decisions. Violence is thus viewed as resistance to the identical aspect within the system. The third and final argument advanced as a justification for the use of violence is that it is the fastest method available to destroy the system. In this view, the system has become so archaic and corrupt that the necessity for its rapid elimination warrants the reliance on violence. In other words, this third argument embodies the maxim that the end justifies the means.

All three arguments are present in the contemporary American environment. Many people have committed themselves to a violent path because they perceive no other outlet for articulating their interests. Many manifestations of violence are present today in a manner and extent not visible in earlier periods.

The full emergence of these factors can be attributed to the appearance of Vietnam as a national issue. Although traces of these new factors were perceptible before the United States's direct involvement in Vietnam, it is that conflict which has crystallized and rendered them environmentally meaningful. While the system has remained operative under this pressure, cracks in the political culture have appeared. The extent of these fissures can not as yet be ascertained; the only knowledge available is that the environment has been changed by the Vietnam issue. This alteration offers a distinct revolutionist potential. At the present time it is not revolutionist because of the existence of sufficient systemic support.

Future developments will depend on what issues the system must face and how it will attempt to resolve them. If such issues as the environmental one create or enlarge previously existing cleavages in the population, the demand for environmental change may well increase to such a degree that a genuinely revolutionist situation could exist. In this event, the demand for change could produce profound consequences. The history of political institutions testifies to the relationship between pressures on political systems and their assumption of a more authoritarian and self-preservative orientation.

A crisis point is reached at that moment when the populace completely loses faith in the legitimacy of its political system. While this can occur because of a decrease in the system's effectiveness, it can also come about when the gap between the respective perceptions of those in the environment and those in the political system becomes dichotomized. If such an eventuality comes to pass, the existing political system will be revamped either through total breakdown—alteration of forms and processes—or through a perversion of democratic tone.

When taken singly, the trends within the American environment might not appear to be revolutionist at the present time. However, when these are combined, the effect is synergic and at least the outlines of revolutionist phenomena have started to make an appearance. Within the environment, certain conditions and attitudes serve as the sources of these particular trends. The United States presently exhibits a deeply disturbed and increasingly fragmented society which differs on whether to maintain the status quo, to redefine the old myths and institutions, or to find something truly new.

Despite the disenchantment caused by these factors, the American political system has managed to weather the two fundamental crises of its viability: effectiveness and legitimacy. While the system has been challenged with increasing frequency on both points, sufficient good will and faith have been accumulated over the years to preserve it. In spite of probing attacks on the nature of the political community and on the relevance of the Constitution, the system has remained essentially unaffected.

One reason for this can be found in the nature of contemporary political man in the United States. He is confused, bitter, and frustrated with his position within the society, a position which he little understands. He is motivated by a desire to participate in political activity, yet he is unable to find adequate means of doing so.

Regardless of his position on the major domestic and foreign issues of the day, he has inevitably been embittered by them, because they have revealed and emphasized inconsistencies in the basic principles of the political community. The major political problems also frustrate him because they defy the solutions he would like them to have. Finally, he is reluctant to assume the risks inherent in the changes he seeks, a factor compounded by his inability to articulate these desired changes to his own satisfaction.

China and Asia

Preoccupied with the "West Wind" and nurtured by the ideas carried on its aerial currents, revolution in Asia has been given its distinct style by the "East Wind." While the theme of Asian revolution has been dominated by man's quest for relevance, its motivating force is rooted in Asian man's desire for his own renaissance.

Asian revolutionists, utilizing both Western and indigenous techniques, eventually perceived that a revolutionist temper could be effected only by devising a formula which accounted for the people, their cultural ties, and their identity with the land. In contrast with the West, where the revolutionist concentration was, and still remains, on the urban areas, Asian revolution has developed in and advanced from the countryside.

The Asian revolutionist experience reveals a continuous, although not always linear, process. While most Asian states are nonrevolutionist, the largest regional actor, China, is the most significant exception; there revolution has become a pattern of life. The pattern reveals both continuity and change. Technology is one reason for this change. While it seems probable that China will not abandon at least limited support of revolutionist movements, its acquisition of nuclear weapons and its potential for developing adequate delivery systems will nevertheless contribute to substantial change in the area. If the wind that blows is indeed an "East Wind," then the unpredictability of China's actions will be increased as it attempts to raise its level of satisfaction through revolutionary means.

The sources of this unpredictability are found in the nature of China's political system. In addition to being a closed system, it is dominated by the will and thought of Mao Tse-tung. His behavior patterns have been repetitive (the Cultural Revolution, for example, is not an isolated event but another—perhaps more encompassing—rectification campaign), and he has sacrificed economic growth for ideological motives; yet even the Soviets were compelled to adopt more pragmatic policies at similar stages of growth. In the conflict between ideology and pragmatism raging in China today, the ideological faction led by Mao and Lin Piao has apparently won the day. Chinese revolutionists invariably have had absolute faith in the validity of their own experiences and judgment.

Two factors tend to account for the behavior and the influence of Mao Tse-tung: his longevity and his lack of first-hand knowledge of the post-World War II West. Since these are not mutually exclusive aspects of the Asian experience, they must be placed in a perspective which is, of necessity, speculative.

Nearing eighty, Mao Tse-tung savors the experience of over forty years of intense involvement in revolutionist war prior to the attainment of independence. Since 1949, the mainland of China has undergone an almost constant and heremetical sealing-off process directed against outside—especially Western—influences. Viewed in a historical perspective, this imposed isolation is an extreme reaction to more than one century of exploitive Western policies in China. Determined that the China of the nineteenth-century missionary and commercial interests would indeed be a phenomenon of the past, Mao quickly imprisoned, expelled, or killed those foreigners who remained after 1949.

If his revolutionary view is projected effectively into the international relations of the area and into the international system as a whole, the desired objective of China will not be a simple alteration but rather a complete change of the system. Other revolutionist experiences thus pale in comparison, for the Chinese leadership would rather create than simply attend its revolutionist moment.

While it is still too soon to evaluate properly the Cultural Revolution, this exuberant manifestation has not been the first rectification campaign conducted by Mao. It has been the most extensive and encompassing of that leader's efforts to create a policy which is truly and totally new. The thrust of the Cultural Revolution appears to have been the prevention of a permanently created elite emerging from the communist party cadres. Mao's desire to avoid the obstacle of an entrenched bureaucracy impeding his line of communication with the people was no doubt an essential factor underlying the Cultural Revolution, yet of no less importance was his fear that the party faithful might create for themselves a new elite class emulating the line of the Soviet Communist party.

Rejecting the party as the vehicle for revolution, Mao began to enlist youths under the aegis of the Red Guards. When he discovered that these indoctrinated youth were difficult to control and that their motivations were somewhat different than his own, he procured the support of Lin Piao and the People's Liberation Army, ordering the latter to disarm the Red Guards and to put them to work on "voluntary" projects. The PLA under Lin Piao thus appear to be the only organization that is still intact in China. As the heir-apparent to Mao, Lin Piao has a vested interest in continuing the revolution—he is, after all, a product of it—and there are no indications that he would be less ideologically motivated than his predecessor.

The Cultural Revolution illustrates the Chinese or, more realistically, Mao's determination to pursue revolutionist goals within China regardless of the cost. The ideology of revolution does not support a modernization program, primarily because reality cannot conform to ideological frameworks. While the Chinese have made significant progress in nuclear weapons, the pragmatism and expertise needed to modernize other sectors have been neglected because of their conflict with Mao's revolutionist values. His attempt to superimpose his own values on reality contributed, more than any other factor, to the failures of his "Great Leap Forward" experiment.

Mao and his supporters care little for modernization in the Western or even the Soviet sense of the term. Because modernization has necessitated bureaucratic elites that rapidly acquire vested interests, Mao has been unreceptive to the general model familiar to most countries. As long as Mao retains power, China will benefit little from modernization if it clashes with the revolutionist interests he seeks to preserve and propagate.

In China, revolution is the dominant aspect of political life. That country has legitimized it as a political system within areas under its control and seeks to extend that system to the Asian continent. In this sense, the Cultural Revolution can be viewed as an internal attempt to fashion power in Mao's image before embarking on a regional program. The recent development of advanced weapons, as well as the probability of an operational ICBM system in the early seventies, will afford China a new capability. Using this capability, or more probably utilizing the threat of its use, China will be enabled to pursue its revolutionist objective of destroying the old regional system and creating one properly cognizant of Chinese influence and hegemony.

If this eventuality occurs, other Asian revolutions will understandably be subordinated to that of the Chinese, for the behavior of China's leaders has indicated their faith in the validity of their own experiences. Believing that tenacity, protraction, and perseverance will eventually secure future objectives as they have in the past, the Chinese leadership seeks to imbue the system with its own revolutionist mythos and institutions.

It appears probable that China, to accomplish these objectives, will evolve a strategy resting on two complementary pillars, one fomenting revolutionist subversion within other states, the other securing advantages through the manipulation of external nuclear threats. Although China's success in the past with indigenous revolutionists has been limited, future attempts might well focus on influencing them to attempt to bring their countries into a Chinese-dominated system.

The implication of these various factors can be seen by the manner in which the Chinese have operated. To create the new order, they expelled all vestiges of the old; even indigenous traces of antiquity were not spared. If it achieved nothing else, Mao's command that "a hundred flowers bloom" further identified dissident elements in the country and thus hastened their removal. The Cultural Revolution is thus but another stage in an internal and ever-present rectification program designed to propel the revolution toward both its internal and broader international objectives. While these objectives do not necessarily assume sponsorship of additional "wars of national liberation," they do include the option to exercise, arbitrarily, sufficient influence to revolutionize the regional system through purge, purification, and, finally, the establishment of new Asian structures. Such objectives have caused even North Vietnam and North Korea to become wary of a Chinese extension of influence, fears evidenced both by the maintenance of direct contact with and by the reception of aid from the Soviet Union.

Latin America

In spite of the powerful social and economic dynamics at work in Latin America today, there is little significant change in the traditional patterns of distribution of power. This is not to say that the present political stability is a tranquil one; the traditional elites are apprehensive and in general capable only of repressive and reactive measures. Perhaps the most disquieting factor in modern Latin America is the incapacity of the dominant elites for imaginative innovation. The greater the problem, often the greater the paralysis of imagination; the more obvious the need for some change, the more determined some of the elites are to maintain the order of the status quo. The general pattern in Latin America today is of an elite that cannot or will not lead, that is still possessed by a relatively static and evolutionary from-the-top-down vision of society and history. The same elites have not been capable of nurturing the birth of evolutionary thought forms and institutions, and of new, more progressive elites.

Perhaps the most forebodingly dynamic feature is the dramatically increasing population in Latin America. "The predominant feature of

Latin American population is its speed of growth. This becomes dramatically clear if we note that at the beginning of this century, the area had a population just over 60 million, and that by the middle of 1960 the population had reached more than 207 million; that is, it almost tripled in the short period of sixty years."[1] This means that Latin American societies must find some way to increase minimal food supplies as fast as the population is increasing. This task is not an insignificant challenge to societies that are not noted for rapid innovations.

The most obvious result of the population explosion in Latin America has been the rapid growth of the major cities and the creation of highly developed centers of industry and commerce which take advantage of the influx of cheap, unskilled labor, and of the new urban market. These industrial centers also have developed a new class of managers and professionals with powerful economic interests. Unexpectedly—especially since the rise of Fidel Castro—this new urban middle sector has not proved to be as reformist-minded as its North American counterpart, and often seems to be more interested in accumulating personal security and/or wealth than in assuring or working for the development of a healthy, expanding national society and economy. Likewise, the majority of the new urban working class has seldom been effectively mobilized for social, political, and economic change, probably because as a group they are satisfied to have so recently escaped the rural worker's peonage, where so many of their fellow citizens still languish.

Only fitfully have the new industrialists and commercial interests dedicated themselves to the expansion of the domestic market and the cultivation of a mass, rather than a specialized and limited, market. The blessings of mass democracy are not as apparent to the newly rich Latin Americans as they were to their North American counterparts earlier in history—especially since a mass, semiskilled (and therefore at least semi-literate) labor force is apparently not as necessary to the creation of a powerful industrial complex as it was at the turn of the century.

The skills of national planning and coordination, generally through one or a series of government agencies, have given the process of change in Latin America added dimensions. With its tradition of the state as the moderating power and arbiter of disputes, it was a natural transition that the state should assume the chairmanship of the economic forces

---

[1] Carmen A. Miro, "The Population of Twentieth Century Latin America," *Population Dilemma in Latin America*, J. Mayone Stycos and Jorge Siras (eds.) (Washington, D.C.: Potomac Books, 1966), p. 1.

working to develop the nation—though often the members of the committee seek to limit severely the powers of the chairman to those of arbitration as opposed to enforced planning. But since the early fifties there has slowly emerged in almost all of the Latin American republics the idea of a national plan of development which has been strengthened by (and in turn strengthened) nationalism.

In the short run, the major force for social revolution will no doubt come from the potential political power of the newly literate groups, most of them in the great urban centers of Latin America. It is this group which moves from "passive marginality" to "active marginality," giving opportunity for enterprising politicians to organize new political blocs. This is the group most susceptible to the tempests of the search for a historical identity, the "rising tide of expectations," and commitment to the populist dreams of social justice and antioligarchical pressures. It need only be noted that no Latin American society has been very successful in blending this new class with the old class, and that probably the static view of history characteristic of traditional Latin American culture has weakened the capacity and the will of the traditional ruling classes to attempt to organize the newly awakening groups into the existing systems.

Relatively isolated from the major currents of world politics, Latin America nonetheless has been profoundly affected by pressures and influences from the rest of the world, probably because its own weakness has left it very vulnerable to any pressures. It is necessary and helpful to distinguish between the measurable pressures coming from other nations, and the Latin Americans' perception of the influences and pressures upon them.

From Bolivar to Castro, Latin American revolutionist sentiment has focused more often than not upon colonialism and neocolonialism as it has existed in fact and fiction in the area. Such a focus has often been encouraged by the national ruling oligarchies through manipulation of a rhetorical antiforeign nationalism. Actually, both the traditional landholding oligarchies and the new industrial and commercial financial groups are often either dependent upon or allied to the very foreign interests they sometimes publicly attack.

In the twentieth century, the United States has been the most common object of antiimperialist feelings. Even though the United States foreswore its practice of intervention in Caribbean and Central American affairs with the Good Neighbor Policy, past interventions and the massive economic penetration that began approximately the same time as the "Good Neighbor Era" were enough to fuel the growing anti-Americanism south of the border. All the old fears were revived and exacerbated with the invasion of the Dominican Republic in 1965. Anti-United States feelings have been manipulated for domestic political advantage by opportunistic politicians of all stripes, and it is not surprising that this particular appeal has not lost its power. On the contrary, from the far right to the far left, there resides at least a little anti-Americanism in almost all Latin Americans, mixed very often with envy and admiration.

One of the major sources as well as targets of this anti-Americanism has been the significant penetration and expansion of United States private capital in Latin America. Though United States corporations such as United Fruit and the sugar companies have for decades been very significant in the total life of Central American and Caribbean countries, it was perhaps only with World War II and its aftermath that United States corporations began to replace the European (especially British) firms in South America. For all their need for capital and skills, Latin Americans nevertheless have tended to resent the presence of these firms, and the profits, sometimes exorbitant, sometimes exaggerated by the Latins, that are sent out of the area.

Traditionally, the government of the United States has considered the Caribbean as an American lake, vital to the security of the United States. Any threat, real or imagined, to the Canal Zone, or the presence of an anti-American power in that area, such as the Castro government in Cuba, has tended to provoke North American countermeasures. Even when the United States government is not devoting much attention to Latin America, its policies and actions (or lack thereof) have tremendous impact on the Latin American nations. The "Nixon riots" of 1958 and the anti-American stance of Fidel Castro excited enough anxieties in the United States to generate the Alliance for Progress, military assistance, and "internal subversion" programs designed to prevent another regime such as Castro's in the area. Castro has the same effect on the traditional Latin American oligarchies and on the newly emerging middle sectors, both of which turned strongly antireformist for fear of spawning another such movement.

Latin American military officers have increasingly been prone to step in to preserve the status quo after the traditional political orders threatened to collapse because of their inability to cope with the successive social, economic, and political crises of the development process. As a result, today more than two-thirds of the people of Latin America are living directly or indirectly under military tutelage. In most cases, these military or military-backed governments must be seen as protracted caretaker governments, but in some cases there seem to be evidences of "militechnocracy," or Nasserism without a Nasser. Such a modernizing military army officer corps, using the appeals of order, development, and nationalism, may well become the most powerful political force for change in Latin America in the next few years if present trends continue.

The Alliance for Progress has been unsure of its basic objectives, which is not surprising, especially because of the multinational nature of the goal-setting machinery and the ambivalence of the United States people and its government. First, it has been designed to promote reformist and evolutionary change, through peaceful and democratic means. Second, it has been designed to provide welfare measures to compete with communist or other promises. Sometimes it has been used to prop up a government incapable of sustaining its own power simply because of the fear of the unknown situation that would arise with its collapse. For example, the decision as to what is subversive has been left to the Latin American military, government, and police officials; and they have sometimes been a bit prone to identify dissent with subversion, legitimate aspirations with treason, and order with progress.

At any rate, the rise of potential urban populism, available as a mobilizing force for political, economic, and social change, coupled with the appearance of Fidel Castro ninety miles from the United States, has caused the Latin American military establishments to "put the lid on" rather tightly in most of modern Latin America. Even so, it is nonetheless true that the Latin American armies, if not terribly interested in the further democratization of their nations, are interested in their modernization and are in their own way nation-builders. The military officer corps is increasingly less allied to the traditional oligarchies, sometimes finding more compatibility with the new industrialists and banking interests, with their common interests in stability (defined as the lack of political agitation) and some sort of national development program.

Except for its impact on Cuba, the Soviet Union has not been an important factor of real political pressure or influence in Latin America. While at least one communist party exists in almost every Latin American state, the pro-Soviet factions have often found themselves engaged in a three-way competition with Castroite and pro-Chinese factions. Recently, the Moscow-oriented parties in many countries have begun to adopt a more "popular front" stance, to work within the existing structures, and to attempt to gain power and influence through legal channels where these are open to them. At the same time, the pro-Castro and pro-Chinese parties are oriented more towards violent revolution through the use of guerrilla warfare and terrorism. But it must be noted that all three factions of the communist movement are increasingly adopting a more nationalistic and less internationalistic stance.

Latin America has always been a battleground of ideas from other continents. Perhaps Marxism as a mystique and method of social analysis has had much more effect on Latin America and its self-understanding than direct political influences from the socialist countries. And although these ideas are still in the process of being adapted and assimilated to Latin American conditions, they represent a real source of revolutionary ferment today in that area.

The Arab World

The Arab world is a dazzling mural of contrasts. It is an ornate mixture of religious groups, a mosaic of people, a puzzle of manifold loyalties, and a diversity of political climates.

It is Islam which has provided the Arab with one of his most crucial dilemmas. While Islam on the one hand has furnished the traditional underpinnings for Arab unity, it has not offered a secular alternative for the Arab seeking to establish his place in the modern world. For Arabs, the question is one of an Islamic revival and secularization to sustain a transcendent Arab myth.

The departure from the Islamic traditional ideal during the Abbasid period between the eighth and thirteenth centuries created an ideological vacuum in the Arab world. Since then, the Arabs have never differed among themselves as strongly on any issue as on holding the reins of power. It was in the valley between racial pride and Islamic fundamentalism that the Arabs split into cultural and political divisions. More recently, nationalism has divorced the newly established states from their Islamic background. Nationalism, being secular (at least in its modern European context), is oriented toward statehood; Islam, having lost its status as a state, is only a religion. In most cases state and religion are no more one and the same, as was the case in the early days of Islam in the seventh century.

For several hundred years the Arabs were subject to ruling elites who, though they shared the identical faith, Islam, were not generally of the same people or culture; few Arabs shared in the authority or responsibility of government. Ruled by Turks, Albanians, Circassians,

Persians, Mongols, and Europeans, the newly emerged Arab states in the aftermath of World War II found themselves sovereign in name only.

The impact of Western technology and ideologies (neither rooted in the tradition of Arab culture) combined with social upheaval and economic changes to create the milieu of the post-independence era. The younger generation, made increasingly aware of the awesome problems of development within their countries and recalling the years of Western rule, found in their concept of Western imperialism a convenient target for the rationalization of their failures and those of their societies. Such a concept encompassed not only the enemy to be defeated, but also served as a catchall explanation for stagnation, both past and present.

It has become a cliché among scholars of the area to view the Arabs as caught up in some vast social upheaval. This growing irrelevance of old-established patterns and institutions has resulted less from internal changes and more from the impact of ideas outside the culture. Indigenous intellectual developments have been sparse, despite those events purported to be a consequence of new mass political awareness.

Fatalism and resignation to the will of Allah—that acceptance of the order of things and men—has indeed been eroded, but sociopolitical consciousness on the part of overwhelmingly illiterate and indifferent masses is slow to develop. Not even the so-called revolutionist regimes have been successful in directing the sentiments of the Arab masses into a confrontation with the problems facing society.

Prior to independence, Arab society was projected into the mainstream of the international system by non-Arab sovereigns and power elites, such as Muhammad Ali and his son Ibrahim in Egypt. These men realized that without some modernization, their societies could not survive the social and political implications of the European onslaught. The search by the West for raw materials, markets, bases and new spheres of influence led to the financial control by European interests of both Egypt and the Ottoman Empire. These influences accelerated the transformation of the region by introducing new economic and social forces. The erosion of communal and local ties led to their replacement by individual and contractual relationships.

Contemporary Arab experience has revealed the strength and intensity of the Arab revulsion against Western political and economic values and ideologies. Ideological changes reflect, first and foremost, various structural inadequacies. The irrelevance of principles and institutions which held together in traditional society have prompted the contemporary revolutionist search for bases of integration. Increasingly, the Arabs assume that such Western ideologies and institutions as democracy and capitalism cannot provide bases for progress.

Spearheading the movement in the Arab world is a group of revolutionists who seek the acquisition and control of governmental apparatus as a revolutionist tool. In Arab societies no institution can wield as much power, capital, and prestige as the state. By presiding over the state apparatus, the revolutionists project with limited success the norms and values they share.

From the outset, these revolutionists have avoided defining or crystallizing their role. Their origins are not, as was true in the past, to be found in a specific regional or social group, but in highly secularized groups oriented toward control and governmental power. Inspired by other than traditional sources, they have become both theorists and practitioners of a concept of revolution which centers on the pragmatic amalgam of nationalism, socialism, pan-Arabism, and nonalignment.

If today in the West we burn what we worshipped at the end of the last century—the nation as a masterpiece of modern history—the Arab revolutionist's collective pride turns upon the assertion of his cultural superiority. Unconsciously seeking diamonds in ashes, he reinforces his drive by believing that the fate of his culture is to be decided on the battlefield simultaneously with the fate of his aspirations.

All groups of people characterized by their own nuances of language and culture cannot, however, mold themselves into a nation through the vehicle of the state. The trappings of modern statehood have been a sort of borrowed finery, fitting awkwardly upon the remains of the Islamic body politic. In the Arab states, the loyalty that statehood can command is flawed by the profound nostalgia for the irrevocable past.

In the past century, the Arabs have been exposed to the force of democratic and industrial revolutions and to the drastic revolution signified in Western history by the Renaissance and the Reformation. At the beginning of modern European history, Islamic ulema (learned men) recoiled from innovation, preferring the shelter of authoritative doctrine of the Shari'ah (Islamic law). When in the nineteenth century Islamic institutions which had been perfected to guard orthodoxy lost their effectiveness, Muslims and Arabs had to pay the price of their passivity by confronting within a single century that complex of ideas and techniques which Europe had developed in the course of five hundred years.

At the individual level, the reaction to the incompatibility between Islam and modern thought has been a rigorous compartmentalization of the mind, a reaction still evident in contemporary Arab thought. Lip service to Islam and to the liberal Western ethic combined with the systematic failure to conform to the precepts of either became the public equivalent of a private duality of mind that many educated Arabs have since inherited. Certain geographic regions and social groups in most intimate contact with the ideas and techniques of the West have provided a disproportionate share of leadership in the process of change. The regional foci of Westernization—Egypt, Syria, Lebanon, Iraq, and Palestine—assumed central roles in the first nationalist movements to question the authority of the Ottoman Empire. Dependent upon groups, Ottoman intentions became suspect. These areas became centers for Western missionary and educational efforts and resource places for political leadership, nationalist movement, and commercial, educational, and administrative skills. Consequently, present boundaries do not coincide with the areas of strongest political sentiment. These arbitrary territorial divisions devised by the European powers may not have hindered nation-state development in all cases, but have created an imbalance by which states are culturally, economically, and militarily dependent upon each other.[2]

Uneven and unequal distribution of natural and human resources in an area poor in both has encouraged rapid development at some points and placed serious obstacles in others. The more advanced state or states have articulated their ideological assumptions in a wider context, attracting loyalties from the citizens of other states. This situation has enabled Egypt, Syria, Iraq, Palestine, and Lebanon to expand their influence over the other parts of the Arab world, both in the Middle East and North Africa. Accordingly, political constellations and alliances in the Arab world are of relatively short duration.

Nowhere else is the definition of an internal affair more anomalous than in the Arab world. Independence and anticolonialism could perhaps be vehicles for the ends of modernization and national assertions, but they become conflicting ones in the milieu in which energies are channeled toward redefinition of the national policy. The relations of

[2] Sidney Lindenberg, "Revolution and Nationalism in the Arab World," unpublished paper, Washington D.C., 1968.

the parties and movements to major political issues and to prominent groups—the army, students, and religious leaders—is one of inter-action, in both cause and effect.

The system of "temporary occupation" mandates and "preferential treaties" reached its height after the elites of the Arab world had been imbued with some idea of liberal constitutionalism. Their ex-perience seemed to show that Western liberalism was not for export. The West relied on force and threat as much as on law and persuasion. The withdrawal of Western presence also came in response to force: the strains of World War II, violent uprisings or guerrilla fighting in Palestine, Egypt, and Algeria. Where an oligarchic group accommodated itself to the foreign presence, the transition was smoother at first, but inevitably was followed by the revolutionary overthrow of these regimes (Syria in 1949, Egypt in 1952, Iraq in 1958, Yemen in 1962, Algeria in 1965 and Libya in 1969) or violent challenges to the traditional order (Jordan in 1956 and 1958 and Lebanon in 1958). Coercion has re-mained a major instrument of domestic politics, and in most states the army as a specialist in violence has been the major power behind, or directly in the forefront of, the political scene.

Within this sociological and intellectual setting, we must note that political development in most Arab states has been diverted into con-spiracy, violence, and personal interests. Political organization among the younger intellectuals began only in the second decade of this century. The short-lived nationalist parties—the Wafd and the Sa'dis in Egypt, the Nationalist and the Sha'b parties in Syria, and numerous similar parties in other Arab states—were frustrated in their aims by foreign occupation and internal struggles for power.

Africa

The environmental changes in Africa have outstripped the institutional structures of the tribal era. Such Western concepts as the nation-state and a progressive as opposed to a static vision of reality have shaken African elites. The promise of higher stages of material and spiritual perfection is competing with the negative condition of primitive African existence. The introduction of new and alien techniques and values into a community ultimately affects its social structure as well as its economic and political patterns. Africa has found her cultural founda-tions threatened, her religious beliefs called into question, and her basic philosophies forced to adjust to new pressure and conditions.

This collision of venerated tribal values, animistic and Islamic traditions, Western concepts, and the realities of the present international environment underlies the existential problem of Africa. The African faces a crisis of coexistence with himself and acclimation to his new political milieu. He is suspended between two developmental phases: a past of tribalism, struggling against extinction, and a future of nationhood, fighting for survival. In order to save his life, he faces the danger of losing his soul.

The colonial period was one of cultural dislocation and, above all, lack of purpose. The colonial sources of power and decision had no relevance to the African heritage. Upon achieving independence, Africa was left with two stark choices: either renounce the relevance of its tradition to its present aspirations, or baptize change within the spirit of that tradition. The first was both impossible to achieve and dangerous for the infant African states to attempt. Hence, it became imperative for the new African states to develop a unique sense of purpose in order to provide the framework within which to interpret their own aspirations.

The conflict of values among the elites has precipitated one of the most pressing political problems in the African states: the establishment of mass support for the leadership groups. Mobilization of the various segments in the population around a systematic framework of national interests is difficult for two reasons. One, a national interest requires commonly held notions of the public good. Such notions have not been crystallized beyond the immediate goal of anticolonialism. Two, there are no established means by which a public consensus can be reached by major segments of society.

There are at least two essential factors for the successful functioning of any democracy: mass participation and a high degree of political consensus. While the colonial powers could encourage mass participation in government, they failed to initiate a realistic process of social integration to develop political consensus. Western political ideas, with which many African leaders are so conversant, never had the chance to be implemented in practice. These ideas shifted into the realm of *ideals* instead of realistic possibilities for an independent African state.

Soon after independence was achieved, African leaders realized the impossibility of imposing alien ideas on a traditional cultural base. Yet, they also realized that traditional methods and values do not meet the requirements of nationhood in a modern world.

African elites are victims caught between the "ideals" of the West and the "realities" of their own societies. They are not at home in the

West or in the East or even, strange as it may seem, in Africa. They must build, through a process of integration, redefinition, and development of purpose, a new conceptual framework in order to acquire a view of the rest of the world and themselves as a part of it.

The domestic political environment in the new African states has been especially conducive to the emergence of small leadership elites that hold effective control of national affairs. African nationalist leaders, around whom the anticolonialist movements coalesced, are identified as the embodiment of their new states. Such a position inevitably leads to an over-concentration of personal power: the African leader becomes the government itself. This increase of personal power is partly the result of the lack of a trained bureaucracy. In the absence of competent subordinates, African leaders assume personal responsibility for governmental action and are bound to accumulate extensive personal powers. Such inordinate power concentrated in the hands of a leader and his personal clique leads to a policy-making process which is nearly always arbitrary. Without a competent bureaucracy, policy decisions are made without regard for differing points of view. There is often little opportunity for the transmission of information which does not support the position of the elite. It is obvious that policy decisions made in such an operational vacuum bear no relevance to actual situations and are destructive of manifest objectives.

The popular pressures and emotions which African nationalist leaders fostered and molded against the colonial regimes are now being directed against them as heads of governments. A major anticolonialist issue was that the colonial powers were inhibiting material and social progress in Africa. The masses were led to believe that once the colonial regime was destroyed, near–Utopian conditions would prevail. Progress was very often viewed as the justification for independence, but just what did the Africans mean by "progress"?

Development and progress are used interchangeably; progress is equated with industrialization, with prosperity, and with human welfare, and is the overall spirit behind African attempts at nation building. But, operationally, progress often means nothing more than the very conspicuous—but generally quite useless—construction of public projects.

Enormous popular pressures for such visible but irrelevant achievements force the governments of the new states into a costly diversion of scarce funds which could be used more effectively in other developmental programs. When faced with a choice between a series of bush hospitals or a superhighway between provincial capitals, the government usually chooses the road, even if there is an insufficient number of vehicles to justify its construction.

It is not unusual for newly independent peoples to look to their nationalist leaders for guidance during the post-independence transition period. These leaders stress national and political unity as being necessary for development and, in doing so, excoriate actionalism. But unity must be predicated upon an active national consciousness, a broad popular consensus, and a homogeneity, all of which are missing from the African scene.

Ethnic, geographical, social, economic, and historical diversity within nearly all of the African states lead to cleavages within their respective political cultures. Factionalism abounds and, as in the Arab revolutionary situation, the various groups too often think and act in mutually exclusive "we" and "they" terms. The spirit of coalition and cooperation is generally lost under such conditions; democracy is interpreted as majority rule with minority exclusion. It is obvious that assumptions can easily lead to destructive political in-fighting and to governmental suppression of the opposition.

It is here where military elites step in. The army has served diverse functions within the African states since their independence. It has been a symbol of national independence and unity and a sword to guarantee newly won independence from external intervention and tentative unity from internal factionalism. In recent years, through military *coups d'état,* the army has been escalated to become the most important wielder of political power and influence within fully half of the African states, thus assuming a comparable status with its Arab counterpart.

A general explanation of the political role assumed by military elites is evidenced by the crisis of African revolutionists. The army has assumed significance because of the political default of revolutionists. African revolutionists, who had been the midwives of independence by pamphleteering, agitation, and guerrilla activities, proved themselves incapable of delivering the goods for nation building. After assuming political office, they preferred facile ideological speculation to the wise allocation of social values, reconciliation of conflicting interests and performance of efficient administration.

It is not difficult to understand why the military stepped in to fill this political vacuum. Trained to implement orders rather than to formulate grandiose goals, they were eager to begin the arduous task of nation building, were intolerant of domestic factionalism, and, most importantly, were equipped with the means of enforcing their will. Outright coups eliminated Ghana's Kwame Nkrumah and Algeria's Ahmed Ben Bella, two of Africa's most charismatic leaders. Even such broadly based civilian parties as Ghana's Convention Peoples' Party and Algeria's National Liberation Front were incapable of saving these leaders. Other African armies have succeeded in a number of "juggling acts" rather than true *coups d'état* and assumptions of power.

In justifying their assumption of political power, military elites have often stated that they are serving in interim the functions normally maintained in the West by the constitutional processes. Nonetheless, such apologies do not fulfill the political necessity for the legitimization of the government. Since military elites rarely relinquish power to the civilians, they must confront the reality that a state cannot be governed effectively by force. Military elites, like their civilian predecessors, must justify their rule by appealing to the various "isms" in vogue in Africa. Nonetheless, such incantations without delivery of the goods of modernization cannot transform power into legitimacy. Since military governments need both elusive ideological justification and hard-won popular support—both of which they rarely receive—legitimacy and nation building are beyond their power.

3

•••••••• **TYPES**
OF
REVOLUTIONISTS

Contemporary political cultures, both international and national, are in a state of transition. The tendency toward more fragmentation of communities and more heterogeneity of interests, values, and goals is evident. Since a core of norms which can condition our approach to these systems no longer exists, the environment has become more permissive and the lack of ordering structures has become increasingly pronounced. As a matter of fact, this phenomenon has become a common denominator of the contemporary political environment.

Evolving from tightly structured systems altered by vast changes in the political, economic, and social spheres, the contemporary trend has exerted a levelling influence upon the international scene. Despite objective disparities, the tendency toward egalitarianism has been the subjective result of a newly permissive environment. This trend has not only nullified many of the systemic constraining factors, but has also permitted revolutionists to have more impact in the world arena. The revolutionist, whether an individual (Fidel Castro), an organization or movement (The National Liberation Front), or a state (The United Arab Republic), has capitalized on the existent diversities in the environment.

Three types of revolutionists have emerged in the contemporary political environment: the revolutionist as an individual, as a movement or organization, and as a state. Quite obviously, these categories are not mutually exclusive and are loosely interwoven in the matrix being presented. While the first two categories of revolutionists generally confine their initial activities to the domestic environment, the revolutionist as a state is operative in the international context. It has been the revolutionist state which has given international articulation to the theories of individual revolutionists.

Throughout history, the individual has challenged the firmly held beliefs of his age. Man's search for faith has been evidenced in his refusal to accept the old "truth" as it was perceived for him. When Socrates chose the hemlock rather than live in a system whose highest value was the city-state, he did so as a revolutionist whose act of faith was nonviolent. In the same manner, Christ, who refused to accept the old faith and reject the new, placed his revolutionist mark on the future of the West. These experiences can be compared to the Marxian dilemma which pits economic man against the economic state in another revolutionist attempt to cope with the human situation.

Thus, the concept of the individual as a revolutionist can trace its lineage into antiquity. If we were to categorize these revolutionists, a convenient method would be to separate the theorists from the practitioners. Marx, for example, was obviously a theorist and did not even participate in the great revolutions of his era. Lenin was both a theorist and a practitioner. As his theories are derived from those of Marx, however, he could well be considered a primary practitioner but a secondary theorist. Mao Tse-tung, on the other hand, is both a primary theorist and a primary practitioner of revolution.

The distinction between primary and secondary revolutionists serves a useful conceptual purpose. Primary revolutionists, be they theorists, practitioners, or both, have a greater purity and originality of thought and action. In those cases where these qualities are combined, there has been a greater correlation between thought and action, as well as more clearly defined objectives and goals.

While the individual as theorist or practitioner represents the origins of the mood of revolution, it is the revolutionist as a movement, or organization which energizes the thoughts and actions of individual revolutionists. Without group action, revolution in practice is not likely to occur. Man may theorize alone, but he definitely is more comfortable when he acts in unison with others toward commonly shared objectives and goals tempered by some consensual values and interests. Thus, the first task of the individual is to identify with those who, like himself, are willing to seek a new beginning and explore the limit of man's faith in the process of rebirth.

The individual revolutionist can endow the group with his identity, and the latter then becomes a corporate personification of the former. This has occurred in the case of Mao Tse-tung and the Chinese Communist party, and also in the case of Lenin and Stalin in the Soviet Union. It has become apparent, however, that this phenomenon can only take place when first-generation revolutionists are involved. There are many exceptions and variations to this: the Vietnamese National Liberation Front, for example, has chosen to remain relatively anonymous (for tactical motives which will be discussed later). Whatever their result, decisions of this nature are initial ones which rely heavily on local conditions.

One of the most striking departures from the past has been the role of the state in the process of revolutionism. It is only by controlling the mechanisms of the state that revolutionist objectives can be realized. Through the agency of the state, domestic and international programs can be surfaced and their achievement hopefully attained.

In the past, revolutionists had a difficult time securing the state for their own purposes. The classic case of the French Revoluton produced Napoleon I, but he was hardly a revolutionist. Even the pre-1789 society which the Revolution had subjected to substantial change was not wholly eradicated, thus enabling the Congress of Vienna to make a partial, if not lasting, restoration in 1815. Since the nineteenth-century world was centered in Europe, both England and the Continental power blocs ensured that no revolutionist states could emerge. This partially explains why violent revolutionists (including anarchists)—both individuals and organizations—of nineteenth-century Europe did not achieve greater results. Since they could not hope to control the state apparatus, their efforts were, at least in retrospect, doomed.

Revolutionists in a Changing Environment

The quintessence of the revolutionist is his search for relevance; he seeks myths and systems which will be appropriate to a changing environment. While it is true that the direction of change might be difficult to predict, the revolutionist is one who realizes that a change in his present circumstances is nevertheless necessary, indeed, mandatory. He cannot maneuver within his present system either because the system will not permit nonrevolutionist change, or because he himself desires a fundamentally different system.

In an era characterized by quantum advances in technology, political institutions are frequently invalidated by the changing nature of the environment. On the international level, the insistence of major states that the new and lesser states abide by the traditional rules of power politics has obviously been nullified by the altered nature of the concept of "usable power." Technology has actually lessened the capacity of major states to apply power in many of the situations in which they find themselves. The Pueblo incident is a case in point: the major participant, the United States, had much greater power in relation to the lesser state, North Korea. Yet the problem the former encountered turned on the factor that very little of its power was usable in coping with the latter. Thus, the old rules of behavior were certainly voided in this particular situation. The new permissiveness of the international system has tended to replace the "great power-small power" myth with a type of egalitarianism among states where "usable power" is more evenly divided; former assessments of real or potential power divergence have become relatively obsolescent. There is, in other words, a propensity toward diffusion and decentralization of power, as well as toward new channels for its application and reassigned objectives.

The new international environment is characterized by a general increase in the number of politically active participants. States operate pluralistically across a broad spectrum of political alternatives in a manner which appears to the outside observer to be both unstructured and unsystematic. The trend is in the direction of complex global patterns of shifting and overlapping loyalties and political obligations. In this complicated international milieu, states often find their interests to be best served by countervailing rather than unidirectional actions and obligations.

Two primary factors have given international life its particular flavor in the post-1945 period. The great-powers no longer govern the dynamics of the state system, and, as a corollary, the small-powers enjoy a wider spectrum of political alternatives.

The great-powers lack the situational capability to deal with the course of events outside their national boundaries and spheres of influence. The very fact that they possess nuclear weaponry compels them to deploy conventional forces cautiously; the threat of escalation to the nuclear threshold is a constant restraint. In addition, a moral stigma has been attached to unilateral interference by the present bipolar powers in those areas of the world formerly dominated by the traditional European powers.

The new states have become less and less the playthings of the great-powers. They often express the fear, or perhaps the conviction, that they are pawns in the cold war. It could also be argued that the United States, the Soviet Union, China, and the other great-powers have themselves become the pawns of the lesser powers. Hence, the power of small, supposedly powerless, states has brought to the fore the issue of the "tyranny of the weak" in international politics.

Domestic environments have been influenced by vast increases in population, by international spillover, and by a tendency toward more authoritarian systems at a time when individuals are demanding more personal liberties. Population explosions have brought about new problems which have hardly begun to be assessed. For the most part, this is an area fraught with unknown implications.

Today's world arena is producing more problems for the domestic environment to cope with than in any previous era. Part of this is the rapid communication of events which enables many populations to be more aware of the world. Many theorists have confused this new awareness with a sense of interdependence. As a matter of fact, the opposite has occurred and separatism is becoming more pronounced.

This factor has also contributed to an increase in the level of popular participation in those processes usually reserved for state officials. In most states governmental reaction to this phenomenon has been manifested in the attempt to centralize its decision-making operations to an even greater degree. Domestically, this new and increased authoritarianism has been made possible by technology and it is increasingly evident even in democracies. The rationale most frequently advanced is that the operational necessity of planning for a big population and international contingencies requires instantaneous response; public interference in the decision-making process would not only delay this response but, in many cases, seriously enervate it. Simultaneously, however, individuals are demanding more participation and more freedom *vis-à-vis* the state.

Briefly sketched, this is the present environment in which states find themselves. An important question is why some become revolutionist in an attempt to cope with it. This can be partially answered by examining some of the issues involved.

It has been assumed that revolutionists evince grievances which the present system will or cannot change. Thus, their attitude toward the present international system is largely negative. They perceive that the system is more beneficial to those Western nations that formulated its standards and means. Although these "founders" are virtually nonexistent today, the level of satisfaction of revolutionist states is minimal, primarily because they believe that existing constraints emanate from them. While they proclaim solidarity with other revolutionist states, they are still depressed by a feeling of extreme isolation when they play the international game. In many cases this impression has intensified their desire to formulate new rules designed to benefit them. The system has tolerated the resultant encroachment thus far, mainly because of the difficulty encountered by the major players in responding adequately to it. Each new successful incursion has tended to illustrate to these revolutionist states that the old does indeed lack relevance.

The trend in the international system toward more independence of action by states previously associated with power blocs, accompanied by the concomitant emergence of new states, has caused the political environment to become increasingly more fragmented and heterogeneous. With polycentrism in the communist world, visible cracks in the Western alliances, and over threescore new state-entities, the vast majority of states operate exclusive of the power centers. While there has been little attempt to compete directly with the power of the United States, the Soviet Union, or Communist China, there have been efforts by small-powers to enter into the contest for influence in the international arena. These states have charted a historically unique course, one determined by the present disparity between power and influence. While not all can be considered revolutionists, those that are—both in their own perception as well as in the estimation of others—have found that they have more space for maneuver than was possible in more traditional systems.

In this century, revolutionists have been identified with two rather distinct types of revolution. The first, with strong antecedents in both the previous century and the industrial revolution, is essentially urban in nature and has been found in the West. The other, with roots in the pre- and immediate post-World War II era, is rural with underpinnings primarily in the less-developed countries of the non-West. Revolutionists in the nineteenth century were concerned with the condition of urbanization. Their thoughts and actions, organizations and movements, and idealized and real states were all predicated on an urban perception and orientation. The revolutionist drive of the Soviet Union between the wars was based on a vision of urban revolution which ushered the Soviet state into existence. The realization by its practitioners that they could not transplant their revolution, or duplicate elsewhere the conditions that existed in their own country, did not become apparent until relatively recently. With the possible exception of certain revolutionists in the United States, the urban revolutionist is in the decline in several areas of the world.

The Revolutionist as an Individual

The revolutionist is one whose sense of physical change is directly correlated with his perception of spiritual change. This melange of physical and spiritual characteristics has helped to weave a web of romanticism around certain revolutionists, of whom Ché Guevara is an immediate example. This is, of course, part of the charisma which these individuals attempt to project in a system where norms and values are in constant flux. The revolutionist attempts to impose his norms and values upon such a transitional system. The environment, because of its permissiveness, is receptive to this effort. In other words, he capitalizes on an atmosphere—domestic or international—in which ordering structures have weakened. This tends to explain why timing is such an important factor. It is obvious that the revolutionist cannot thrive in any environment other than one which he has deemed to be no longer relevant. When this occurs, his spiritual exploration takes him into an unchartered and previously prohibited area, but one in which he is uniquely qualified to enter, since it provides his *raison d'être*. As a theorist, he senses the issues and parameters of conflict; as a practitioner, he energizes the theoretical constructs and attempts to exploit them. While effectiveness is not dependent upon a single factor, the revolutionist will be ineffective if his moment for action has not truly arrived. He thus must have a sense of the dynamic involved in his situation; he must possess that elusive sense of timing.

As an individual, the revolutionist must be acutely aware of the milieu in which theory and practice are to be interrelated. While he does not have to be indigenous, he must be aware of the distinctly local conditions which modify the environment. Although many revolutionists seek to universalize in both thought and action, they are nevertheless creatures of distinct conditions which cannot be duplicated in time or space. They have found it difficult to transplant their essence because of its situational uniqueness.

When viewed in this analytical context, none of the existing Soviet leaders could be considered revolutionists. They are clearly not theorists of revolutionism, nor have any been its practitioners. The Russian communist today lives outside the framework of revolution which gave him birth; the old Soviet revolutionists are virtually all extinct. Contrast this with Communist China, where the new man is very much a revolutionist; the thought and deed of Mao are still vibrant. Disciples such as Lin Piao are very much alive to incite the flames of revolutionist thought and action. For Soviet man, the mythos of the revolution is alive, but fixed in history, and it has supported his domestic institutions which have become equally fixed. In China the human situation is in flux, and the myth of revolution is the living ideology which promotes the fluid conditions characterizing that country.

As an Individual in the Non-West

Non-Western revolutionists have been deeply influenced by Western sources of thought. The vast majority have received their education in the West and are partially products of the mainstream of that particular influence. This experience has been conditioned by circumstances as well as the situational milieu in which they have found themselves. Most have experienced colonial regimes, independence, and post-independence situations, all of which required cognizance of the differing circumstances which each of these phases implied.

The preindependence revolutionist had one primary objective. In the quest for freedom from the colonial power, a great variety of strategies and tactics were utilized, each as necessity dictated. In this respect, there were two general categories of action undertaken: one involved a combination of military, psychological, and political means; the other utilized primarily psychological and political maneuvering. Essentially, the means used dictated the type of revolutionist who finally emerged in this first phase. Those who led a struggle were not content merely to gain independence, but also aspired to restructure the society itself prior to independence. There were exceptions to this of course, Nkrumah being one of them. Those who did not have to use armed force, however, were initially content with the mere gaining of independence. Consequently, many of these could not be characterized as revolutionists since revolution implies the transfer of more than one power.

In order to secure the implied objectives of independence, a different sort of revolutionist emerged in the initial independence phase. Physically, he may have appeared the same man, but his perception had been altered. The myth of independence had to become the myth of the state, although, in fact, the latter did not exist. Independence revealed to these revolutionists the need for new structures and relationships to support the state. In so many cases, this task proved to be impossible, and the visionary was swept out of office on a tidal wave of discontent.

In the post-independence phase, the revolutionist is struggling to find meaning in his novel creation—the state—which often exists more in theory than in fact. Intense feelings of frustration have deadened revolutionists to the point where some have lost faith and are no longer committed to revolution. Men such as Nkrumah and Sukarno became so immersed in their own charismatic mystiques that the revolutions which they created bypassed and then discarded them.

The Revolutionist as Movement, Organization, and Party

The group is responsive to the local environment which has generated its existence. It delineates gaps caused by the lack of alignment between changing environment and staid institutions. Although the revolutionist individual has perceived that the old myths are no longer relevant, it is the revolutionary group that must activate this concept. It must also initiate new myths which will support the new institutions and structures it seeks to establish. In the final analysis, grievance identification does not by itself enable the revolutionist organization to capitalize on the revolutionist mood. Ultimately, it will have to come forward with a message of hope that prophesizes something truly new— something that makes the destruction of the old worthwhile. In symbolic terms, it must issue a promissory note for rebirth.

Revolutionists as groups normally have two sets of objectives and goals. One of these, which has already been discussed, is the symbolic goal generally constructed around the concept of rejuvenation. The objectives to which we shall now address ourselves tend to become very specific in the political, economic, and social fields. One shared characteristic of these objectives lies in their comprehensive nature. If the revolutionist goal is rebirth, then the objectives must necessarily be far-reaching. It matters very little that the implementation of programs designed to secure these objectives is postponed until the future, since the group is not now in a position to act upon them. Indeed, it is far more preferable that they remain in a future context, as they can then be modified to meet any contingencies that may arise.

These programs are also modified by the supreme revolutionist value—Change. Under different guises and in as many different languages as there are peoples, this aspect is not only the meaning of revolutionism but is its most important value as well. The perception of change is, after all, the *raison d'être* for the revolutionist. The irrelevance of the old and the relevance of the new are the stimulants for the movement, organization, or party which, by the very act of incorporation, has given change both form and substance.

As Movement, Organization, and Party in the Non-West

In Africa and Asia, revolutionists as organizations and movements legitimized themselves by trying to appear as mass organizations when, in reality, they were elitist movements. The preindependence phase of these organizations was dedicated to the proposition of independence, and this commitment provided the cohesive element which bound together what were otherwise rather diverse segments. Naturally, not all of these organizations were revolutionist, so it becomes essential to define those groups that did constitute revolutionist movements.

On the first level, there are those organizations which fought for independence. While this in itself does not make them revolutionist, it nevertheless did force such groups as the Viet Minh in Indochina and the FLN in Algeria to wage a revolutionist war utilizing the tactics of revolution. Conceptually, they were revolutionist, since the type of conflict waged demanded a framework centered around both a complete restructuring and an attempt to fabricate something truly novel. This may be contrasted with the Mau Mau in Kenya, who waged guerrilla warfare without a framework of revolution.

Preindependence movements that could also be characterized as revolutionist were those that did not resort to physical force, but whose organizations stressed the adoption of a different form for the society. Specifically, we are referring here to the Parti Démocratique de Guinée (PDG) in Guinea, and the Convention Peoples Party (CPP) in Ghana, where, in both parties, the organizational objectives went beyond independence. These organizations were engaged in a two-tier struggle directed against the colonial power as well as against traditional authority. It was the second aspect that distinguished them as revolutionist, because their attempt to destroy the old was viewed as a comprehensive one. In this respect, we are not referring to ultimate success or failure, but rather to the objectives of these organizations. The great majority of preindependence organizations, when judged by this criterion, could not be considered revolutionist *per se*, yet one of the ironies of recent history has been the lack of understanding of this factor.

As Communist Parties

At the present time, most scholars have acknowledged the polycentric nature of communist states. Less discernible, but of perhaps greater significance for the future, is the even greater diversity among communist parties in the world today. At one time, almost all communist parties owed their allegiance to the center of communism which had given them birth or inspired their founding. Although the existence of some of these parties predates the Russian Revolution of 1917, their special character came after that event. Virtually every nation during the inter-war period had such a party which, depending upon local conditions, was dedicated to a variety of intermediate objectives; their unifying factor, however, whether they were located in Germany, or China, or the United States, was close connection with Moscow. In most cases, the Stalin regime used them more for Soviet purposes than as a revolutionist vanguard.

After World War II, the roots of polycentrism were progressively solidified as the Chinese Communist party under Mao gained control of the mainland. As this party and its leader were dedicated more to Chinese interests than to those of Moscow, the inevitable tension of a dichotomy of objectives caused a strain in Sino-Soviet relations. The parties, following the lead of their respective states, competed initially on the party level for allies, not only in an ideological, but in a temporal, struggle as well.

The Soviet Union had recognized by this time that the existence of occasional local communist parties had to be sacrificed in order to facilitate the pursuit of policies perceived to be in her interest. This was true in the Middle East, and in certain African countries such as Ghana and Guinea, where local leaders feared the existence of any meaningful competitor party. In essence, the Soviets decided to work with nationalist groupings which attempted to use Marxist principles in their organization.

In Latin America, the nature of local communist parties began to change. While they had used the methods of revolution in the past, they had never really been revolutionists, and in retrospect their past role seems almost pathetic. The lines of communication from Moscow were long, and conditions operative at the time of their founding had changed considerably. They were never able to mobilize suitable revolutionist individual elites, let alone any illusion of mass support. In addition, there were never any realistic attempts to adopt policies suitable to their indigenous circumstances, and they remained aloof from the political process. The concept of guerrilla warfare was confused with its tactics, plunging Latin American revolutionists into an abyss of meaningless and outdated objectives.

An exception to this model was the communist party in Cuba. When Castro gained power, the party, which had not fought with him as a party, became the indispensable catalyst in his consolidation of power. As the Castro regime evolved, the party became his instrument in a sweeping, but not yet fully completed, reorganization of the state and its society. In doing this, the character of the party once aligned to Moscow assumed the peculiar personality of Castro and consequently became a different entity. Its prime quality became revolutionist at the same time that communist parties further south were trying to integrate themselves into their respective indigenous political processes.

Communist parties in both North and Sub-Saharan Africa have never been able to organize effectively. In the preindependence stage, nationalist movements, which undoubtedly included individual communists, were oriented toward the one goal of independence. The great majority of these movements cannot be considered revolutionist within our definition; their objective was mere replacement or substitution of power rather than the development of truly new institutions and structures. Yet all too often these movements were considered revolutionist, an evaluation based solely on their desire for independence. In any case, local communist parties played a negligible to nonexistent role in this process.

There were several reasons for this inactivity. The first was the willingness of the Soviet Union and, to a lesser extent, Communist China, to acquiesce to the jailing or political banishment of indigenous communist parties. The reluctance of local leaders to accept communist participation was due to their desire to maintain a one-party system which faced no opposition. Both the Soviets and the Chinese have tended to accept this desire, and have consequently refrained from direct aid to fledgling communist parties in Africa. This decision of the two major communist nations has pertained, ironically, to Communist parties in such countries as Algeria, the UAR, Guinea, and Ghana, all of which had originally been considered among the most revolutionist of states, and which received a large part of the Soviet aid allocated for Africa.

Asia posed a different problem: here the influence of, first, the Soviet party and, until the Cultural Revolution, the Chinese party was significant as a revolutionist force in certain countries. The present status of these parties in Asia cannot be generalized, however. In the Democratic Republic of Vietnam (DRV), the Lao Dung party is and has been a revolutionist force, but the influences upon it today are self-generated. The Lao Dung party has also influenced the behavior and character of the National Liberation-Front (NLF) and the movements in Laos (Pathet Lao) and the communist party of Thailand (CPT).

The Chinese-influenced PKI in Indonesia has been weakened by the army's forcible ejection and replacement of Sukarno. Communist party influence in the remainder of non-communist Southeast Asia is marginal and not revolutionist at the present time. The party exists in India and Japan, but plays a role in, and not outside of, the political process. In North Korea, the party is more revolutionist in its direction of external activities than it is internally. Its links to the Chinese party are vague, since considerable evidence exists that the Chinese Communist party as a force in China has been minimal since the Cultural Revolution. But the Chinese party's reconstitution, if engineered by the forces behind the Red Guards, could once again make it a formidable revolutionist organization.

Not all communist parties are revolutionist; at the present time, very few are. They exist, but in many comparative cases their goals are certainly not revolutionist simply because they are communist. When they are revolutionist, their character is different because indigenous ingredients have molded the party into a vehicle for revolutionism. The perception of the former force of monolithic world communism has been superseded by socialist revolutionist nationalisms. Although some revolutionist parties, by adopting Marxist organization principles, resemble the classic organization, their interests are tending to be more pragmatic than ideological.

Revolutionists as States

For revolutionists as states, the revolutionist ideal is the supreme value upon which the legitimacy of the state is predicated. The revolutionist state seeks change in either the domestic or the international milieu, or, upon occasion, in both. It has rejected many of the traditional norms of international life in favor of revolutionist ones which may or may not be obtainable. Such actors view revolution as a vehicle for bettering their position both domestically and abroad. Their satisfaction evolves from the pursuit of revolutionist policies primarily designed to achieve a "place in the sun."

The revolutionist state views itself as the most appropriate vehicle for the symbolic, as well as literal, rebirth and restructuring of its institutions, economy, and society. Rejection of the old was, after all, the *raison d'être* for its appearance and formulation. The evolution of this type of state has generally proceeded from individual to group to state. There is a cumulative experience factor inherent in this transition. It is an important objective of revolutionists to be able to seize control of the state apparatus, for the state, with its powers, can alone bring success to the process of generating something truly new and giving it political structure.

As a historical phenomenon, the revolutionist state is a relatively recent occurrence. While it is true that revolutionary France, in the period between the fall of Louis XVI and the emergence of Napoleon, did constitute an historic example of the revolutionist state, this example was nonetheless a rather short-lived and isolated one when judged by the revolutionist qualities of eighteenth-century France. Although many of the revolutionist ideals and aspirations survived that regime or series of regimes, the international environment in which France found itself was a tightly structured one with a rather homogeneous setting. This environment continued until World War I, when the forces that have shaped and are shaping the present international atmosphere were set into motion.

The Soviet Union emerged onto the world scene and, at least initially under Lenin and the Third International, attempted to project the revolution externally. This effort was unsuccessful, however, because it was confronted by a relatively hostile international environment, and by unsettled domestic conditions as well. After Lenin's death, Stalin sought to strengthen the Soviet Union and chose to operate more through its foreign apparatus than through the Comintern. While the operational milieu still remained hostile, the Lenin-Stalin state was a truly new state. Yet the early recognition that fundamental changes were taking place in the international system did not enable the Soviets to capitalize upon them. In all probability, the reason for this stemmed from two basically different sources. First, the Russian Revolution was a unique event which proved impossible to export. Second, and most important, the other states in the system had not yet adjusted their own way of thinking to a changing environment, and consequently the old, somewhat tired myths retained sufficient resilience to carry the day. By the time the environment became more permissive, the Soviet Union had assumed a greater preoccupation not only with the restraints imposed on her by advanced weapons but also with the rapid advancement of her own economy. The U.S.S.R. thus became a status quo state in the system, at least in the perception of those states that viewed themselves as revolutionist.

In an almost symmetrical sense, the Soviet Union, since its own development of advanced weapons systems, has become less revolutionist at a time when a host of states have become increasingly dedicated to revolution. When it became apparent in the mid-fifties that the "usable-power" inherent in the bipolar nuclear balance was not relevant to most states, the cracks and flaws of the international system created a new permissiveness for states not involved with the new technology. In other words, the level of necessary toleration of deviant states in the system has been raised to a threshold which is the highest in history.

The characteristics of these novel states are based upon a dual perception, consisting of the manner in which they perceive themselves and, in turn, the way that others perceive them.

As States in the Non-West

It is not difficult to discern revolutionists as states in Africa and Asia. The new international order has already been characterized as a crude but vital form of international democracy, as contrasted with the essentially aristocratic state system it is replacing. The entry of dozens of new and small states into active participation in world politics bears similarity to the sudden eruption of the bourgeoisie into post-feudal politics. Like their middle-class predecessors, the new states find the long sanctified aristocratic values of international life irrelevant to their concerns. These states have no roots in the system.

The international political stage has been beset by a virtual horde of new "bit players" whose demands for prominent roles remain unfulfilled. They incorporate a vision of the world which is almost entirely nonpolitical, where distinction among states is to be replaced by cooperative efforts to elevate the misery of the human race. As the level of satisfaction in many of the new states is relatively low, most of these actors are deliberately seeking to alter their conditions. Many have organized along the Marxist model, all are intensely nationalistic, and their attitudes toward the great powers are filled with suspicion and mistrust. However, it is not the existence of these factors alone which accounts for the proliferation of revolutionists among this particular grouping.

An understanding of what defines revolutionists among these states can only follow a discussion concerning the nature of their societies. Upon gaining independence and facing the problem of organizing a society suitable for their new state, the leadership was confronted with two general choices: complete reorganization or, alternatively, acceptance of a partnership between the new and traditional authorities. Those who opted for reorganization were among the most intensely nationalistic, and legitimized their behavior as an attempt to structure genuinely new, or what they believed to be new, institutions founded on their assessment of internal needs and external threat (i.e., "neocolonialism," "neoimperialism"). Such states as Touré's Guinea, Nkrumah's Ghana, Ho Chi Minh's North Vietnam, and Mao's China fit this particular model. The degree to which these states may be termed revolutionist is determined by the intensity of their social reorganization, a process envisioned as necessary to further their respective goals.

The delineator of the revolutionist process initially had more concern for the society than the state. It was mandatory for the state to come into existence, however, before this process could take place. The political objective of the reordering process has been the elimination of competitive elements to the primary organization or party which identified its aspirations with those of the new state. This process, once instigated, has assumed a momentum of its own and, while initially confined to the domestic sphere, provides a revolutionist fervor which has often flooded over into the international arena.

The dynamics of the revolutionist process predominate over static characteristics in the evolving nature of the revolutionist. The factors of time and experience form a matrix with the environment to produce a constantly changing revolutionist. In those cases where the revolutionist undergoes the metamorphosis from individual to organization to state, only the understanding that change is the highest value will assist in comprehending this evolution and its development. This perception is tempered by the process of change. If we do not recognize that the institutions of yesterday do not satisfy today's needs, then we shall be surprised by tomorrow and the revolutionists who may be operative then.

Viewed in this framework, the evolving nature of any revolutionist must be constantly scrutinized for changing trends and characteristics. We must be alert to changes in the conditions which spawned the revolutionist. In addition, altered values and objectives must be detected if they exist, and the ability of the revolutionist to satisfy his goal must be evaluated. In this respect, the level of further change cannot conflict with the level of satisfaction if the former is in predominance. Yet satisfaction may decline in the revolutionist process which is not unidirectional. If a multidirectional process occurs, the revolutionist temper provides the impetus to carry on the revolutionist struggle. The North Vietnam and Communist Chinese revolutionists, and their respective parties, all serve as an illustration of this dynamic.

Only a belief in change, and the necessity for change, is the characteristic which links all revolutionists. When they believe that change is no longer desirable, they are then no longer revolutionists. This occurs when the objective and subjective factors responsible for their emergence disappear or are modified in such a manner as to make them invalid. We have seen this in the case of the Soviet Union where a general level of self-satisfaction, which became sufficiently high during the late fifties, conflicted with the old revolutionist myth to which only lip service was being paid. This phenomenon has been caused by the Soviet perception of threat emanating from the very revolutionists to which it gave birth, rather than from the so-called "enemies" of the revolution.

As individuals, organizations, or states, revolutionists have only one shared characteristic. Many scholars, however, in trying to place these revolutionists into prefabricated models, have formed linkages that do not exist and that have consequently been misleading to student and practitioner alike. Much of this scholarship has been highly colored because it has confused the manifestations of revolutionist behavior with the characteristics of the revolutionist. The concept of revolution is quite different from the tactics involved in the revolutionist process. Revolutionists are difficult to compare because they exist on a conceptual level which is conditioned by local situational and dynamic environmental factors. Attempting comparisons on this level does not increase our understanding of the revolutionist; it can only be comprehended as a model for itself. In this sense, each revolutionist is unique, but the manner in which they all express themselves has common characteristics.

4

•••••• PATTERNS
OF
REVOLUTIONIST
THOUGHT

Contemporary revolutionist thought adds a new contribution to man's philosophical history. While the appeals vary, its essence contains a clarion call to combine thought and action. It is no accident that the major revolutionist theorists are its major practitioners. Mao Tse-tung, Fidel Castro, Ché Guevara, Vo Nguyen Giap, Lin Piao, and Gamal Abdel Nasser are not armchair theorists.

For the most part, revolutionist thought appears empirical and analytical rather than normative. While it seeks converts, its primary purpose is intended for those already converted to the master's teachings; it communicates a message of faith and elucidates the direction that must be taken in its quest. It is not a literature of despair but of hope and fulfillment.

Contemporary revolutionist thought can be traced to Plato, since the image of reality expressed in "The Allegory of the Cave" is a fundamental one in today's milieu. The minor prophets of the Old Testament, the zeal of the New Testament, the writings of Dante and Luther, and the Enlightenment, and Lenin, Karl Marx, and syndicalism, and fascism are benefactors of the revolutionist tradition.

While its lineage spans the history of Western thought, contemporary revolutionist thought differs from that of the past. Its theorists are mainly non-Western and they write about the non-West. They have selected aspects from the Western tradition and placed them in their own operational milieu; they differentiate between revolution as a concept and a tactic as well as between communication as a process and a dialogue. Their theories have an operational alertness heretofore unknown.

Most of present-day revolutionist theorists combine both conceptual and tactical elements in their writings. Their conceptualization is directed at the overlying theory of revolution, and it stresses the particular framework which will give the tactical ploys form and direction. Their tactical schemes concern the means of conflict of revolution: guerrilla, political, and psychological warfare. While all revolutionist theorists advocate these tactics, the latter is not by definition always violent. Even guerrilla warfare can be nonviolent if the conceptual approach stresses such an orientation.

Nonviolent revolutionist activities have always been well planned and executed by the revolutionists themselves. These revolutionists maintain the conviction that the particular path of nonviolence fits the moral teachings advocated by their sponsors. Tactically, nonviolence as a method reflects the perception of *force majeure* and the existence of approbation (domestic as well as international). In many cases, such as in preindependence India and, most recently, in the United States, nonviolence has been utilized to provoke violent responses from the authorities. These responses presumably augment the moral position of the revolutionist and correspondingly downgrade that of the authority he seeks to challenge.

Violence is more representative of contemporary revolutionist experience. Its proponents see no alternative to a violent path and thus adhere to it wholeheartedly. Violent tactics may be divided into two stages: visceral violence, caused in many instances by an extended revolutionist situation; calculated violence, dispassionately planned to effect the desired change. This preplanned use of violence normally signals that the revolutionist has reached the point of no return in his quest for change. Since revolution has frequently been violent, there has been a natural tendency to equate it with violence. Yet Christ, Gandhi, and Martin Luther King were revolutionists who stressed nonviolence.

Whether violent or not, revolutionist theory is goal oriented. Its aim is the transfer of state power which will enable the new recipient to restructure the unit so that it is substantially different from previous entities. If such a plan is not in the theoretical outline, then it is not a revolutionist theory but rather a philosophical or political scheme designed for the present system.

The revolutionist behaves in a highly energized political manner. The key to his behavior can be found in his value orientation: his conviction that change is necessary. This conviction is rooted in a messianic view of what is wrong in the old system. In assessing political systems, there is always an unquantifiable point where the revolutionist will take the leap of faith. As he is a creature of habit, man is reluctant to change his structures except in the most stringent of cases.

Destruction of the old does not necessarily imply that a vision of the new exists. While aspirations for the new but untried is indeed a motivating factor, the most powerful incentive is still the extirpation of the old. Order is readily sacrificed for a particular perception of justice which can only be obtained through the process of revolutionism.

Development of Revolutionist Thought[1]

The infusion of science into the European community during the seventeenth and eighteenth centuries contributed a new facet to revolutionist thinking. The conscience of the West had been exposed to millennial thinking for centuries. The minor prophets of the Old Testament had introduced the idea of transcendent life as an attainable earthly goal. The Middle Ages witnessed a host of chiliastic crusades, all under the banner of imminent parusia. Passages of the Old Testament are replete with eschatological obsession. Notice the mood and implications of the opening of the Book of Micah: "For behold, the Lord is coming forth out of his place/ and will come down and tread upon the high places of the earth/ and mountains will melt under him and the valleys will be cleft like wax before the fire, like waters poured down a steep place/ And this is for the transgression of Jacob and for the sins of the house of Israel."

The religious fanaticism of the Middle Ages was supplanted by a new level of expectation and Sorelian "social myth" that was brought about by the Industrial Revolution. Invention clashed with tradition; and the resulting impact, still being felt in our time, was a reassessment of the foundations of society. Many traditional societies were proven unviable in the face of a new economic order with wide ranging political ramifications. The transformation from peasant to worker and lord to capitalist signalled the doom of traditional Europe.

An additional and alluring force were the democratic credoes ad-

---

[1] The authors acknowledge their debt to Professor J. L. Talmon whose many and distinguished works on political movements have provided them with invaluable insights.

vanced by writers of the Enlightenment. New dogmas, partially based on the heritage of Greek and Christian humanism, identified equality and fraternity as synonymous notions. In their zeal to upset the traditional order, many writers of the period found little validity in the old assumptions of hierarchy, and thus interpreted equality in its most absolute forms as requisites for contemporary thinking. Fraternity was abandoned, and the concept of equality became an enduring myth of Western democracy.

The French Revolution made equality and fraternity coordinates. In so doing, it provided respectability to an exaggerated level of expectation. Equality is a disrupting concept; insofar as human relationship is based upon order, it is order without design. It establishes a meaningless regimentation.

Fraternity directs attention to others, equality to self. And the drive for equality is simultaneous with the growth of egotism. The sense of duty which fraternity stimulates is itself the source of ideal human existence. Where men feel that society means station, the highest and lowest see their efforts satisfying joint requirements of the human condition in harmony rather than in competition.

Rousseau, Montesquieu, and Locke questioned the basic groundwork of societies rooted in antiquity. Their writings were resoundingly applauded by an intellectual audience that decried against the fundamental and outmoded institutions of Europe: the monarchy and the Church. Already thrust into a state of disequilibrium by the Reformation and the two succeeding centuries of unrest, the French Revolution was the culmination of the development of antihierarchic and anticlerical ideas.

The monarchies of the West could no longer remain complacent as the pillars of Europe crumbled under what Hegel termed this "glorious mental breakdown." Napoleon's chant of "liberty, equality, and fraternity"—a curious mixture of inconsistencies with electrifying appeal—heralded the birth of a new social outlook. The ideas of liberalism and socialism—celebrants of man's potential perfection and independence—dominated the nineteenth century. Marxism, anarchism, syndicalism, and fascism offered new interpretations of the Enlightenment ideas, gave unprecedented emphasis to science, and eased the transition from rigid monarchy to the displacement of tradition intrinsic to democracy.

The discordance of the nineteenth century produced a peculiarly anti-Western strain of thought that reacted to the dehumanization and social upheaval that were the consequences of political and economic innovation. The Hegelian outlook, as incorporated in the Marxist philosophy, was a synthesis of antirationalism and antistructuralism. The idea of the self-determining individual was superseded by the position that freedom could be found only in collectivity and that restraint, not self-emancipation, is the elemental desire of mankind. The individual personality could not be fully discerned unless it was viewed in the context of the group. Deviation from established group norms was tantamount to treason—for the meaning of the individual was dependent on conformity and submission.

The eschatalogical nature of Marxism and its concentration on the scientific achievement of the Benthamite ideal of mass happiness distinguishes it from the more moderate and evolutionary goal of the American and French Revolutions. The substance of Marxism is found in history. In the Marxist view there is no meaning, no value, and no reality to human life other than its meaning as an item in the on-going historical process.

Prior to the nineteenth century, revolutionist thought possessed little structural emphasis. To be sure, men such as Paine and Voltaire provided many of the ideas and justifications for their respective revolutions, but plans for the realization of these ideals certainly did not assume an aura of immutable holy writ.

Marx introduced politics into the realm of economics, for he viewed poverty as a political rather than a natural phenomenon as formerly perceived. According to Marx, with the onward march of industrial capitalism, man was being dominated by his products. Marxist theory proposed violent political revolutions as the most efficacious means to terminate this domination. For Marx, economic and political revolutions are inseparable; the former achieved by the political revolution of the working class, is of the highest priority.

The band of trained and dedicated revolutionists projected by Lenin and actualized in the Bolshevik and communist parties is not a concept found in Marx. Lenin proposed the direction of the revolution by a nucleus of revolutionist intellectuals and demanded total commitment from his upperclass leaders of a proletarian movement.

Lenin bypassed the bourgeois democratic state to the soviet of workers, peasants, and soldiers without considering the need to endure all the stages of large-scale capitalist exploitation. He converted a trained band of revolutionists into perpetuation of Party-Government practicing. However, the same secrecy, ruthlessness, and persecution which they had learned as thoroughgoing revolutionists remained prevalent in their actions upon their achievement of the revolution-state and in their attempts at consolidation of the revolution.

For the successful implementation of this revolution, strict party organization and a highly detailed and developed plan are essential. The ultimate goal of the Marxian theory is a collective system, under the auspices of the dictatorship of the proletariat, where each man would produce according to his ability and receive according to his needs.

All of these Marxian concepts sharply contrast to previous revolutionist ideas. The impoverished working masses became the focal point of revolutionist thought for the first time. In contrast, previous revolutions had been implemented mainly by the middle class. For example, one of the main causes of the American Revolution was the fact that political institutions could not keep pace with the changes caused by the rising economic and social ties of the colonial powers. This same situation occurred recently in Algeria.

Previous revolutionist thought had emphasized the ideal of "liberty, equality, and fraternity" as a means of propagating economic and social concepts. The inherent dignity and natural rights of man functioned as the focal points of the theory of those revolutions, as their advocates never tired of pointing out. The Declaration of Independence proclaims: "We hold these truths to be self-evident, that all men are created equal, that they are endowed by their Creator with certain unalienable Rights, that among these are Life, Liberty and the pursuit of Happiness," an affirmation which echoes the Declaration of the Rights of Man and Citizen.

With the coming of the nineteenth century, however, individualism as the focal point of revolutionist programs diminished. Abundance replaced freedom as the motivating force in the progress of revolutionist ideas, for poverty is viewed as a political force of the first magnitude. The life of society and the perpetuation of its process is the highest good, with the individual being regarded as important only so far as he fits into the pattern of the new state.

After the mid-nineteenth century, the articulation of the concept of a highly disciplined and organized mass-based party distinguishes present from past revolutionist thought. Previously, revolutions had never been "designed"; they happened. Although the creators did attempt to give them direction, they possessed no clear-cut plan for organizing and instituting the revolutions.

As a corollary to the concept of the highly organized party, the nineteenth century also gave birth to professional revolutionists. The initiators of previous revolutions for the most part had been men of means whose primary interests were not revolutions. Toward the middle of the nineteenth century, the revolutionist leaders constituted an entirely different entity, for their vocation and avocation were to study and create revolution. Consorting with their own kind, even while in jail or in exile in Europe, they developed and refined their doctrines.

Bolstered by the same forces that popularized Marxism, anarchism reached its full fruition in the nineteenth century. Never an integrated or unified philosophical school, anarchism nevertheless had certain general discernible characteristics, such as civilization of the self. Replete with stratification and authority, the idea of an ordered social system intrinsically violated the natural equality that is the basis of the anarchistic outlook. The fundamental antiparticipatory political nature of anarchism precluded the institution of change from above and destined anarchism to remain outside the realm of viable systemic alternatives.

The anarchist rejected the Hegelian collectivity idea and accepted the highly rationalistic ethics of Kant. The movement was implicitly antitechnological. Echoing the Rousseauian and Thoreauvian tradition, the anarchists rebelled against man's compartmentalization and alienation from the sources of his labor. Not limiting their attack to class as did the socialists, the anarchists saw technology and its by-products as major evils. Anarcho-syndicalism, as an exception to the aloofness of anarchists toward unionism, adhered to the Marxian idea of salvation through organization and the quintessence of worker disaffection—the general strike. The bourgeois state was now to be disrupted more by the proletariat than by the ideologue or peasant.

The origin of syndicalism as a separate philosophy from anarchism is found in the writings of the Paris Commune, Bakunin, and Sorel. Syndicalism resembled anarchism in its rejection of the state and view of imminent revolution by the masses. Revolution was to be accomplished by the general strike, which was to paralyze bourgeois industry and enable the workers to assume control of the state.

This idea of "direct action" was borrowed from the Marxian concept of the eternal clash between the two irreconcilable and heterogeneous classes. The general strike was considered the only alternative to a political structure that systematically excluded the interests of the working class. The strike takes on connotations of a holy crusade, and violence is justified as a requisite for the vision of post-revolutionist millennium.

The major organized expression of syndicalist sentiment was the

Confédération Général du Travail. The Confédération was founded as a temporary but necessary exponent of revolutionist organization; its purpose was simply to channel revolutionist energy until the revolution made politics a phenomenon of the antiquated past.

Another movement that became prominent as a result of the excesses of industrialism was fascism. Rooted in the late nineteenth century, fascism rejected the traditional view of man as a creative and rational thinker, and developed an outlook that subordinated the individual to the state, robbing him of all pretenses to individualism.

Fascist thought embodies a basic distrust of human reason and a denial of human equality. Logical outgrowths of these assumptions are a code of behavior based on violence and lies, government by the elite, national chauvinism, imperialism, and opposition to international law and organization. The fascist state stresses the permanent mobilization for war and, consequently, maintains strict authoritarian relationships in all national and personal affairs. Mussolini said that "war alone brings up to their highest tension all human energies and puts the stamp of nobility on the peoples who have the courage to meet it."

Fascism developed in Europe as a popular philosophy among increasingly impoverished lower-middle class, who feared an economic plunge into the proletariat. It arose as a response to the outward failure of democracy in societies which had a tradition of autocracy. It also sought to fulfill alleged historical national destinies that have been either trampled by other nations or are simply a part of the nation's mythical past.

The nineteenth- and early twentieth-century revolutionist saw man and society not only as changeable but on the verge of imminent transformation as well. The militant zeal and totally uncomprehending nature of their visions are reminiscent of the wars of the Reformation. All millennial movements—religious and political—share a common belief that they embody the last, best hope of mankind.

Revolutionist Thought: The Old and The New

Throughout history, revolutionists have aspired for change and/or progress. Rhetoric aside, for the contemporary revolutionist, progress means emulating Western achievement. Hence his goal has been to grasp the latest developments of Western thought as reflected in liberalism and the parliamentary system.

Western concepts of democracy, freedom, equality, representation, and, above all, the central importance of the people have a powerful appeal to him. However, while their fascination continues to hold, the contemporary revolutionist has given these concepts drastically different forms and meaning.

At first, the dominant model for most revolutionists was that of Western parliamentarianism. However, disillusionment with parliamentary democracy grew within one non-Western country after another, becoming synonymous with corruption, favoritism, factionalism, and continuous political struggle. Wherever such disillusionment occurs, an amalgam of Leninism and fascism emerges, for the situation enables the revolutionist to invoke the broad, theoretical values of democratic forms and practices.

The new state which revolutionists desire to create is based upon a tutelage of the masses by the highly organized elite. Theoretically, the people continue to be the object of worship, the source of supreme authority, the foundation of truth. In practice they become the subjects of intensive indoctrination, of mass mobilization, and of total commitment to the purpose of the state as defined by the vanguard.

The people are forced to participate in politics on a more intensive scale than at any other time in the past. But this organized participation is under the close supervision of the vanguard party. Hence, representation is scientific, participation is vicarious, elections are rituals of support.

Contemporary revolutionists have superimposed a political doctrine on the non-West that posits authentic mass participation in government as a requisite for political legitimacy. The development, however, of a political aristocracy that seeks to delineate, translate, and mobilize mass opinion should not be interpreted as a failure of parliamentarianism. Even in the West, parliamentary and representative government remains more of an ideal than a common practice. Philosophical commitment to representative government does not mean that the political environment or public state of mind will be receptive to such a radical departure from a more autocratic tradition. This pattern is remarkably reminiscent of that experienced in the West. Only Westerners with little appreciation for their past can superciliously condemn non-Westerners for being unable to implement parliamentary democracy.

Contemporary revolutionist thought assesses man in terms of his utility to the collective. Man is viewed as a series of groups, i.e., nations, classes, and religions. There are many corollaries growing from this assumption, but this perception is central. Revolutionists view the people as groups—"the masses," the peasants, enemies, and followers.

The revolutionist of today calls for unity and for voluntary, or even forced, supression of individualism. Nasser puts it this way: "Political revolution demands, for its success, the unity of all national elements, their fusion and mutual support, as well as self-denial for the sake of the country as a whole."[2]

A major corollary of this is the view of man as either good or bad. The familiar example of charges levelled against "counter-revolutionaries" illustrates this assumption. Lin Piao talks of "U.S. imperialism and its lackeys" and calls for a never-ending struggle against them, as though they were all-evil.[3]

Modern revolutionists speak fondly of the masses, instead of man or the individual. Lin Piao speaks for all revolutionists: "In order to win a people's war, it is imperative to build the broadest possible united front and formulate a series of policies which will ensure the fullest mobilization of the basic masses as well as the unity of all the forces than can be united."[4]

Why and how the masses act is another question entirely. The leaders tell the masses that their movement is spontaneous. Lin Piao continues:

> The liberation of the masses is accomplished by the masses themselves— this is a basic principle of Marxism-Leninism. Revolution is people's war in any country and should be carried out primarily by their own efforts; there is no other way.[5]

The leader tells his followers that the masses can achieve social consciousness and are capable of governing themselves. He, however, believes that they require leadership, and recognizes their natural submission to leadership in any form.

To stir the masses, the leader must convince them that they are being oppressed; hence, the overuse of that term and the amusing attempt of intelligentsia to call themselves workers in order to promote identification with the masses. Propaganda becomes a central function of modern revolution, and only with modern communication can revolution succeed. It becomes the task of the revolutionist to bring the

[2] Gamal Abdel Nasser, *The Philosophy of the Revolution* (Washington, D.C.: Public Affairs Press, 1955), pp. 36–37.

[3] Lin Piao, *Long Live the Victory of the People's War* (Washington, D.C.: Foreign Broadcast Information Service, 1965), p. 4.

[4] *Ibid.*, p. 12.

[5] *Ibid.*, p. 38.

masses to submit to him rather than to the old order. He does this by disrupting the old order and perpetuating the revolutionist process.

The revolutionist sees an intrinsic value in revolution itself. Nkrumah lost sight of his powerbase in the joy of promoting social change. Ché Guevara went on to other nations and death. Most revolutions claim to remain such even after achievement and institutionalization. Revolutionist elites want to preserve the momentum and the power of the revolution.

The leaders must guard against the feeling of revolution for its own sake on the part of their followers. There is a joy in being out of power—escapism. If the revolutionists become escapists, the power will not come to their leaders. For the leaders themselves, overidealism will lead to disillusionment, with its inherent dangers.

A corollary to the assumption of revolution as a value in itself is revolution as an emotional experience. The essential difference between reform and revolution is most probably the emotional involvement of its participants, not the changes desired. Emotions are expressed in violence, which becomes a symbol of revolution. Violence is not essential to revolution, but there is a probable relationship.

If we accept that the revolutionist changes may not be fundamental, and that revolution is actually an emotional experience, then the societal value of violence and revolution is a purge of fire—a refining process. For the individual in society, it is an emotional rebirth or renewal of relationship.

In contemporary revolution, terror is directed at the people as a whole. For example, organized terror suppressed counter-revolutionists between 1950 and 1953 in China. Widely publicized Chinese suppression ended with large-scale executions, for Mass Accusation Meetings had inflamed the public for mass executions.

The behavior of the revolutionists in their attempts to seize and consolidate power undoubtedly is one of the characteristics of present revolution that has not been affected by Marxism or previous revolutionist thought. Although contemporary revolutionists have usually been more systematic and thorough at this stage, all revolutionists appear to engage in strict surveillance of the participants, both morally and politically, so that all effort and concentration is directed toward the revolution of ideas and objectives. The banning of smoking, campaigns against alcohol, the censorship of the press, and the secret police are only a few evidences of such practices. When the revolutionist state has become relatively institutionalized, these restrictions are relaxed. Yet a period of dictatorial authority is established before this institutionalization is achieved.

The domestic political environment of revolutionists has been especially conducive to the emergence of small groups of elites who hold effective control of national affairs. Such centralization of power has had obvious effects on the structure and processes of their political life. This increase of personal power is partly the result of the lack of a trained bureaucracy. In the absence of competent subordinates, revolutionists assume personal responsibility for governmental action and are bound to accumulate extensive personal power. Such inordinate power concentrated in the hands of a revolutionist leader and his personal clique leads to a policy-making process which is nearly always arbitrary. Without a competent bureaucracy, policy decisions are made without regard for differing points of view. There is often little opportunity for the transmission of information which does not support the position of the revolutionist elite. It is obvious that policy decisions made in such an operational vacuum bear no relevance to actual situations and are destructive of ultimate objectives.

Revolutionists stress national and political unity as being necessary for development and, in doing so, denounce factionalism. But unity must be predicated upon an active national consciousness, a broad popular consensus, and a homogeneity which are missing from the scene. Ethnic, geographical, social, economic, and historical diversity lead to political regionalism which is in direct contradiction to unity. Factionalism abounds, and the various groups too often think and act in mutually exclusive "we" and "they" terms. The spirit of coalition and cooperation is generally lost under such conditions; democracy is interpreted as majority rule with minority exclusion. It is obvious that such assumptions can easily lead to destructive political in-fighting and to governmental suppression of the opposition. Although it is the task of the governments to unite rival factions, men in power are greatly tempted to impose from above a consensus which generally reflects their own or their party's position.

In adopting the most obvious of democracy's tactics, majority rule, revolutionists overlooked its corollary: minority participation in the decision-making process. Rival and opposition groups are suppressed simply because they challenge the "in" position of the ruling party. Yet it could also be argued that the reason they challenge the ruling party's position is precisely because they are totally excluded from the government. Where coalition and interparty cooperation are generally ignored, the opposition is forced to turn to obstructionism, if not outright revolution or secession.

In such a political environment, the uneducated masses play a primary role. Linking progress (or the lack of it) to the party in power becomes the main occupation of the ruling and opposing groups. Eventually the party finds it necessary to establish itself as the only legal party, thereby further distorting the political process.

It should be obvious that such situations are highly unstable. Instead of actual elections, polling is reduced to simple referendum. Real changes in government become possible only through *coup d'état* and assassination. The ruling groups resort to further suppression in an effort to retain control. But, in so doing, they completely transform the democratic concept of rule by majority into an authoritarian tyranny of a self-declared majority, actual or not.

Contemporary Revolutionist Doctrine

Contemporary revolutionist doctrine is nationalist, antisupremacist, and socialist. Its edifice is a multiform of differences. There is no blueprint for world revolution. The principal universal element in contemporary revolutionist thought is man's articulation of faith and his hope for rebirth—it is his determination to move his superstitions from the realm of theology to that of politics. In the contemporary environment, as in the past, it is man's reaffirmation of his existence.

The revolutionist's romanticized versions of past greatness and of the traditional values of his society include an idealized picture of individual freedom in a sort of pure, primitive democracy. The symbols of status, wealth, power, and prestige are declared alien to his society, primarily because these elements have been introduced by foreign powers and have caused a corruption of the basic culture.

The revolutionists' concept of nationalism ranges the full spectrum from tribal factionalism, the blind fanaticism of terrorist groups, the racism of absolute superiority, to supranational Panism. It is factional, yet federal. It is reactionary, but also radical. No two revolutionists envisage the same nationalist goals, and their concepts of organization, development, and democracy are unclear. In some cases nationalism is seen as a means of recapturing a romanticized history, while in others its primary emphasis is on the immediate and future problems of building modern states. It is a refutation of what foreigners, whites, and Westerners have been saying about them for centuries, and it proves that they can and will take their rightful place in the world. It offers a means of proving to the revolutionist that their inferiority was not a fact, but an enforced foreign myth. Nationalism also provides part of the spirit and drive necessary for the achievement of what is seen as a specifically national well-being. Despite their emulation of Western technology and progress, there is a fundamental desire to avoid the materialist/neurotic by-products of technology that have radically transformed Western thinking since the onset of the Industrial Revolution.

One way that the revolutionist can overcome this enforced inferiority in a Western and white man's world is to exclude "them" from his states, create a new nation, develop a modern society, and act in concert with other revolutionists at home and abroad—all these things to prove that he is just as competent as Westerners and whites in anything that he attempts. The inferiority which was forced upon him has left a deep emotional scar; it is causing him to assert repeatedly his nationalism today to prove that he really is what he is not: modern, progressive, and flexible.

These facts give a visionary quality to the nationalist expressions of the revolutionists. Their nationalisms generally lean to the grandiose and dreamy side of life. They are untroubled by the incompatibility of ideas tinged with reactionism. Through nationalism, they recoil from the trials of modern existence and assume an attitude of admiration, self-containment, and exclusiveness. In this context, nationalism is a tool of disengagement which reverberates the defiance and resentment born of their present frustrations.

In the West, revolutionists found institutions to be emulated, one of the most obvious being the Western nation-state. The achievement and maintenance of national unity and independence became their central values. They assumed the cloak of Western nationalism in their independence movements. But Western thought and values had not penetrated deeply enough to give these leaders a grasp of the principles upon which the nation-state rests. They assumed only the outward manifestations, the language and apparatus of statehood, but the real bases for unity were ignored.

The application of these standards to their situation, where national consciousness hardly exists, has been very difficult. The dichotomy between freedom and authority has virtually necessitated the consolidation of power at the expense of individual freedom. No matter how they are spoken of and pointed to by the revolutionists, the conditions of Western democracy do not exist in their societies.

Revolutionists are the mediators between the old and the new. They are usually products of the modernization and education which have not yet touched the mass of their countrymen. They must set the ends and employ the means of modernization. Yet the values and techniques which they have adopted are often inappropriate to their traditional societies.

In their own lands they are strangers, subverting the existing order and society. They quite naturally want to change it in order to satisfy their own needs. Their desire for changes is in part a narrow personal wish, but it is rooted in an intense desire to bring the "better" life which they have seen elsewhere to their own countrymen. However, the amount of change needed to lead to political and cultural awakening necessarily disrupts orderly transition. The endeavor to create a united nation-state through common effort usually runs into traditional patterns which strengthen factionalism and division.

It is here that the concept of antisupremacy is realized. Anti-supremacism serves the double purpose of creating a rationale for nationalist desires and a mass support for performing the role of the revolutionist. Twentieth-century nationalism, rooted primarily in anti-colonialism, needed something positive which could structure the principally negative movement against the colonial powers. It needed anything which could give purpose, direction, and force to the "morning after independence."

In the past, the societies about which revolutionists spoke were denied racial equality and national political freedom. They claim that this forced inferiority stifled the creativity and dynamism of their people. They resent the barriers of Western power and white superiority which barred them from participating in the international system. They demand equality more and more loudly. They would prove themselves only if given the opportunity; whites and Western peoples' thought dominate them. Gradually, the drive for acceptance and racial equality developed into a revolutionist movement. Nonwhite and non-Western characteristics were proclaimed to be the framework of a unique personality, something to be proud of, not to be hidden under a cloak of shame. What began as an attempt to give the revolutionists a sense of personal worth and self-respect rapidly changed into an emotional reaction to white and Western domination which could easily be distorted into non-Western racism and extremism.

As the basic ingredient of nationalism, antisupremacy serves two primary functions. It provides the unity and support necessary for a successful liberation movement in areas still under great power domination; and it provides the perceived common threat which revolutionist actors invoke to preserve their domestic and international positions. It must be remembered that revolutionists gained their independence at a time when sovereignty had become compromised by the technological necessities of interdependence. Self-sufficiency was not possible, no matter how passionately sought. As the ideals of this nationalist movement were comprised by the realities of the situation, ambitions remained unfulfilled and the new states were beset by problems of development.

Proceeding from the premise of equated West-white supremacy and capitalism, it is asserted that these interests continue in a post-independence attempt to exert *de facto* political power by economic means. They see that the independence and progress of the new states are threatened by continued foreign economic domination. This form of covert control is denounced as the direct cause of the immediate failures of the post-independence period.

At the same time that many revolutionists are passionately derogating these interests, they are actively attempting to imitate Western achievements. In such cases antisupremacy provides a convenient screen for their contradictory attempts to achieve what they believe to be the hallmark of modern statehood.

Mass poverty is the revolutionist's predicament. The lack of relevant skills and managerial talents, inordinate income differentials, medical pluralism, and the desire to overcome a Marxian, colonial self-image are the intertwined problems of the revolutionist's society.

Socialism has become the a priori solution for the revolutionist's maladies. He believes that without such generic ideology, there could be no consistent response to social needs. He asserts that economic, political, and social reforms can be best advanced when his society becomes ordered by common ideological principles.

Revolutionists believe that socialism will arise from the conviction of the majority that it answers the need for a moral and just social order. The elevation of human dignity, the provision of social justice, and the equality of opportunity are foremost among social values. To fulfill these, revolutionists advocate the elimination of class distinction and privilege. They emphasize that this can be accomplished without violence and class warfare. Marx's assumption that capitalism necessarily leads to the impoverishment of the working class is not acceptable to most of the revolutionists. They assume that it is more likely for the proletariat to become indistinguishable from the middle class than for the middle class to fall into the proletariat.

Socialism is a program as comprehensive as the revolutionist's problems. Although it emphasizes improving the lot of workers and peasants, it gives more consideration to the problems of the latter because of the agrarian base of nonindustrialized states. While it believes in democracy and individual freedom, it invokes state power more often than do Western socialists, because the revolutionist's world is in a less advanced stage of political consolidation. Socialism is concerned primarily with agriculture, national unity, and international politics.

The revolutionists view capital formulation and accumulation as a responsibility of the government. It is possible for a centralized government agency to aid in the formation of institutions which will permit capital growth at the same time that it will maintain careful control over the use of that capital. Governmental manipulation and planning are very much a part of the socialist program. However, their situation necessitates a degree of flexibility to make possible the most effective use of resources and capital at the same time that a socialist basis is established for society. The role of governments in encouraging private investment can be almost infinitely varied, as can the degree and range of governmental controls and planning.

Most of the revolutionists have inherited a one-crop agricultural economy from colonial days; they are actively committed to industrialization and to a reduction of continued economic dependence on a metropolitan power. Such a dependency on revenues from a fixed market leads to problems that must be solved pragmatically. They have a vested interest in continuing good relations with the metropolitan states, both to assure continued imports and to gain the influx of much needed capital and trained personnel. They readily accept a mixed economy, which unites central planning, state operations, joint state-private enterprises, private enterprises cooperatives, and state controls over profits and reinvestment.

Virtually all revolutionists are confronted with serious post-independence problems of control, which are a direct result of the drive for independence and for economic and political development. Foremost among these problems are gaining and maintaining strong public support for continued economic activities that will aid in capital formation and accumulation without creating new economic, political, and social imbalances in already precarious situations.

In the realm of control, the socialists' program functions much the same as nationalism did before independence. It stresses the basic unity of the state's population, and it tries to imbue the whole population with the desire to work and cooperate in programs of economic development. Such popular support and unity is necessary for the establishment of socialized, independent, and industrialized states. People must be intimately involved, or development and stability will not follow. Most revolutionists are firmly convinced of this, though the means of gaining support and involvement may vary radically from state to state.

Socialism is trying to create in all elements of the population a will to work, to sacrifice, and to cooperate. It is trying to transfer traditional loyalties to the larger unit of the nation-state, and to mobilize energy and resources for the good of the state and its citizens. It has the unifying goal of sacrifice and work by the individual, not for selfish gain, but for the good of the collectivity.

The revolutionist's self-image is collectivist and egalitarian. He asserts that only in a society based upon such principles can the individual find fulfillment. Such a society is seen as having a collective mind which conditions the behavior of all individuals in it. This collective mind, similar to Rousseau's concept of the general will, gives the society the right to force individual deference to the collectivity. This strong assertion of egalitarianism, when united with the assertion of classlessness, defines political rights which do not flow from wealth, status, or power, but are and must be equal for all members of society.

Socialism serves another very important purpose for the revolutionist. It helps to define an important role for him between East and West. Both Marxism *per se* and capitalism are generally discarded as inapplicable to his conditions. Socialism thus lends itself to the politics of nonalignment and speaks with an independence of mind which augurs an independence of action.

It is important to point out that while many people in the West do not make the distinction between revolutionist socialism as a program of "development" and Leninism as an organizational process for change, revolutionists themselves do.

Most revolutionists are, if we delve beneath their rhetoric, impressed by the achievements of the Western world. They attempt—whether consciously or not—to assimilate the fruits of that civilization into the frameworks of their own states. However, with regard to an organizational structure and developmental process, they have turned to Leninism and militarism.

5

•••••• **REVOLUTIONIST VISIONS AND MODELS**

No other factor has influenced the contemporary era more than revolutionism, for its spirit extends from the urban areas of the United States to the coasts of Asia, from the jungles of Latin America to the Arab world, to Africa. Its proponents include revolutionists of all nationalities, backgrounds, and styles. Its thoughts differ, but they are united by a common desire for change which cannot be accommodated within the context of the established political process.

The specifics of revolutionism are unique to an area and are firmly rooted in its socio-economic milieu. The search for a master factor or analytic philosopher's stone is therefore futile. If in the past little has been written which can account for the revolutionist process, it is because one must examine dissimilarities as well as similarities. Different geographical areas deserve different treatment.

From an analytical viewpoint, this lack of a single model for revolutionism limits the range of inquiry. Since there are as many models as experiences, contemporary revolutionist activities can only be evaluated on a case-by-case basis. The case study methodology, however, is only relevant for the specific situation under examination. Many have been led down a path hazardous with pitfalls because of the virtual absence of identity which characterizes contemporary manifestations of revolutionist experience. Guerrilla, political, and psychological warfare are visible components of each revolution's action program, but they do not constitute the essence of its experience.

In an ideological model, these components are integrated and structured so that the action program supports and secures the objectives of the revolution. The waging of the revolutionist campaign should not be considered as an objective *per se*, but rather as the means or the vehicle of revolution. It should also be noted that these are elements which tend to receive the most study when the subject of revolution has remained predominantly obscured.

When viewed separately, neither guerrilla, nor political, nor psychological warfare could be considered revolutionist. It is the combination of these three elements that constitutes revolutionist warfare from the tactical viewpoint. The experience of Ché Guevara in Bolivia, where there was inadequate political and psychological preparation, illustrates the ineffectuality of guerrilla warfare when conducted in a vacuum. However, there have been many types of revolutionist warfare where the three components have been combined in differing proportions and degrees. The extent and composition of this combination have been determined by the revolutionist's perception of the operational situation and the degree of exertion required to alter it. It has been relatively impossible to transplant models of revolutionism from one environment to another.

There are many factors which account for this particular difficulty. The most significant ones are derived from an individual operational assessment which stresses the specific combination of tactics to be used. Unsuccessful operations by revolutionists who demonstrate little understanding of their own situation tend to be initiated in areas where they have lacked relevance. From this viewpoint, a tactical prerequisite must be an appraisal of the political and societal flaws which have caused the conviction that the old order must be destroyed.

It is more useful to analyze the fundamental flaws of a society than the manifestations of its corruption. Compilation of catalogues of specific grievances is valuable only when the origins of these grievances are taken into account. There are grievances, both articulated and unarticulated, in many societies; but the revolutionist temper is absent because their institutions are not lacking in perceived relevance. When the grievances are based on the irrelevance of the basic structural beliefs, a revolutionist situation emerges. Once discredited, the old myths cannot be revived or restored. Viewed from this perspective, revolution may be examined as a competition for replacement of the myths and values which structure the society.

Another generic model of revolutionism which has recently resurfaced is that of anarchism. Displaying deep roots in the late eighteenth and nineteenth centuries, anarchist models are linked to an overromanticized notion of the nature of man. A corpus of thought from Proudhon and Bakunin advocates the reduction of authority and of the governments which enforce it. Most anarchists emphasize the destruction of structures which would be replaced by individual effort. Viewing political behavior with both mistrust and apprehension, the anarchist seeks an order based on the individual because that of the community has no meaning to him.

The anarchist model, seeking the destruction of order and justice, envisions the will of the individual as the only legitimate guide to action. In the most dogmatic terms, the anarchist pursues change for the sake of change. The contemporary tactics of anarchism stress the objective of destroying the irrelevant status quo. Since its current manifestations have been observed primarily in American and European groups, anarchism certainly does not lend itself to the themes of revolutionism which are charged with a high degree of programmatic political content. A linkage between contemporary anarchists and revolutionists can be demonstrated, since both desire destruction of the old. Yet the former seeks a dispersion of power and the breakdown of society, while the latter stresses power transfer.

Unfortunately, more scholarly energy has been expended on the techniques of revolution than on the actual phenomenon itself. The revolution in China, for example, provides little insight about Castro's revolution. Although a revolutionist mix was utilized in both situations, the environment as well as the proportion of ingredients differed greatly. The Malayan experience differs from the Vietnam conflict; each one of the situations introduces a new chapter in the art of revolutionism. If revolution is to be understood, it must be viewed within the framework of its own distinctive terms.

It must be determined what it is that is irrelevant in the old structures. Although every revolution has been against something within a system, the actual reason that revolution occurs, however, is that the system could not accommodate or accept the demand for change. From a logical vantage point, this change should be articulated in a program which stresses the extent and direction of the proposed change. While most revolutionist manifestos have contained these programs, several have not. With increasing frequency, the sole prescription of revolutionist programs, particularly by revolutionists having low tolerability of the traditional order, is that the old should be eliminated. Replacement becomes an issue only after this is accomplished.

Scope and Dimension

Until the Russian Revolution of 1917, revolutionists who sought to modernize and industrialize had available to them only one comprehensive blueprint for development: nineteenth-century capitalism. The Bolshevik Revolution of 1917, however, brought with it an alternative blueprint, i.e., Marxism-Leninism, as a model of development.

Revolutionists have before them the success story of a Marxist-Leninist society. They can point with some justification to the development of the Soviet Union over the past decades and can conclude that were it not for their Leninist organization, the extensive development which the Soviets have achieved would not have occurred. Of course, in saying that Russia in 1917 was a totally backward, agrarian, peasant state, they neglect embarrassing facts. Pre-Bolshevik Russia had already constructed an infrastructure for development. Nonetheless, the Soviet Union has certainly impressed revolutionist actors. The Communist Chinese experience has acted both to modify and strengthen this image.

Impatient to achieve their goals and to realize development, unimpressed with the capitalist model of nation-building, revolutionists have rejected a considerable portion of the Western organizational process of development. While most revolutionists reject Marxist economics, they favor the centralization of power and authority within a Leninist model of a one-party system.

It should be understood that most revolutionists have not adopted a purely Leninist model. They are reshaping the export to fit their own unique frameworks, traditions, and modes of life. They are seeking to adopt the "relevant" and the "desirable" so as to achieve their own ends and goals in their own fashion. They are borrowing from both East and West—revising and readjusting in order to meet their own needs. Impatience, the desire for rapid development, the lack of an agreed upon criterion, and the search for dignity and status, all account for many of these contradictory choices and decisions.

The United States of America

Although United States history is replete with radical movements, the contemporary dimension is new. This is reflected in the youth of its practitioners. If this is something to be done by those under thirty in the United States, revolutionists in other areas are far older. Their triumphs as well as frustrations are more durable. In a sense, revolutionists in the Arab world or Africa know what to expect within broad parameters. Those in the United States do not, and herein lies the difference. This is a new phenomenon in the United States, where the degree of real revolutionist commitment over a sustained period of time is simply unknown.

One of the few accepted hypotheses of political theorists from Aristotle to Gabriel Almond is that political systems are characteristic expressions of their socio-economic settings. The Marxian assumption, that political man is economic man in disguise, is simply a doctrinaire formalization of this hypothesis. Historically, man's political responses to the socio-economic "facts of life" have been to a degree Pavlovian.

Nevertheless, man ultimately relates himself to these facts of life by creating myths. Myth both shields and makes comprehensible the realities of social life. Political society is sanctioned invariably by myth. Even such theorists as Hobbes and Locke, who appeal to reason as a basis of political society, posit "rational man" and "natural rights" in leaps of faith.

The myth of American politics, the liberal-democratic ethos, has been described variously as the American "genius" by Daniel Boorstin and the "liberal tradition" by Louis Hartz. Boorstin and Hartz have diagnosed a quality peculiar to America: its national political tradition has remained within the hazy bounds of the liberal-democratic faith. Nevertheless, contrary to its intimations, America is not the "city of God"; it is no spiritual kingdom of everlasting love (or consensus).

America's uniqueness is that traditionally it has belied the Marxian dictum that political man and economic man are synonomous. In fact, America's political dialogue has been conducted in a sacred vein. As a corollary, the American political myth, as institutionalized in the political system, has failed to reflect the socio-economic dimensions of American life. In the period since the Civil War, characterized by those secular phenomena—the revolutions in urbanization, industrialization, and immigration—there has been a divorce between the challenges of the socio-economic facts of life and the responses of the political system. Even in the 1930s the response of the political system was inadequate to the crisis in the socio-economic order. This almost total failure of the political Pavlovian reflex has been both a blessing and a curse.

The myth has been a blessing because, again contrary to the Marxian assumption, the consequence of myth is not solely alienation; that is, the myth of American politics has been creative as well as de-lusive of reality. The myth has endowed American life with a tradition of political freedom and stability unparalleled by any society, including the British. The American political system has never reflected the manifold socio-economic needs and splits which, having been articulated in many lands since 1789, have generated cycles of revolution and reaction. The situation of men possessing socio-economic power without political power, which de Tocqueville saw as the prelude to the revolution in France, has been inverted in America; ever since the foundation of the Republic, political power has been diffused on the basis of an evolving interpretation of the liberal-democratic myth of human rights, rather than on the basis of ascribed or achieved socio-economic status. Consequently, the American socio-economic order has been cemented into a politically homogeneous monolith. In other words, the myth has been the substance of American political consensus.

The myth has been a curse because, possessing a compulsion in political life which truth lacks, it has confounded appearance and reality. Americans believe that the myth reflects the quality of their society and is a relevant guide for political action. They elevate their mythical postulates to the rank of scientific laws for political freedom and stability and prescribe them at random to an errant world. Public officials are elected to articulate and guard the myth; the sincerity of a politician catering to the general will is a political asset.

Self-interest, even in its crass form, cynicism, is alien to this mythical political world of ritualistic adherence to an absolute faith. Where transcendent absolutes rather than the ideologies of competing factions are the bases of political life, how can men recognize, let alone pursue, self-interest? Beyond cynicism, political man in America is a hypocrite inhabiting a world of self-deception and self-fulfilling prophecies. It is therefore understandable that the American lacks the acumen to recognize his predicament: never before has the dissolution of a myth, the basis of American uniqueness, appeared as imminent as it does today. The consensus upon which uniqueness depends did survive the challenge of rapid industrialization and urbanization surrounding the Civil War, the second wave of immigrants, and the Great Depression. Today it is being strained and perhaps will be fragmented by the Black Revolution.

The black's demand for access to the mainstream of American life is causing some Americans to repudiate the myth. Those who perceive their status threatened by blacks are falling back upon what they consider to be their more reliable affiliations. They become "whites," "white Protestants," Irishmen, or Lithuanians, asserting identities which were thought to have been diluted in the "melting pot," if not shed in the "transmuting pot." They join with those to whom they feel safe granting equal rights and duties; but this number does not include those of alien identities—today, particularly blacks.

The exploitation of the blacks during the heyday of the American political myth was undeniable, yet, as has been discussed, understandable hypocrisy. Activists in the Black Revolution imagine one of their most compelling weapons to be the exposition of the facts of black life to the glaring light of American principles. By the ostensibly innocent act of revealing hypocrisy, however, activists, such as the Black Panthers, have begun a witch hunt that might prove to be nihilistic.

To purge American political society of its hypocrisies is to assault the myth which transforms more than 200 million individuals into a political society. It is to denude American political man of those rights and duties which cloak his truly inalienable attributes: his objective identity and his biological passions. The discrepancies between mythical America and the plight of the blacks—hypocrisy—perhaps is the price of preserving the American myth.

In the South it would seem that, given a heavy infusion of Jeffersonian agrarianism, the myth still can be twisted to rationalize the exploitation of the black. In recent years, however, the whites in Northern cities have found hypocrisy a burden and defy publically the American political myth.

If the response of whites to the Black Revolution is to be a spiralling factionalism and repudiation of the liberal-democratic ethos, American consensus will be forfeited. Were several groups in American society to desert the myth, others might be compelled to follow. It is almost axiomatic that the few, and not the many, initiate the dynamics of political life. As medieval Christendom disintegrated finally into ethnocentrism, so might the seamless web of American political life unwind to reveal a discordant pluralism lacking any transcendent myth; American uniqueness would vanish.

Then the black man would lose the one source to which he can appeal for his "rights." Rights are derived only through participation in a society whose political myth allows them to be granted. Herein lies the black's dilemma: when he claims the rights he has been told he possesses, he fractures the consensus upon which the myth depends for its very existence.

Does the integrity of the myth, it might be asked extraneously, depend upon the black's resignation to his traditional lot?

Evidently, some might retort, the Irishman, Italian, and Jew found a status in the indigenous society when he arrived around the turn of the twentieth century. Yet, he was tolerated, it might be suggested, only because he could be integrated functionally into the American socio-economic system. Further, this functional integration precluded his entrance into certain spheres of American life reserved to the dominant groups.

A less auspicious situation confronts the black. Unlike members of other minorities, he seeks entrance to the socio-economic dimensions of the indigenous society at a time when automation and bureaucratization are making men generally, and the unaccultured in particular, superfluous. And it scarcely needs to be said that to a greater degree than other minorities, the black lacks cultural and physical affinity with the dominant groups.

Closely associated with the nonrevolutionist temper of revolutionism in the United States is an amorphous group known as the New Left. While united by a common belief that change is needed, and by general agreement on the tone that should be taken regarding certain major issues, the members of the New Left are nevertheless split as to objectives, the means for their attainment, and their priority of emphasis. Throughout the twentieth century, there has always been a group on the Left, which has invariably tended to be both issue- and cause-oriented. Prior to World War I, the issues generally turned on labor problems; the emphasis between the wars was directed to socialist economic reforms, many of which were associated with the Depression while some were simultaneously characterized by a flirtation with communism. During the present decade, the issues have been concerned with international and domestic relations, as well as with the relationship of the individual to the state.

The New Left of the present may be differentiated from the Old Left by its involvement with the major issues of American life. Indeed, it was the surfacing of these issues that enabled the Left, after being dormant for over a decade, to become once again a highly audible and visible part of the political culture. Domestically, the New Left has been more concerned with policy regarding poverty than with civil rights. While they see a connecting link between the two issues, they have nonetheless been interested in economic alternatives to the poverty culture of the less privileged Americans. Their thesis has been grounded on the postulate that alleviating the conditions of poverty will enhance prospects relating to civil rights.

In this respect, the New Left and Black Power groups view domestic programs from different perspectives. While the former tend to view these programs from a socialist viewpoint, the latter are highly concerned with promoting their cause as a special interest. Since the New Left is not ideologically committed to the concept of Black Power, few blacks can identify with its aspirations and they tend to exhibit a neutral or hostile attitude toward its socialist programs.

The other major issue concerns the international relations of the United States and its concomitant role as a major power. More specifically, the New Left has launched a crusade against the Vietnam conflict. On a larger scale, it has utilized Vietnam as a springboard to question the relevance of the political system as well as of United States foreign involvement in general. Some of this has occurred as a result of new interpretations regarding the first decade and a half of the cold war; revisionist historians have now claimed that it was the United States rather than the U.S.S.R. which was the provocative power. Their conclusion, in this respect, has been highly cause-oriented: their purpose has been to influence foreign roles which have proven offensive to them. If the involvement in Vietnam has highlighted the New Left's concern with United States foreign policy, this same involvement has also increased their intense concern with the relationship of the individual to the state. It has questioned assumptions relating to the necessity of individual obligations to the state and, in so doing, has interwoven the Vietnam conflict with one of these obligations embodied in the draft. This, coupled with the concern for the relationship of the individual to technology and its state-oriented uses, has caused them both frustration and anger.

The issue of individual conscience versus the public ethic has compelled the New Left to adopt policies emphasizing the former at the expense of the latter. This confrontation has been raised to the philosophical plane by Herbert Marcuse and applied on the action level by a host of diverse personalities including Benjamin Spock and William Sloane Coffin. Closely identified with this issue is the attitude of permissiveness that pervades the society. Attitudes based on the premise that "anything goes" so long as it conforms to the individual's belief of what is right, tend to condone behavior whose only norms are individualistic.

This has created problems for the American myth as well as for its societal institutions. The deep probing and agitation of the liberal ethos has caused many of the New Left to lose faith in the system. Indeed, the most militant among them are the revolutionists whose antecedents can only be linked to the nineteenth-century anarchists rather than to twentieth-century programmatic reformers. While the more prominent members of the New Left have no revolutionist illusions at this time, such neoanarchism still cannot be definitely ruled out. The logical extensions of their thought and action may create the social gap that would indicate the environment's readiness for a revolutionist thrust. When viewed in this perspective, the New Left projects the impression that they are not only waiting for the revolutionist circumstance in the style of Lenin, but also are trying to create that moment in the style of Mao.

By making the invisible visible, the New Left has deepened the public cleavages in American society. While it has not yet created a revolutionist situation, constant attacks on the American ethos, the political system, and its institutions could result in a revolutionist atmosphere. The extension of its advocacy, which is based on change, is of course revolution—something truly novel. At the present time, the dual dilemma of the members of the New Left is that of all intellectual revolutionists—the direction of the revolution once it is realized and whether or not they will be among its first victims.

Like the New Left, the current student protest is both cynical and idealistic. It is a function of intense concern over social and political inequities as well as of a solitary desire to provoke consternation among and thus to disrupt the staid and "stagnant" older generations. There are issues at stake that have acquired great salience in the students' perception of the world they live in.

While social and political inequities are old facts, they were not translated into issues during the 1950s. Then, college students were silent and apathetic. Their disregard of any type of political involvement was near total. At the beginning of the 1960s new issues were made out of old facts. These issues were exacerbating enough to merit political concern and action. The necessity for their rectification had been revealed and the cure had been discovered. Two events that occurred in 1960 delineate the apathy of the students of the 1950s and the diametrical commitment of the student protest of the present.

The civil rights movement in Greensboro, N.C., manifested in the sit-ins of February, 1960, revealed to students the extent of prejudice and inequality in a society that they had formerly accepted as humane and equitable. The election of John F. Kennedy in the same year and his promise for reform imparted to the nation, and to students in particular, a feeling of the necessity for change. While the first event alerted students to the need for reform, the second provided them with the opportunity to do so. In addition, this second event seemed to reinforce the first, for once again it apeared to sanction the civil rights movement as legitimate and necessary. This movement, in turn, was of assistance to its benefactor, for its own pursuit of reform served to extend the conducive atmosphere for such actions generated by the administration.

With the passage of the Civil Rights Act of 1964, the students discovered that through exertion of effort and intentness of commitment they could produce positive, appreciable results. It was perhaps at this point that the awareness of "student power" was first formulated. And although the assassination of President Kennedy had supplanted the paramount advocate of reform with an administration that appeared to travel at a more deliberate, cautious pace, former success and a growing conception of power persuaded the students to continue their efforts and at the same time to broaden their areas of concern.

One of these issues, destined to replace civil rights as the predominant question, was the accelerating United States involvement in Vietnam. Initially, it provided an alternate rallying point after the death of President John F. Kennedy, but gradually, as the related intentions of the United States to prosecute the war and of the students to oppose it simultaneously increased, it became a self-sustaining and perpetuating end in itself. Opposition to the war was transformed into opposition to the system that waged it. But the war was not the only issue that confronted the students, even though it eventually assumed primary importance in their calculations. Other areas of discontent demanded satisfaction; the commitment to civil rights would still maintain its high priority, but it would be accompanied by other interests occupying similarly important positions in the student hierarchy of values.

Various political organizations were developed on separate campuses to facilitate the prosecution of these demands. The student membership in these organizations and the number of self-proclaimed student activists have induced some analysts to discount any significant or influential effect they may be able to exert, primarily because of the small minority of students involved. Yet such assessments neglect a most important consideration which renders them essentially irrelevant. For what should never be minimized is the realization that despite their paucity of numbers, the students activists articulate the feelings and emotions of many quieter and less assertive students. They are, as it were, the self-appointed spokesmen for their fellow students, self-assigned expositors of their complaints and desires. And although the students they represent did not select or request them to do so, still the issues they advance and the inequalities they decry are those of the student body as a whole.

Although student dissent is obviously formulated on the campus and expounded by students, this does not automatically consign its attention and purview solely to campus issues. Though this admonition may perhaps be unnecessary—it is admittedly impossible to attribute the civil rights movement or the Vietnam dispute, with all its "coeval" ramifications, to an entirely student or university context—a reiteration of its basic premise may prove useful in comprehending what the essence of student protest entails.

The university, despite the fact that it provides sanctuaries for the plotting and theorizing of student activists, cannot be isolated as the main sight or focal point for their protests. The university is merely a staging area for revolution. It alone has not produced the conditions which antagonize and alienate the students; indeed, it is incapable of doing so. Rather, student dissent is directed against more awesome and more powerful entities, against the bureaucratic intricacies otherwise recognized as the United States government and against the societal system it has spawned.

The students perceive the crisis, or crises, as originating within the society as a whole, not solely within the university. As a product of the system, the university has some of the same defects that are characteristic of the larger aspects of society. In many instances, the university is subjected to the most strident attacks of the student dissidents, not necessarily because it is partially responsible for the inequities they protest and seek to redress, but because it is conceived as a miniature reproduction of the society in general.

This concept of a "miniature society" university provides the premise for the second reason that students turn their most vituperative attentions to the campus. Activists view the university as an instrument of a corrupt society, as an institution generated by the latter to advocate its values and expand its influence. Thus, the attitude of activists toward the university is characterized by disgust and condemnation. Not only does it reflect the immorality of society, it also attempts to rationalize, defend, and sustain it through the imposition of a vastly irrelevant and indoctrinal curriculum. Education is conceived as yet another tool of society, designed to acclimate the students to the standards it wishes to promote but which they do not respect.

A third reason why the university appears as an irresistible magnet attracting the most vehement student protest is based almost entirely upon a tactical consideration. Essentially, the university presents a more tempting and realistic target than does the whole of society. For the latter is so massive, so amorphous, that attack against it would almost inevitably evoke no response. Protest against such a society is useless, for its immense size, like that of the government, guarantees both anonymity and intractability. Initially the students encounter frustration only because they are unable to centralize around a focal point, and later because coordinated efforts appear unproductive.

The university, on the other hand, is extremely vulnerable to protest, not only because its functions and responsibilities lie primarily with the students, thereby rendering it more sensitive to their complaints and demands, but also because of its availability. It is, simply, there—permanently located—unabetted by extraneous devices that serve to camouflage it. And since the entity of the university can be perceived, as that of the society cannot, it becomes that much more malleable and responsive to incitements for change. Since it is a visible target, the university presents a potentially more fruitful area of action than does the society.

This direction of activist protest to the campus arena can also be explained by another factor, that of the students' fear that in a few years the society will divest them of their crusading passion and concern. There exists among them the anxiety that, after graduation, the society will inexorably assimilate them and acculturate them to its prevailing dictates. Thus there is the paramount necessity for immediate action, lest the resolve that prompts it evaporates or atrophies.

Initially, student protest can be viewed on the political level. It is in essence an anti-establishment movement that denounces the inequities in American life and seeks their rectification. It especially condemns the United States involvement in Vietnam, which it regards as yet another stage in America's attempt to construct an international empire. The student movement believes that the U.S. could, instead, by applying the intense resources it expends in that effort, improve the adverse conditions and minimal opportunities that pervade the lower strata of its citizens, as well as improve the quality of its environment for the entire population.

The second level of student protest is conducted on moral, rather than political, grounds. There exists, as it were, a revulsion against a society that is becoming progressively more corrupt, that inexorably is increasing the distance between the theoretical pretensions and its practical performances. It is this disparity between professed principles and actual achievements that has antagonized the dissidents.

Viewed on its "subterranean level," student protest is an existential rejection of the distant, impersonal mechanisms that increasingly permeate the society and, because of their remoteness, do not satisfy human needs. It is, in effect, a revolt against bigness, the bigness generated by the growth of a progressively more complex welfare state. As this state expands, a person's sense of individuality is gradually curtailed. Any attempt at self-definition becomes increasingly more difficult, and the prospects of success even more improbable.

These three levels together constitute the foundations of student protest. To categorize them as a single entity would be impossible. In reality, student dissent is directed against a proliferation of targets and is conducted on disparate levels. Paramountly, it is an existential revolt, a revolt culled not so much from the injustices and failings of the society, though these are definitely persuasive, but rather from the fact that these conditions exist at all. They exist, but they should not. They should be eliminated, but as yet they have not been, and undoubtedly will not soon be. It is essentially a revolt stimulated by the factors of authority, the traditionalism it preserves and the complacency it instills; it is a rejection of their influences, the intention of effecting their change or demise.

The ideology of student dissent can be said to be constructed around those factors that elicit their disapproval. Yet, while their ideology is well grounded and the validity of most of their complaints can be readily acknowledged, the student protestors have presented no viable programs or alternatives to replace the system they detest. While there is agreement on which conditions antagonize them, there is little unanimity on what they advocate or what would be acceptable to them.

This strange situation in which the reconstructors of society have advanced few remedial suggestions has been viewed in various perspectives by different observers. Many critics have interpreted student dissent as primarily interested in the eradication of the system. Whether this proposition, which appears to condemn the students summarily, can be substantiated or rejected depends upon the individual spectator. This judgment, which is perhaps too questionable in its impartiality, gives little credence to the possibility of altruistic concern on the students' part.

Another consideration is that the students desire only fewer rules, not their total abolition, that they are averse to seizing power, but would rather obstruct it in the hope of obtaining worthwhile concessions. But whatever the actual cause, it is incontestable that the majority of the protests are not tangible or politically oriented. Rather, they center around the feelings of morality and dedication that pervade the movement.

Obsessed by the belief that the system is characterized by ethical depravity, the students have developed their protest within the abstract values of truth and morality. They insist that morality and politics are indivisible and mutually interrelated, a concept which has sometimes been labeled as the post-Nuremburg ethic. The foremost postulate of this ethic can be summarized as a belief that each and every individual is completely and morally liable for everything he does. A man must assume full responsibility for his destiny, and he must alone arrive at decisions which will influence his life. From this concept springs the participatory idea of democracy; a man can only be worthy of the mantle of citizenship by participation. But this participation must be generated by his own concern and moral values. Only in this way can he liberate himself and reconcile himself with his conscience. That is really man's primary political purpose—to seek individual respect in an age dedicated to its discredit and destruction.

In the panoply of attempts to disrupt the American ethos of its mythical unity and "justice for all," another group, the women's liberation movement, has emerged, challenging the domination of the male ruling class and the contented image of mother confined to the kitchen. The American woman, comprising one-third of the country's work force, has only recently begun to demand an equal role in industry and society—no longer satisfied by a deceiving electoral equality. Western society, once awed by the vision of the Virgin Mary, has —since the end of the nineteenth century—been transforming its essential outlook on women.

The rejection of unwanted domesticity differs in style and character from previous historical movements in which women participated as happy ideologues. The new feminism has centered in a novel and compelling issue: Is the only position for women in our society—as Stokely Carmichael of SNCC has said—prone? In modernizing cultures it is already evident that a transition of roles for both men and women will produce simultaneous disorientation but not necessarily an appetite for women to aspire to roles traditionally and exclusively held for men. This appears possible only in an environment characterized by technological reductionism, where the complex and sophisticated dimension of roles and functions are being reduced to the least common denominator of human function. These roles, such as a man the provider and woman the child-rearer, may lose all cultural significance in a society which will conceivably be described in the distant future by technological unemployment and the flourish of child-care *kibbutzim*. It is not a fortuitous coincidence that the sociological decay of the family has been attended by the increasing absence of both mother and father from the family. A technological society is, by definition, one which forfeits experential knowledge for the prepackaged security of the tried and proven.

Theoretical and philosophical influences on U.S. revolutionists are diverse, encompassing both indigenous and foreign origins. Although these revolutionists claim to be guided by certain theorists, the influence acknowledged is one more of the image rather than the substance of thought.

This is particularly true of the Black Panthers, where images of beneficial systemic change affecting their group are important. As a theorist, Eldridge Cleaver conveys an image of the black man perpetually the victim of a white system. His language and personal experience contravene, at every opportunity, the white man's codes and conventions. His book, *Soul on Ice*, is an evocation of violent images which call for a change in the system.

The New Left is perhaps the most philosophical of U.S. revolutionist groups. While there are many who presume to speak for the New Left, Herbert Marcuse has achieved the greatest influence in recent years. By speaking about systemic depersonalization and the alienation of the masses, he has addressed himself to those concerns which intimately affect a great number of young people. Here, again, image is important and *One Dimensional Man* conveys it.

The student radicals are perhaps the most cosmopolitan of U.S. revolutionists. They have certainly been influenced by Cleaver and Marcuse, but also by Ché and Mao Tse-tung. In the case of Ché, especially, there is the image of the romantic-cum-revolutionist vanquished by a contemptible system. While the supposition is difficult to confirm, one suspects that radical students read very little although they definitely have access to reading materials. Theirs is a visual, not a reading, generation. Unlike the New Left, the students form their ideas from a kind of group dynamic rather than from inner reflection.

In comparison with other areas, a very real problem for U.S. revolutionists has been the lack of theorists intimately acquainted with the

United States as an entity. Cleaver speaks of blacks, Marcuse is a philosopher who abstains from prescriptive remedies, and both Ché and Mao simply cannot be transplanted to this country's environment. Thus, a very real theoretical gap exists which has reduced the level of persuasive articulation for the black, the New Left, and the student radical. There is a discipline for revolutionist theory that has been utilized elsewhere and has frequently become the precursor to revolution. Such a discipline is not likely to occur in the United States until the hedonistic images yield to the sterner stuff and substance of which revolutions are made.

China and Asia

Unlike revolutionists in the United States for whom modern revolutionism is relatively new and not institutionalized, those in Asia are experienced with it as a tool of political management and organization. It is the only tool with which they are familiar. Since their experience has been predicated on revolutionism, they tend to use the lessons derived from this experience as guides to both present and future actions. Primary Asian revolutionists, Mao Tse-tung, Ho Chi Minh, and Gandhi, have written about their own experiences. The written word has been utilized both as a guide and as a type of catechism for the faithful. The impact of these works has been significant in establishing the revolutionist criteria to be followed in a specific country.

Revolutionists in Asia differ from those in the West in that they have sought to mobilize rural rather than urban masses, the latter having only recently begun to emerge. From a sociological point of view, the nuclear family remains the basic social unit in Asia. If changes were to occur, they would of necessity emanate from the countryside rather than from the essentially polyglot, urban areas of the region. In addition, the colonial powers were strongest in the urban areas and maintained only token forces in the countryside.

This rural orientation of Asian revolutionism was itself a revolutionary idea (if not in Asia, at least in the West) of considerable conceptual and tactical magnitude. The rural populace, whose existence was so tied to the land of its ancestors, and whose horizons were limited to the village, were thought to have no other awareness. Yet, they were aroused by the revolutionist cadres of Ho Chi Minh and Mao Tse-tung, who spoke persuasively in the people's own idiom, and who stressed ideas such as social justice and economic measures such as land redistribution.

Asian revolutionism has been directed both against Western influences and traditional Asian forces that have tolerated and acceded to those influences. Asian revolutionists have been vigorously anti-Western in their behavior. This attitude has been due to nationalistic feelings on the one hand and to a certain amount of political ineptitude of the West in its past dealings with Asia on the other. The realization that Western nations were not invincible came in 1905 when the Japanese defeated the Russians. Together with the impact of the Japanese shock wave of World War II, Asians experienced a profound disillusionment with their former subservient acceptance of Western hegemony.

More attention has been devoted to Asia's revolt against colonial and imperial powers and to the coeval revolutionist reaction against traditional authority (which had been co-opted by Western authorities). Throughout the area, the old hierarchical patterns have been co-opted by the revolutionists. Whether the point of reference is the Brahmins or the Mandarins, the various structures of power which they represented no longer operate as they did before. The anti-Western tendency directed against these institutions was produced because they were identified with the Western powers.

The assault on internal structure has shaped Asian revolutionism. For the Asian revolutionist, the traditional powers were a target which had to be supplanted if progress were to be made. Revolution had been predicated on theories of the redistribution of power and on the reconstruction by that power of the political, social, and economic foundations of society. Because the vast majority of the traditional authorities were in a state of dry rot, their low level of resistance simplified elimination. They had survived the conditions which had created them as institutions; and now, divested of their mythological basis, they were indeed vulnerable to revolutionist assault.

Mao has his own mandate not unlike the Emperor's "Mandate from Heaven," and, when he speaks, it is with similar authority. His certainty, consequently, penetrates the villages. In like fashion, Ho received the veneration of the scholar-leader and had replaced the moral aspect of the old Mandarinate. And, while repudiating the caste system, Gandhi followed the Brahmin tradition of being an interpreter and teacher to the masses.

Aside from the differences in revolutionist methodology, Mao, Ho, and Gandhi share common characteristics. Their thought is deeply rooted in the realities of their own nations. They correctly assessed their enemies and employed tactics which were effective against them. As philosophers, they constructed a message which was new to Asians. They recognized the value of propagandizing for internal and external consumption.

Of most significance is the fact that these three revolutionists knew their own people and seized opportunities as they arose. In many ways, they created and engineered them. All three recognized the value of personal example, dedication, and sacrifice; and they set the tone for others to emulate.

On the other hand, there are important differences between Asian revolutionists in terms of alignment, orientation to basic communist tenets, and violent struggle. Mao and Ho certainly share characteristics that Gandhi does not share with them. In terms of a continuing revolutionism, the impact of Mao and Ho are more contemporaneous in China and North Vietnam than that of Gandhi in India.

Asian communist revolutionists have no reason to doubt the validity of their own experiences. They have been at least moderately successful against significant odds in many situations. The essential theme of these experiences has been the belief in the inevitability of the fruition of their political objectives. In the pursuit of their objectives, such figures as Mao and Ho are historical determinists who believe that the key to these objectives can be found in survivability. So long as the revolution can endure and survive, its final accomplishment and the realization of its goals are inevitable.

It is the revolution that must survive. Although the nation and its population are of obvious importance, survivability pertains to the revolutionist cadres. In generic terms, these are the men and women who shared the hardships of the "Long March" with Mao and who fought the French with Ho. The cadres form the nucleus of revolutionism, but continuation is ensured only as long as they remain revolutionist.

As was true with Ho Chi Minh, Mao, Asia's leading communist revolutionist, is among the most respected communists. Both survived them all—Lenin, Stalin, and a succession of other Soviet leaders. Despite the ideological differences with the U.S.S.R. expressed by Mao, they are legendary figures in the communist movement. Having held positions of leadership longer than any other living communist—or Western leader for that matter—their tenacious control of the center of power, the revolutionist cadres, has afforded a certain perspective from which their respective world views have been molded.

The primary characteristic of Mao is his durability. Mao has endured through hardship and adversity. From the early 1920s to 1949, Mao fought four wars—three revolutionist civil wars and one against the Japanese. Despite the setbacks that he suffered before World War II, when he and a small number of cadres survived the "Long March," Mao played a significant role against the Japanese and was able to gain control of the mainland in 1949. In one sense, this was where the revolutionist struggle really began, with Mao's effort to reconstitute Chinese society.

While Mao is basically a Marxist, in the Leninist sense of the word, the Chinese sources of his thoughts and methods cannot be overlooked. These sources may be traced back to China's dynastic cycle and the romantic tradition associated with it. There is a type of antitradition associated with the dynasties which can best be seen in *Romance of the Three Kingdoms*. This forms an ideological basis which is as ancient as the Chinese. The most important of these tenets is the belief in the authority of the corporate unit over that of the individual. The old Confucian historical ideology, like the Marxist, was grounded in the notion of natural or materialistic forces as the determinant of the historical process. Finally, the Confucian belief that man could be perfected on earth was held in old China (before neo-Confucianism in the thirteenth century modified this notion) just as strongly as it is in the new China.

If Mao's brand of Marxism is not completely alien to Chinese culture, he has introduced new concepts based on his own revolutionism. These were designed not to be merely theoretical propositions but to be theories placed into action as well. Mao, the theorist, and Mao, the man of action, cannot be easily separated.

The law of contradictions is a distinctly Maoist-action concept that stresses moral progress through conflict and struggle (as did Confucius). In this context, progress refers to the historical process that Mao has formulated. This process is similar to Marx's historical determinism, with the condition of communism as the ultimate goal. One dissimilarity with Marx is Mao's fusing of feudalism and capitalism as one period for China because it had not gone through an indigenous capitalist stage of development. When Mao talks about capitalism, he means imperialism and colonialism, since foreign enterprise was the only real form of capitalism in China.

From a tactical viewpoint, Mao's historical process makes reference to a two-phase revolution: the bourgeois democratic and then the socialist. In this case, the process is one of tearing down and rebuilding the society along Marxist lines. This entails an eventual purge of anti-revolutionist bourgeois elements so that only the "people" remain. It is only when the bourgeois remnant of imperialism and feudalism are expunged that the process of socialism can begin. The law of contradictions reinforces this tactical view of history.

Mao speaks for the masses and is of the masses. Those who disagree with "the mass line" are by definition enemies of the people. They are in need of reeducation through rectification or elimination (a Confucian process). On a mass scale, the Cultural Revolution is an example of this phenomenon.

The attempt at total politicization has been made in contemporary China, and the thoughts and writings of Mao are all-pervasive. They can aid all manner of things from agriculture to industry. Technical expertise is not nearly as important as political expertise based on a knowledge of Mao. It is much more important to be red than to be expert.

Before turning our attention to Ho Chi Minh and Vietnamese revolutionism, the question of the role of the Chinese Communist party qua party is an open one at this time. One of the net effects of the Cultural Revolution was the decimation of the CCP party structure. Mao established alternate links of control using many of the party cadres but, as an organization, the party no longer exists. The reason for this was that Mao feared the CCP would become as the CPSU had: a new, elitist class with privilege and a vested interest in its maintenance. In his view, the effect of this would be a satiated perspective that would cast off revolutionism in favor of its own position, thus creating a situation that would retard revolutionist progress.

Like that of Mao, Ho's experience stressed patience and protraction to gain objectives over a broad time spectrum. Since he was effective in this, there is little reason to believe that these tactics will change; his principal associates, Truong Chinh, Le Duan, and Vo Nguyen Giap, were also committed in various degrees to a philosophy which emphasizes endurance and survival.

By far the most enigmatic actor in Asia, Ho Chi Minh was a unique figure in twentieth-century revolution. With the exception of Mao Tse-tung, Ho outlived the first generation of revolutionists and yet, in many respects, must still be counted in their number. As a witness to the first strains in the old colonial system before and after World War I, Ho attempted to present a petition stressing the plight of the Vietnamese people at the Versailles Peace Conference in 1919 to President Woodrow Wilson without success. He was instrumental in the founding of the

French Communist party and worked in China for the Soviet Comintern during part of the interwar period. His activities in Indochina were short-lived until World War II, and he spent most of the time in exile. He was the best-known political figure within Southeast Asia and therefore symbolized revolution in much of that area.

Ho's total image, formed from his political writings and the simplicity of his dress, was that of a revolutionist. As the symbol of the new Asian man, he spoke with the virtue of a Mandarin, but without their affectations. Disdaining to remain aloof from the people, he attempted to be one of them and conveyed this identity at every opportunity. This identification was a unique aspect of the Asian approach. While it had been attempted in the early days of the Soviet Revolution, it did not endure. In Asia, it became the style not only of Ho but of Mao and Gandhi as well.

Closely identified with Ho Chi Minh and somewhat unusual in the annals of revolutionists, the members of the National Liberation Front (NLF), as they term themselves, or the Viet Cong (VC) as they are called by their opponents, have remained relatively anonymous as individuals. Although most revolutionists such as Mao or Lenin, or even Gandhi, have placed considerable emphasis on the charismatic qualities of individuals, the NLF has chosen to stress organizational charisma. Although the leadership of the NLF is nominally known, the majority of its adherents are anonymous and lack the visibility normally accorded revolutionist actors. For perhaps the first time in history, the NLF has coordinated a managed revolution carried out along organizational rather than along personality lines. Besides, there was no figure in Vietnam, North or South, who could compete with Ho.

Although the political relationship between the NLF in the South and the Lao Dung Party in the North is both close and hierarchical, the revolution itself does exist in South Vietnam, a factor which necessitates an examination of the NLF as an independent revolutionist actor. The presence of relatively large-scale military operations should not obscure or invalidate this analysis. South Vietnam has essentially four distinct political populations: (1) the lowland Vietnamese from the DMZ to Binh Thuan; (2) the polyglot population of the Saigon megapolis; (3) the peasants in Cochinchina or the Delta region; and (4) the tribal population or Montagnards, which comprise about 12 percent of the South's population. When the clashing socio-religious mix is superimposed on this already disparate matrix, the diversity of interests in a relatively small population (approximately fifteen million people) becomes apparent. As a matter of fact, the *composition* of the NLF in 1960 included both regional and religious representatives. (In Chinese *and* Viet history, the state has viewed all organized religion as subversive.)

But for the possible exception of the *first* few years of Diem's government, no Saigon regime could cope with such an explosive situation even if the latter had not been exacerbated and utilized by Hanoi. The prevailing need for change was augmented by the lack of rapport between the population and the government. Unlike the North, where independence had produced hardship but also constructive change, the conditions in the South, also an independent state, had succeeded in obtaining the former but had failed to achieve the latter. The existing institutions, which exerted little relevance in the urban areas, enjoyed none in the countryside.

Much of what has been said concerning Asian revolutionists is relevant to Gandhi. With the exception of his methodology and circumstance, Gandhi's approach to revolutionism was similar to that of other Asian revolutionists. Against the British, his nonviolent tactics were quite effective. He understood the revolutionist's need to capture world opinion, and this he did, by provoking the British to harsh reprisals. If nonviolence as a methodology is viewed as camouflaged violence, since it seeks to incite violent reaction in others, then conceptually Gandhi fits into the general Asian pattern.

While much of Asian revolutionism has been notable for its violence, it also exhibits nonviolent examples. The contrast between the two extremes has been particularly marked in Asia. As a revolutionist whose behavior stressed nonviolence, Gandhi developed techniques of civil disobedience. Although he first used these tactics in South Africa, it was in India that the Nationalist movement under Gandhi became converted to nonviolence as a methodology against the British whose normal response he predicted.

The vision of Gandhi transcended the objective of independence and stressed the issues of faith and rebirth. In this instance, he was a highly nationalistic figure, extremely antisupremacist, and one whose doctrinnes were socialist and whose organizational techniques were in the Leninist-Marxist tradition.

As a master of political and psychological operations, Gandhi in this sense was the Asian precursor to contemporary Buddhist militants in Vietnam. But his concept of nonviolent revolution did not attract adherents elsewhere in Asia.

Part of the reason for this rejection stems from differing internal circumstances, but another portion is explained by the observation that Gandhi was a synthesis of both Western and non-Western ideas. He was essentially a humanist, borrowing freely from Christianity and Marx as well as from the teachings of his own culture. His vision of a society free from suffering, fear, and want underlined even his earliest efforts. That he chose the political path to accomplish his ideals illustrates his keen awareness that political change had to occur if socio-economic change were to be accomplished; the former antedated and was necessary for the latter.

Latin America

In contrast to Asia, Latin America is still at the beginning of its revolutionist process. Except for Cuba, revolutionists control no other Latin state. However, the influence of Mao in Asia is analogous in kind rather than degree to that of Castro in Latin America. In both cases, their rhetoric has been sharper than their actions. But in Asia, Latin America, and elsewhere, the crystallizing focus of revolutionists is the antisupremacist feelings that all share. This gives impetus to their theories.

In Latin American revolutionist thought, there is a dichotomy whose essence can be approached through an examination of Aprista and of Castroite theory. Although elements of both have an obvious linkage with revolutionist theories outside Latin America, they are essentially indigenous adaptations of revolutionism. Before discussing them in detail, it is important to note that no Latin American government has wholly adopted the ideas of Aprismo, nor have those of Castro been able to take root (outside of Cuba). Our purpose here is merely to illustrate two essentially different revolutionist alternatives which were conceived in Latin America.

For the present and the future, Latin theorists believe that the search for identity will have to be defined from its own indigenous wellsprings. The two mentioned approaches or reactions to change attempt to do so in a radically different manner. While there have been other revolutionist inputs which have emanated from the region (viz., the Mexican experience), these two programs, in their conceptual form, are ones which seek converts. Although the future might not belong exclusively to either, both concepts have attracted considerable interest in the area.

THE APRISTA MODEL

Many of the concepts of Aprismo have been embraced by a number of Latin American political parties.[1] Significant elements of the Aprista program have been incorporated into the platforms of Acción Democrática of Venezuela, the Christian Democratic party of Chile, the Christian Democratic party of Costa Rica, the Christian Democratic Party of Brazil (it helped elect Janio Quadros to the presidency), and the Union Cívica of Uruguay.

The Aprista program has had a substantial impact on the more revolutionist parties of Latin America. Apra parties, *per se*, have disappeared or have been labeled with different names, as is the case with Peru, where it was recently renamed the Democratic Front (1962 elections). Nonetheless, Aprismo captured a significant group of Latin leaders during the late 1950s. The members of this small group claim to be disciples of Victor Raul Haya de la Torre, Peruvian founder of Aprismo. Former Venezuelan president Romulo Betancourt claims that he was inspired by the Cubans' Prime Minister, Dr. Carlos Prio Socarras, the leader of the Aprista organization there, called Partido Revolucionario Cubano. The same claim has been made by Juan José Arevalo of Guatemala, José Figueres of Costa Rica, Juan Bosch of the Dominican Republic, Victor Paz Estenssoro of Bolivia, and Arturo Frondizi of Argentina. All of these men were Latin American presidents who pursued vigorous programs of social and political reforms. Their parties have been labeled "brothers" because of the similarity in their political platforms.

Developed in the years following World War I, the Aprista movement was conceived as an indigenous movement. No longer relying entirely upon Europe for its ideas, Apra commenced during student unrest in Argentina and Peru. In the latter state, the workers supported the students in their demands. At the same time, intellectuals, particularly in Peru, were searching for indigenous cultural forms to serve as sources for new patterns of political, social, and economic thought.

Aprismo was born out of a loose alliance of students, workers, and intellectuals, the three groups who are traditionally in the forefront of the whole gamut of revolutionist activity in Latin America. They opposed religious fanaticism, the *caudillos*, and the lack of status and

[1] The authors acknowledge their debt to Professor Brady Tyson for sharing with us many of his insights on Latin America and to Marta San Martin for the use of portions of an unpublished paper dealing, *inter alia*, with Aprismo.

nonintegration of the Indian population. Haya de la Torre was the leading theorist of the movement which was in reality a nonmovement, because his scheme was generally conceived in the instance of Peru, where Aprismo had a specific program that was not adopted due to the resistance of the established powers.

For our purposes, Haya de la Torre's program for Peru is less important than his ideas for Latin actors collectively. Keenly aware of external intervention of all kinds in domestic affairs, the Aprista program was antiimperialist. Here, imperialism was initially considered to be an economic rather than a political phenomenon. However, the economic aspects in this concept began to influence the political situation. Apra sought economic cooperation and infusion of foreign capital in such a manner that sovereignty was maintained. Thus, the first step was to control and regulate economic imperialism so that it could not subvert the political sphere and so that foreign capital cannot exercise joint sovereignty with indigenous powers.

Clearly allied with the first part of Haya de la Torre's maximum program for the continent was a concept of involving political unity. For the Aprista leaders this meant looking inward and essentially called for a sense of a continental solidarity: the creation of a "continental consciousness" which would enable the Latin nations to view themselves as a whole unit. In a most fundamental sense, Haya de la Torre called upon Latins to create their own destiny—take control of their own history—which would certainly be a new phenomenon. It is the idea of a selective break with the past (i.e., exchanging internal for external sources) that represents the revolutionist input of the Aprista program.

Aprismo is essentially committed to a theme that stresses nonviolence and democratic techniques of organizing and exerting popular political power. In the Aprista creed, power acquired by violence cannot foster the programs of social justice which are, in their opinion, necessary to promote the type of order sought. For Aprista theorists, mass education, especially for the Indian population, would be one of the preliminary first steps in their program.

In this sense, Aprista leaders are dedicated to attaining power by legal means. They abhor power begotten by the *coup d'état* and revolt, as well as that retained by the personalism inherent in the *caudillos*. The Apristas seek a myth rooted in their very Latin phenomenon, in order to build institutions which reflect the indigenous temper. One of their problems concerns whether the new can be created if the old is not completely eradicated. But Apra has not been concerned just with the creation of new political institutions; it has never forgotten that ideas have a power of their own. In this sense, Aprista theorists, like Christ and Gandhi, seek a spiritual change which can alter basic attitudes and values in a revolutionist manner. They seek a permanence of concept, which can only be brought about by the fertilization of ideas. In Latin America, the direct challenge to contemporary Aprista ideas is the terroristic violence of Castro who, like Fanon, believes that revolutionist concepts can be energized only by violence, and that the old must be destroyed to make way for the new.

For all revolutionist actors, timing is important. For Marx and Stalin, the critical historical moment had to be seized and acted upon, while for others, including Mao, the revolutionist moment is relative, and depends upon the relationship of space and time. Whereas space is the socio-political culture which encompasses the entire history of a people, time is the particuar context which exists at any given point of history. Thus, the space-time theory of history has permitted Apristas to adopt a theory of historical relativity. In this theory there are no absolutes, no moments to be seized or moments to be created, and no irrefutable historical processes.

As we shall see, Castroite theorists, unlike Aprista theorists, especially Haya de la Torre, view man as the sum of his influences at a particular moment in time. Nothing has been preordained, in that there is no historical determinism, a common feature of many theorists of revolutionism. The processes and influences of history are many, and they can be approached from different points of view. From this perspective, history becomes inseparable from its own space-time motion.

Latins must follow their own historical rhythm, which is not rigidly fixed in the Marxian sense. There is no essential parallelism in the development of peoples or regions. The perspective from which this motion is observed will determine the view seen. This theory helps to explain the Aprista concept of a "continental consciousness" so central to Aprista thought.

THE CASTRO MODEL

In considering indigenous revolutionist alternatives, Fidel Castro's revolution deceptively allures Latin America. While there is no denying the fact that the Cuban experience has been closely watched by Latins, it is increasingly obvious that it is a unique experience not likely to be repeated in detail. As has been previously explained, the specifics of the revolutionist experience are unique and cannot be transplanted. Both the Soviet and Chinese revolutions were not exportable, *per se*, and we suspect that the Cuban phenomenon cannot be repeated. However, the theoretical output in terms of tactics and strategy is exportable. Castro, in fact, has made considerable efforts in this respect. The Cuban leader stands diametrically opposed to both non-Communist actors of the left as well as to old-line Communist parties. His theories stress both military tactics and his nihilistic perception of Latin America. Seeking to destroy the old myths by replacing them with those which attempt to legitimize the revolution, Castro's ideas smack of personalistic policies. These have proven to be fertile soil for the building of Latin institutions.

Much of Castroite thought is contained in a short treatise called *Revolution in the Revolution?* by Regis Debray, a young Frenchman. As Juan Bosch has written, "It is clear that he (Debray) is expressing the opinions of Fidel Castro . . . and for that reason, his book is of tremendous importance."[2] Essentially, this work is a polemic directed against the communist parties of Latin America for their lack of militancy and inability to seize power. The pattern of revolutionist activity advocated by Debray may be categorized as a theory of violence through which the political process is replaced by the guerrilla armies. "A successful ambush, a torturer cut down, a consignment of arms captured—they are the best answers to any reformist faint-heartedness which may arise in one or another American country."[3] In this concept, political activity would deaden militant revolutionist activity. Therefore, its existence must be denied during the phase of armed struggle. Debray's sociology apparently consists of violence which can never be structured or even brought to a conclusion.

Since a political framework is lacking and political philosophy is placed in a subordinate position, the goal will never be reached because it can never be recognized. The multiplication of the guerrilla groups is a goal in itself in Debray's thought. Revolution is a tautology which exists for no other purpose, and Debray reflects the frustration inherent in this theory.

However, it is apparent that his appeal has been taken up by some. In the United States, militant blacks have expressed similar concepts

[2] Juan Bosch, "An Anti-Communist Manifesto," *New York Review of Books*, (October 26, 1967), p. 3.

[3] Regis Debray, *Revolution in the Revolution?*, trans. Bobbye Ortiz (New York: Monthly Review Press, 1967), p. 126.

to describe their own situation. This explains the views of H. Rap Brown and others on violence without a program or objectives. It reflects a deep feeling that something should be done and that violent activity will answer all problems.

In this sense, Debray, as well as black militants in the United States, has missed at least one essential point of successful revolutionist warfare. Violence may be used extensively in order to achieve its political goals; yet, when used without political structure, violence becomes an end in itself.

Contemporary revolutionist theory is deeply rooted in a viewpoint which emphasizes historical determinism. Indeed, the revolutionist in this era is caught in a conceptual squeeze because the leap of faith which he desires is shackled by his view of the historical forces. From Mao Tse-tung to Regis Debray, the rationale, the style, and the methodology advocated vary greatly; but the revolutionist dilemma is omnipresent. It is a *sine qua non* that revolutionist theorists start with a deterministic view of history. Without this, there would be no rationale for the revolution itself. However, this puts in motion the contradictions found in most theorists since they become prisoners of their own framework. Historical determinism lacks the buoyancy needed for a Nieztchean leap of faith which is inherent in the revolutionist ideal.

Regis Debray and Fidel Castro are historical determinists, and they share the contradiction that is found in revolutionist dialectics. This explains why Debray may argue "hence, an historic responsibility which the Cuban Revolution has never hesitated to accept." Debray's appeal is put in historical terms. For him, the true revolutionist cannot "hold back" from the armed struggle. If he does, history "will see to it that they are left by the wayside."[4] This view of history is both violent and preordained, but it is the outlook of revolutionist youth and has had its effect in other areas. Fidel Castro, for one, has capitalized upon this type of iconoclastic stimulation of youth.

His concept of freeing the present from the past is based on the premise that revolutionist events will take place. This accounts for Debray's being able to state that the "armed struggle is on the agenda of history" in some countries (Peru, Bolivia, and Brazil are mentioned specifically).[5] In order for the agenda to be acted upon, "revolutionary politics, if they are not to be blocked, must be diverted from politics

4 *Ibid.*
5 *Ibid.*, p. 123.

as such."[6] The historical process can be unclogged only by militant behavior which will permit its natural flow.

The difference between the determinism of Debray and traditional theorists is in the balance of the historical image. For the traditional Marxist, the sweep of history is a relatively uninterrupted process of stages with little or no revision necessary. Debray has perceived a revisionist tendency and deplores its existence as an impediment to the inevitability of revolutionist activity. In effect, history is poured into a dialectical mold which will turn out a perfect model once the impurities are removed.

Fidel Castro says simply that there is no revolution without a vanguard; that this vanguard is not necessarily the Marxist-Leninist party; and that those who want to make a revolution have the right and duty to constitute themselves a vanguard, independently of these parties.[7]

If it is the vanguard who will constitute the armed movement, who or what will give structure and concrete purposes to the revolution? This is the question to which Debray fails to give a satisfactory answer. One might suggest that the reason for this turns on his complete repudiation of political activity as precursor to armed struggle. In this sense, there is an almost mystical belief in the triumph of militancy within the operational milieu.

The disparity between this theory and practice has been shown recently in Bolivia. With no political preparation in the zone chosen by Ché Guevara, the armed struggle was immediately launched with immature optimism. While its defeat is history, the reasons for its failure fall into two categories which can be related to Debray's theory. These include lack of political means and objectives and no psychological preparation of the region. The recent Bolivian experience demonstrates that guerrilla activity outside of a political framework is doomed to failure because it lacks the expression and form which political direction normally provides.

On one level, Debray appears to be following Mao Tse-tung's axiom that "every communist must grasp the truth, 'political power grows out of the barrel of a gun.' "[8] However, this quotation derives its meaning

[6] *Ibid.*, p. 124.

[7] *Ibid.*, p. 98.

[8] Mao Tse-tung, *Quotations from Chairman Mao Tse-tung* (Peking: Foreign Language Press, 1966), p. 61.

from the factor that Mao views revolution as the servant of politics, not as its master. For Mao, the revolution will progress from political considerations which dictate the course of the revolution and not vice versa.

Traditional communist control of both revolutionist and conventional forces has been intimately linked with the party through the use of political officers. In Debray's scheme, this process would actually be reversed, since the party would be directed by the armed revolutionist force. The thrust of party efforts would be in support of the armed struggle and would subordinate any political objectives that were not compatible with the struggle. To extend this thesis logically, members of the guerrilla force should, in effect, serve in an analogous capacity to the party as, for example, a political commissar serves with a military unit in China or North Vietnam.

The guerrilla mystique permeates Debray's thought. In this, he is not alone in the feeling that the guerrilla band is unbeatable. From a historical point of view, this can be disputed by examples from Greece, Kenya, Malaya, and perhaps Vietnam. However, the important point to consider is that the guerrilla band is the nexus of the armed revolutionist struggle. Its license to conduct operations comes from its cadres in the name of the people. The cadres are all relatively militant, and it will be they who will take over the political direction and movement of the party. In this argument, it is the party which exists for the guerrillas, whose leadership will serve as the party leadership when the military objective is in hand. The reason that Debray rejects this stems from his frustration over the milieu of Latin American revolutionist activity. The apparent rejection, by many Latin American communist groups, of armed warfare in favor of political struggle has incited Debray's attack on them.

> In Latin America today a revolutionary is not defined by his formal relationship with the Party, whether he is for or against it. The value of a revolutionary, like that of a party, depends on his activity.[9]

The antinomies between Fidel Castro and the traditional communist parties in Latin America are more easily comprehended against the backdrop of their respective historical experiences. Debray emphasizes this separation and it serves as the *raison d'être* for his militancy. The party had very little to do with the success of Castro in his struggle

[9] Debray, *op. cit.*, p. 104.

against Batista. However, as Juan Bosch points out, the party had everything to do with his consolidation of power in Cuba. The paradox arises from Debray's analysis, since the utility of party apparatus comes as a successor, not a precursor, to armed struggle. Furthermore, the party will gain its strength from those who take part in the armed struggle rather than from those who are mere political activists.

The attack on the old-line communist groups in Latin America reveals the radically different aspect of Castro's ideas for the struggle phase of the revolution. "We will undertake the revolution with the masses . . . they will say who are most capable and most revolutionary . . . it is only the people who can judge . . . the old guard must know that it is doomed."[10] Revolution becomes a value in itself and not a vehicle for political goals and objectives.

"In some countries, revolution is a continuing and permanent symbol, furnishing legitimacy to an established regime in which, by itself or with other vital symbols, it provides the foundation of national identity."[11] This identification serves as a sanction for the Castro regime in Cuba as well as for his attempts to interpret revolutionist activities and themes in other states. There has been an attempt to link militant Castroites' themes with the revolutionist history of Latin America. As Debray states, "a reading of Bolivar's biography reveals an enormous amount about war and about America—including a valid lesson for today's American revolutionary wars."[12] By establishing a link between successful revolutionist leaders (Bolivar, Castro), Debray hopes that revolution, as a symbol of legitimacy, will be reinforced by "a union of communists and nationalists [which] will come about through guerrilla action."[13] In his scheme, it is "guerrilla action" which is legitimitized for its own sake and becomes his revolutionist goal.

In comparison to other revolutionist contemporary theoretician-participants, Debray is inadequate because he really does not advocate revolution, but rather directionless conflict. He has taken the Orwellian principle of continuing external war, and has put it in a milieu emphasizing violence *qua* violence as means, values, and goals. The failure is

[10] Fidel Castro, "Fidel Castro versus the Old Guard," *Excelsior* (Mexico City), 2 November, 1966, reprinted in *Translations on Cuba*, No. 532, UPSR, 39, 175 (19 December, 1966).

[11] Charles W. Anderson, Fred R. von der Hohe, and Crawford Young, *Issues of Political Development* (Englewood Cliffs, New Jersey: Prentice-Hall, Inc.), p. 149.

[12] Debray, *op. cit.*, p. 21.

[13] Bosch, *op. cit.*, p. 4.

a lack of perception that guerrilla warfare cannot be legitimized as a system projected into infinity. While this phenomenon has been a tool of a larger political process, it has not had an independent existence of its own.

While Debray has a comprehension of revolutionist activity, his thoughts lack a clear perception of the meaning of politics. The political process is one which has as its goals the maximizing of values. If it is "the duty of every revolutionary to make revolution,"[14] then revolution for its own sake must be a value. Is it always a value? Does it have an objective? Is it a means or an end? For Debray, it is apparently an end, but for others such as Ho Chi Minh, Mao Tse-tung and Kwame Nkrumah, it has been a means (i.e., a propellant of the political process). For these theorists, revolution has been a path toward a utopian vision. There is no stopping point for revolution in Debray. The title of the book, *Revolution in the Revolution?*, betrays that one revolution contains the seeds of another. Debray's vision of the "heavenly city" is simply revolutionist activity. Thus the inadequacies of Debray as a revolutionist theorist are based on his inability to see beyond the revolution. He does not provide a concept of a political process, but only one of armed struggle.

As we have previously stated, the revolutionary model for the area will be cast in a distinctively Latin manner. While each actor will engage his dreams and promises by a different means, there will be an underlying philosophical base which they will share. In the past, the quest for Latin rebirth was founded upon too many utopias which were imported from the outside. The failure of the old-style communism, the newer Castroism (for actors other than Cuba, we consider Castroism as an external source), the *Civitas Dei* promised in the Alliance for Progress, and the stability promised by the military technocracies have all created a spiritual wasteland from which few relevant ideas have emerged.

It has seemed to us that the concepts of Aprismo represent an indigenous attempt to cope with change. In fact, except for the Mexican revolution which predates Aprismo, the majority of nationalistic revolutions in the area have had substantial input of these concepts. While few of these revolutions can be considered complete, they are in varying stages of continuance. Bolivia, for example, has attempted to integrate the Indian population, has nationalized the primary sources of wealth

---

[14] Debray, *op. cit.*, p. 12. (From the Introduction to the Spanish edition by Roberto Fernandez Retamor.)

which were formerly in external hands, and has bettered the lot of the masses. Here we have a case where continuing sequential reforms might well dictate additional revolutionist changes. Although many of the old institutions are still present, the myths supporting these institutions are weakening.

The failure of Guevara in Bolivia must be considered on the basis that one revolution could not dislodge another, more indigenous one. The same might be said for Venezuela during the 1965–1967 period, when that country was threatened by guerrilla and terrorist activity. The platform of that country's "Acción Democrática" was not only a more attractive alternative, but it was also of their own making and adapted to local conditions fairly easily.

Latin American actors seek more than the manifestations of change (i.e., reforms, redistribution, etc.) to correct the existing gaps. They seek the ideas from which true change may emanate. These ideas must be tailored for a particular environment. The twin rejection of Castroism and North American paternalism may well be the beginning of a new revolutionist mood (perhaps emanating from a more socially oriented military) for the continent. While the future is obscure in this respect, the rekindling of man's spirit, of his pursuit for faith, and of his desire for change are the variables in Latin America today where there are converts seeking ideas. In this sense, there is no old myth to destroy, but a new myth to create.

The Arab World

Revolutionism is least understood in the Arab world. Unlike Asians (Mao) or Latin Americans (Castro), the Arabs have no single dominant revolutionist who can personify the revolution. Yet the desire for rapid transformation is as strong in Arab lands as it is in any other area in the world, but dedication to change is lacking. In the final analysis, it is the man of conviction (right or wrong) who becomes the revolutionist. While such men have existed in Arab states, the present political realities of the area favor conservative institutions such as the military and religious institutions. Additionally, there is a sheer lack of other indigenous political structures which can be assailed by revolutionists.

The retrogressive tendency to verify the impotence of the present by the glorification of the past is an all-pervasive element in contemporary Arab revolutionism. Interjected among these strands is the messianism of Arab revolutionist thought, which would carry to the immediate present that which was in the past the reward of the other world. Faith and rebirth are transformed from the universality of Islam to the university of a secular movement unable to cut the bonds with the religion. Specifically, Islam emphasizes a universal concept of community regardless of nationality.

Even the concept of "Arab" has had a different meaning in different contexts of time and space. Traditionally a somewhat pejorative reference to the Bedouins, in the early expansion of Islam it identified the Arab-speaking peoples of the Arabian Peninsula as opposed to the non-Arabic converts to the religion. After the decline of the Ummayad empire in the middle of the eighth century, the term returned to its pejorative context. The Arab, whether arabized or native, whether urban or rural, became identified along tribal, provincial, or city lines— a Shammari, a Cyrensican, or a Baghdadi.

A great deal of energy and time has been consumed in defining the new Arab identity. Arab scholars, mainly Christians, spearheaded the movement to develop a secular Arab consciousness. In Lebanon, in the middle of the nineteenth century, such Christian Arab thinkers as Nasif Yaziji and Butrus Bustani, attempted to reform Arabic as a vehicle of social change within the Arab community of the Ottoman Empire. From the Syrian Scientific Society of 1857 to the secret societies of the early twentieth century, the drifting aspect of literature came to politics.

The literature on Arab identity has since become boundless. Arab writers have spared little effort to isolate those components intrinsic to Arab culture. At the Arab Congress in Paris in 1913, an Arab was identified as any person who lives in the Arab world, speaks the Arabic language, was brought up in the Arab culture, and takes pride in Arab history. Sometimes definitions have been restricted—qualified by language, culture, and religion—and at other times widened to include anyone who considers himself an Arab.

The Arabs wish to idealize a non-isolating concept to define their political personality. Such a concept, it is held, would form an Arab secular community to replace that of religious believers. However, the encompassing cover of such a community has had few takers in the Arab world.

When the Renaissance began to secularize the thought of Western man and the Reformation nationalized his concept of religion, the original contradiction in the political attitude of Christianity was gradually resolved. Such was not the case in Islam. From the thirteenth century on, Muslim elites became increasingly traditionalist; innovation in religious and social matters was discouraged. The idea that man is solely created for the service of God became predominant. In subsequent practice, this notion has produced in the Muslim mind the implication that social welfare is not the concern of the government. The Western concept of the state is alien in such an Islamic framework, where the political community as such has been mainly interested in leading the good life, and less interested in who administers it.

In effect, the fragmentation of the Arab world into independent states, together with the traditional division into Sunni and Shi'ah religious sects, has stimulated the desire for a return to the fundamental organic unity of life which Islam once conveyed. Confronted by change and division, internal competition, and secular rivalries, the Arab looks to his leaders to rehabilitate the conditions for the restoration of the short-lived unity during the early period of Islam.

Conceptually, Arab political and revolutionist thought could be divided into various and overlapping stages of development: a period of religious revivalism from mid-nineteenth to early twentieth centuries; the pre-independence nationalist stage—the interwar years; and the post-independence nationalist stage. The early period is exemplified by the focusing of attention upon the thought of the prophet Muhammad by reformers of the time: Rif'at al Tahtawi, Khayr al-Din Tunisi, Abd al-Rahman al-Kawakibi, Jamal al-Din al-Afghani, Muhammad Abduh, Mustafa Kamil, and Rashid Rida.

The reformers of this period credited the West with superiority over the Muslim world due to Western political and military organization and systems rather than to Western Christian ethics.[15] They observed that sound government emerged out of the combination of liberty and justice, adding that this leads to hope, which in turn leads to initiative.[16] Western Christianity, these reformers concluded, did not concern itself with temporal and political matters, so it represented no barriers to rationalism or secularism. But Islam, they averred, corrupted by superstitious elements which were not worthy of the message, inhibited the Islamic trend toward innovation. Some of these reformers argued that Western political systems accounted for the efficiency and

[15] Khayr al-Din al-Tunisi, *Aqwam al Masalik Fi Ma'rifat Ahwal al Mamalik*, cited in Khaldun S. al-Husri, *Three Reformers: A Study in Modern Arab Political Thought* (Beirut: Khayats, 1966), pp. 33–53.
[16] *Ibid.*, p. 98.

progress in Western Europe, and thus they urged the Arabs to adopt their structures.[17]

The following stage of growth in Arab revolutionist thought produced more heat and less light. It was stimulated by the alienation of the Arab nationalist thinkers from emerging trends in the Ottoman Empire: the ethnocentrism of the Young Turk Revolution of 1908 and its departure from traditional Islamic institutions. Arab thought found expression in societies which turned from cage literary clubs to political groups such as al-Fatat and al-Ahd and to the Arab insurrection of 1916.

The Arab revolt of 1916 has appeared highly symbolic in the eyes of Arab nationalists as the first concrete manifestation in modern times of their desire to re-create an independent and unified Arab state. The insurgency arose—not in the land of the intellectuals of Lebanon and Syria—but in the vast deserts of Arabia. A synthesis of Arab nationalist aspiration, dynastic ambitions, and British strategic interests in World War I, the revolt sparked a movement which won the liberation of Damascus, the ancient center of Arabdom, from centuries of Ottoman domination. The entry of Amir (Prince) Faysal (son of al-Sharif Husayn, guardian of the holy places of Mecca and leader of the Arab revolt against the Ottoman during World War I) into Damascus made the dream a reality for a brief moment, but this dream was soon smashed by the Western partition of the Arab world into the Mandate System. The interwar developments added to the frustration of the post-war generation of nationalists, who were plagued by impotence of ideas and insufficient means. The harsh political realities of the interwar period produced a milieu of competing nationalist schemes and apologetics. Polemics was used to persuade the already convinced and to anger the already engaged. Little attention was given to issues of reform and social justice.

The body of Arab thought in this stage can best be understood in terms of the introduction of Western thought into a society just set free from scholastic theology but not yet certain of the direction of its goals. Arab thinkers called for rationalism and secularism, not as a repudiation of Islam, but rather as a reformation of it. Islam could be reformed by a return to its roots in its Arabic background. But for many this process, aside from its remote possibility, seemed an

---

[17] *Ibid.*, p. 122; see also Abd al-Rahman al-Kawakibi, *Tabai' al-Isti'bad*, Aleppo (publisher not cited), 1957; Rif' at al-Tahtawi, *Takhlis al-ibriz Fi Talkhis Baris* (publisher not cited), Cairo, 1834; and *Manahij al-Albab al-Misriyah Fi Manahij al-Adab al-Asriyah* (publisher and date not cited), Cairo.

outmoded explanation of the ills of the Arab society, if not an apology for the failure of Islam to match the dynamism of the West.

The works of such thinkers as Sati al-Husri, Constantine Zurayk, Abd Allah al-'Ala'ili, Sami Shawkat, and Ali Yusuf Nasir al-Din strove to refine basic concepts new to their respective societies. Explaining the meaning of nation and nationalism, they devoted much space to arguments about the components of Arab nationhood and the delineation of the geographic boundaries of the Arab nation. The particularistic nationalisms so pervasive in the various Arab countries at this time combined with a neo-Islamic revival to reduce these efforts to bitter polemics.

The Syrian Social National Party (SSNP), founded by Antun Sa'adeh in 1932, represents an important development and departure in the ideological context. As the first doctrinal party in Syria, and with the exception of the Arab communist parties, it ushered in the era of mass-party organization and well-defined social reform platforms. By advocating the concept of geographic Syria (based on the closer affinity of the peoples of Iraq, Jordan, Lebanon, and Syria, and a common historical era that preceded Islam) and by adopting a rational and positive approach to social reform (the corporate state, separation of church and state, and the re-education of the masses), it departed from Pan-Arabism and Pan-Islamism in its regional stance and cultural inspiration. Elite-oriented and opposed by all religious sects in the area, the SSNP failed to achieve power and is proscribed today in Lebanon, Syria, Jordan, and Iraq.

In the post-independence nationalist stage, change in emphasis ended the concern and polemics involving the more basic concepts. After the first victories of the Arab national struggle at the conclusion of World War II, the task of achieving self-definition projected questions of content. The independence of several Arab states and the birth of the League of Arab States in 1945 ushered in new issues.

With the evacuation of British and French troops, it became more difficult to blame imperialism for each successive failure. The political thinkers of the period began to suspect that Arab society had been weak and corrupt prior to the imperialist onslaught. Arab thinkers urged their governments to effect changes in the societal and economic spheres.

The writers of this period, including such men as Musa al-Alami and Constantine Zurayk, exemplify the call for reform and innovation in the Arab world. Their writings, along with those of many others, attempted to examine the ills of Arab society and to explore the means best suited to alleviate them.

The 1948 Arab-Israel war and the subsequent Arab defeat added urgency to this movement for reform. Unfortunately, analysis concentrated mainly on a diagnosis of the societal crisis in the Arab world and not on realistic remedies. While writers were in close agreement on the genesis of the dilemma, there was little consensus on an appropriate response. This is, of course, not a uniquely Arab weakness—intellectuals everywhere seem far more able to accurately describe a problem, while having little in the way of a substantive, realistic course of action to recommend.

Constantine Zurayk's *Ma'na al-Nakabah* (*The Meaning of Tragedy*) explains the meaning of the catastrophe relative to the necessity for revolutionist change. He analyzes several immediate causes: inadequate Arab understanding of the danger posed by Zionism; insufficient utilization of their human and material resources; Arab disunity; nonparticipation of the Arab masses in the political process; and a failure to develop and sustain alliances with strong states. The defeat was seen not as that of one people over another, but of one kind of system over another. Zurayk envisioned a society united and progressive, directed toward modernization, separating state and religion, and demonstrating a scientific attitude and receptivity to the spiritual and intellectual values of other civilizations.

Warning the Arabs of the consequences of the forces of reaction, Musa al-Alami called for renovation in all aspects of Arab life and the reintegration of the Arabs into the community of advanced nations. Al-Alami in *Ibrat Filastin* (*The Lesson of Palestine*) placed the Arabs at the crossroads from which change and development were to be inevitable after a self-betrayal by division and slackness.

These thinkers developed their ideas along Western rather than Arab patterns of thought. Their writings reveal the splintered psyche suffered by the Arab revolutionist theorist. He has carried religious concepts into a secular framework. From his grasp of modern life he has been affected by the crisis of modern man so that the closer his concern with problems, the wider the gap between the normative ideas that govern his social expectations and the scientific thought that forces these philosophies to submit to inquiry.

The values of the European Enlightenment and the troubled response of the nineteenth century could be only artificially superimposed in the Arab world. The force that acted as a catalyst to the ideals of democracy, nationalism, and liberalism, and the reactions of communism, fascism, and totalitarianism were all alien in a political milieu that was first emerging from the provincial shackles of a social transnationalism.

Thus, with the acquisition of independence, came the challenge of nation-building; the problems of the parts of the Arab world thereby assumed larger proportions and had an impact upon the area as a whole, far greater than expected. The answer to the fundamental question as to whether democracy is to follow or accompany socialism and Arab unity found its logical conclusion in the gradual rise of several revolutionist models.

When viewed superficially, there is no scarcity of revolutionist models in the Arab world. The Ba'th in Syria and Iraq, the Destourian Socialism of Tunisia, the Front of National Liberation (FLN) in Algeria, the Arab Socialist Union of Egypt (ASU), and the Palestine Liberation Movement, all compete for revolutionist leadership. At best, however, Arab revolutionism flounders betwen the luxury of a self-assured past and the immensity of an uncertain future. There has occurred little innovation in institutions.

In the Arab world, revolutionism is merely a medium, and the medium is the message until a new medium appears. As a medium, it is a justification for the rivalry of competing groups rather than a process of significant change. The Arab is too comfortable with his identity; hence it is very difficult for him to sustain a revolutionist model. Rejecting the political messianism of modern Western philosophies of history, and unwilling to abandon his life-style, he is not easily susceptible to radicalism in action. Imprisoned in seemingly hopeless economic and social conditions, his anger is similar to the howling of a caged wolf, as it is less a demonstration of virility and more a function of self-preservation and a release of frustration.

The Ba'th Party (Resurrection), until recently the most potent Arab revolutionist model—and here one must use the term "potent" in a relative sense—finds its roots in an Arab environment which was reflected in the message of the prophet Muhammad to the world. The cofounder of the party, Michel Aflaq, emphasizes that these roots are social and political justice, and he rejects the Marxian economic deterministic approach to social and historical developments. Aflaq asserts that the overriding problem in the Arab world is not economic exploitation of the many by the few; rather, it is the division of the Arab land into weak, antagonistic units. Aflaq thus parts company with Marxian socialism, a universal, rather than a nationalist-minded, dogma.

Aflaq understands revolution to be the "awakening of the Arab spirit."[18] The use of the Arabic word *inqilab* (overthrow) has been employed by the theorists, while *al-thawrah* (revolution) has been widely used by the practitioners. Revolution must not necessarily entail blood and fire. What is necessary, however, is the revolution in thought and precepts by changing the roots of the public way of thinking.[19]

The unity of the Arab world is possible, Aflaq says, through the unity of the workers and the intelligentsia with the Ba'th party at the top. Aflaq foresees this as the only means for an *inqilab*, which would bring into power socialist Ba'th regimes throughout the Arab world. Aflaq's revolutionist process, which does not accept the class struggle of Marxism, seems to be vague. While he does not call for a violent overthrow, asserting that what little exploitation does exist in Arab lands could be remedied by legislative and not revolutionist means, Aflaq leaves no explanation as to what he means by an *inqilab*. The Arabic word does not necessarily imply a violent revolution, but neither could it be used within a context excluding the use of force. Aflaq seems to advocate force for obtaining control of governmental machinery but not for the allocation of power to the masses who would insure social justice—the absence of which Aflaq laments.

The Ba'th has represented at times in its early history a different type of party, with some popular support and a definite program. Having spread its Leninist-patterned organization from Syria into Iraq, it has suffered from its involvement with the frustrating question of Arab unification. The Ba'th has competed for power less by electoral methods and more by the prevalent techniques of intrigue and violence.

The Arab Socialist Union (ASU) in Egypt is an eventful process aimed primarily at preserving the Egyptian revolution from internal opposition rather than at providing it with a popular vehicle for the implementation of social reform. Contrary to Aflaq's academic socialism,

[18] Michel Aflaq, *Fi Sabil al-Ba'th (The Path of Resurrection)* (Beirut, 1963), p. 175.
[19] It must be noted that Aflaq wields little influence over the Ba'th today. Another important work of Aflaq's is *Ma'ra kat al-Masir al-Wahid (The Struggle of One Destiny)*, (Beirut, 1959.)

Gamal Abdel Nasser's is a pragmatic one. The sources of Nasser's socialism are the experiences of the ruling Egyptian Revolutionary Council which in several periods of time acquired different status and names. The cleavage between Nasserism and Syria's Ba'thists—there is no longer one Ba'th revolutionist thought in Syria—centers around the sensitive issue of whether or not democratic rule should follow development toward a socialist system.

Nasser believes that democratic freedoms must be suspended until the socialist experiment has reached certain stages of success. Aflaq and his supporters, hoping that Nasserism could provide a vehicle for the spreading of the Ba'th doctrine, called for a simultaneous development of both democratic freedom and socialism. The logical conclusion of their fundamental difference found its end in the breakup of the United Arab Republic in 1961. Since 1961, Syria's revolutionist jargons and ideals have mainly been for public consumption. There is near-complete ideological sterility. The exigencies of the time now determine the level of revolutionist jargon in Syrian politics. It is not difficult for the military with its monopoly of power and the intelligentsia with its intellectual ability to advertise a regime as a revolutionist model in the Arab world.

The demise of the United Arab Republic in September, 1961, two months after the nationalization decrees, led the pragmatic revolutionist doctrine of Egypt to reorient itself toward state socialism. The replacement of the National Union with its basis in revolutionist ideology by the Arab Socialist Union projected a notion of priority for the success of the socialist effort in each Arab state individually before the next formula for unity could be attempted. The ASU served as the basis for the 1964 elections, and its membership included peasants and workers. Theoretical bases for the new constitution dwelt in the never-never land of Arab socialism through the 1962 Pact of National Action.

If Nasser has been the leading pragmatist in the socialist endeavor, he has followed Ba'thist doctrine, among others, to the extent that they represent plausible reactions to the existing situation and the great pressures he faces in the area of internal developmnt. Rationalization of such policies in the ideology of social reform is a consequence of the role such concepts played at Bandung and Nasser's prestige in its wake. The socialist-democratic cooperative is a convenient term for government direction and control of an increasingly dominant public sector within a flagging economy. Nasser's model has had a few half-hearted attempts at achieving legitimacy by founding a government party, but its repeated failures indicate that the regime can survive by relying more on contact with the populace vis-a-vis the bureaucracy and policy than by popular enthusiasm for any hand-picked party.

Ahmed Ben Bella's socialism, as embodied in the Front of National Liberation, and his use of the left-wing French intellectuals, the *pieds rouges*, to amend the failures of his system of direct government management of farms aggravated the conflict between him and his successor, Houari Boumedienne. While Minister of Defense, Boumedienne utilized soldiers as his labor force in military colonies, the only state farms to show a profit, and formed the Army of National Liberation (later renamed the National People's Army, ANP) by drawing upon the Algerians, who had formerly been career soldiers in the French Army.

Boumedienne's socialism is aimed primarily at achieving internal consolidation through a revitalization of the structures of the Front of National Liberation. The new structure appears to be more pragmatic than the previous one, with emphasis upon greater representation. Externally, Boumedienne has utilized sweeping rhetoric, propelling Algeria to the front rank of the Pan-Arab crusade to restore Arab rights in Palestine and accumulate for himself both international prestige and some popularity with mainly non-Algerian Arab masses. The incontrovertible fact is that independence has not yet produced the expected and much-promised economic and political relief for the people.

Habib Bourguiba's revolutionist temper is a moderate one. This contrast with extreme Arab revolutionist thought is explained partially by the fact that Tunisia moved toward independence from France by means of negotiation rather than prolonged violence.

Bourguiba is neither a follower of a specific doctrine nor the creator of any. In this respect he emphasized that he is neither a man of doctrine nor does he feel a need for one. Bourguiba's concept of revolutionism is purely pragmatic.

Bourguiba's goals and aspirations are more like those of bourgeois nationalists than of revolutionists. He hopes to improve the Tunisian standard of living through large-scale industrialization, irrigation projects, and land reform. This would open the way for the Tunisian middle classes to exercise the dominant role in the economy and society that the French *colon* played prior to 1956.

The Destourian Socialism of Bourguiba is supported by labor unions and the most effectively organized mass party in the Arab world. The "Tunisification" law of 1961, the Bizerte crisis, the long-range planning, and the farming cooperatives of Ahmed Ben Saleh in the late sixties, led the doctrine of Destourian socialism into intricacies increasingly not related to her economic problems.

Ultimately, the various revolutionist models in the Arab world merge in the overriding context of the single-party state with an ever-widening public sector. No early solution to the problem of national identity is in sight for these revolutionist models. Public authority remains precarious; political personnel often untrained and inexperienced. A general impatience for political participation by certain groups is evident, but "the transformation" has yet to come.

In effect, every Arab revolutionist state perceived itself to be weak and protests the existing societal, inter-Arab and international stratification. As they are subject to subversion and internal opposition, their political insecurity functions in their mutual relations on a continuum between winning support from each other to countering violent attacks on their respective legitimacies.

None of the Arab revolutionist models has been able to institutionalize itself firmly, to create lasting structures, to establish liberal or popular institutions, or to relax its vigil against subversion, imagined or real. Stemming from their overreaction to such forces, these revolutionist models are constantly at the mercy of counterproductive consequences.

Africa

In contrast with other areas, African revolutionism is unique. Power was transferred to Africans without the benefit of such practitioners as Mao and Castro. While revolutionists in China and Latin America are concerned with mobilizing the masses and revolutionizing their indigenous systems, the Africans are most troubled by their search for identity. This quest for distinctiveness is the first stage of revolutionism and one that other areas went through before our era.

At the heart of the African revolutionist temper lies the problem of direction and the concept of a uniquely African personality. The present dialogue expresses the troubled psychological ambivalence of the new Africa: a pattern of attraction to, and repulsion from, reason on the one hand and submission on the other. It connects the rational with the irrational and joins objective circumstances with the consciousness of new Africans. It searches for ideal and spiritual elements of African character and origin.

Some African revolutionists, such as Kwame Nkrumah, whose revolutionist theory conceives of history as the spirit's progress towards liberation, have adopted an outlook similar to that of the earlier utopian socialists. Nkrumah believes in some kind of transcendental justification of the free spirit in necessary rebellion against all restraints. However, Nkrumah's impact upon African revolutionary thought was as ephemeral as his dominance over Ghana.

Then there are revolutionists such as Leopold Senghor and Julius Nyerere who insist on an organic African reality in culture, law, politics, and economic development. Others like Frantz Fanon and Ahmed Sékou Touré portray an Africanism which takes the form of a new romantic idealism: they conceive of African national problems as a contest between good and evil—the evil of colonial environment and an undefined African good. They call for total Africanization in society, politics, and culture. There is also Jomo Kenyatta, who is not quite as immersed in romanticism. He retains the idea of progress and inclines toward a moderate liberalism which is optimistic in its faith in the African future.

African revolutionist thought is best illustrated in the attitudes of African elites toward the nature of the revolutionist process, the role of political parties, and the relationship of violence to the revolutionist experience. The tendency of African revolutionists is to view change as a dialectic process. While there are parallels in their thinking, African revolutionists are in disagreement on the essential forces in operation in the dialectic process. On the one hand, there is the view represented by Fanon, who, although Western by training, through his association with the FLN became very much a part of the African revolutionary experience. He contends that the African revolutionist process is a contest of "good" against "evil." On the other hand, there is the philosophy of Nkrumah which conceptualizes the African revolution in more Marxian terms. Still others, like Touré, suggest that Africa's revolution is a combination of "good" against "evil" within the context of a Marxian struggle toward socialism. Julius Nyerere disavows the Marxian process completely, illustrating the absence of a class struggle in the African environment while searching for an African personality to revolutionize the contemporary setting. Leopold Senghor develops a theme of pragmatism, blending Marxism with a trial-and-error methodology.

One of the most humanistic of Africa's revolutionist figures was Fanon, a leading political theoretician in the Algerian independence movement, as well as one of the principal activists in the Algerian Liberation Front. In Fanon's philosophy, decolonization is a violent dialectical process. It will create a synthesis of new men with fresh mentalities. Fanon calls for a complete overhaul of the old system of relationships between nations, a process which he describes as having a "political philosophical objective which seeks to conform to the dictum: the last shall be first." This idea has the logical consequence that the "last" must be made to climb "the well-known steps which characterize an organized society, and they can only triumph through violence."[20]

Fanon says that the world of colonialism is divided into two parts: that of the colonialist and that of the native. The former is a good one with values, ease, and comfort. The latter, according to the colonialists, is a world without values; it is in fact a negation of values. The colonialists see the native as a destructive element, destroying, deforming, or disfiguring whatever comes his way. The result of this colonial categorizing is that the native is dehumanized. Yet, the moment the native realizes "that his life, his breath, his beating heart are the same as those of the settler," a "new revolutionary assurance of the native" appears.[21] In a sense, the appearance of the colonial settlers caused the death of aboriginal society, which in turn brought on a widespread cultural lethargy.

Nkrumah seems in agreement with Fanon on the point that decolonialism is a dialectical process. However, Nkrumah is more committed to the use of violence, for the former first president of Ghana subscribes to a philosophy quite similar to the dialectic of Marx. Following this thesis, Nkrumah asserts that for Africa to jump from its present state to socialism, it must skip the interim stages. This feat must be done rapidly and sometimes violently. Yet, Nkrumah with all his charisma, was unable to leave behind a relevant revolutionary legacy.

Nkrumah asserts that progress from communalism to socialism could have been achieved in Africa through normal processes of reform, since the underlying assumptions and principles are the same. But, as in Europe, the communalistic societies have gone through feudalistic, capitalistic, and colonialistic stages of development. Consequently, revolu-

---

[20] See Frantz Fanon, *The Wretched of the Earth* (New York: Grove Press, 1963), p. 30.
[21] *Ibid.*

tion is indispensable to the establishment of socialism because the antecedent socio-political structures have been animated by principles which negate the assumptions of socialism.[22]

Like Fanon, Touré, the president of Guinea, sees the struggle for decolonization as a fight of "good" against "evil." Yet, unlike Nkrumah, Touré sees the need for a firm commitment to move rapidly from the current state of African underdevelopment to a more productive society. Like Nkrumah, Touré's reality is that of a Marxian struggle.[23]

Nyerere of Tanzania shares the belief of Touré that the party is the vehicle for change. Like his contemporaries, Nyerere seeks to bridge the gap between the African past and the African present. He views the African past almost in a sense of prenatal cleanliness uncorrupted by the influence of the European colonialists.

To Senghor, president of Senegal, revolution means a socialization of society—a blending of the past and the present with the future. His early reading included Marx and Engels. It was particularly Marx's concept of humanism and his sociological analysis of man's alienation which attracted Senghor. He was quick to draw an analogy between the alienation described by Marx, and the alienation of African man by the colonialist powers.

Senghor used Marxism over the years as a framework on which to hang his changing concepts of socialism. He constantly insists that new methods must be chosen, new techniques tried, if one hopes to face the realities of the modern world. He foresees a third revolution causing "a reaction against capitalistic and communistic materialism that will integrate moral, if not religious values with the political and economic contributions of the two great revolutions."[24] In this third revolution, Africans could play a vital part. Senghor asserts that Africans must build their own development plan, based on European socialist contributions and also on the best of black American civilization.

African revolutionists differ among themselves upon the role of the political party as a vehicle for change. Touré and Nyerere are

---

[22] See Kwame Nkrumah, *Africa Must Unite* (New York: Praeger, 1963); *Ghana: The Autobiography of Kwame Nkrumah* (London: Thomas Nelson & Sons, 1957); *I Speak of Freedom: A Statement of African Ideology* (New York: Praeger, 1961); *Consciencism* (London: Heinemann, 1964); and *Neo-Colonialism: The Last State of Imperialism* (London: Thomas Nelson & Sons, 1965).

[23] See Ahmed Sékou Touré, *L'Afrique et la revolution*, Tome 13. This publication carries neither date nor place of publication.

[24] See Leopold Senghor, *On African Socialism* (New York: F. A. Praeger, 1964), p. 36.

firmly committed to the use and maintenance of strong political party structures. Other leaders, like Nkrumah, are less committed to the party as a vehicle for change. Fanon is critical of his contemporaries in regard to political parties.

Touré's vehicle for change is the P.D.G. (Parti Démocratique de Guinée). Like the chiliastic philosophies of many other leaders, the Jacobinism of Touré is predicated upon metaphysical assumptions of dubious consistency and relevance. Touré defines true Guinean consciousness in terms of an effective motivation to improve the entire society. In the good society, says Touré, all the restraints wrought by colonialism will be replaced by this conscience of social justice.

Through the party and education, the individual and collectivity are harmonized. There is no need to repeat the European experience of feudalism and capitalism in Guinea; the inherent moral stature of the true Guinean and the revolutionist struggle by the party guarantee social equilibrium. The construction of a socialist society, rooted in the communal African past and guided by the vision of a Marxist heaven, can begin.

For Nyerere politics is the organization of consensus. Both within his state of Tanzania and on the continent of Africa, he assumes that the basis of this consensus exists. Nyerere speaks of the precolonial African characteristics of equalitarianism and humanism. With the attainment of independence, all Africans can regain these traditional political modes.

Because there is a basis of consensus within the state, Nyerere believes that the European "isms," as well as such notions as interest, coercion, and elites, are superfluous. The nation is a preexisting reality coterminous with the state, which the party alone can represent. The party provides the sense of freedom within which differences are reconciled through dialogue and consensus is generated. After the party synthesizes the differences, however, no opposition can exist. Nyerere heralds democratic centralism in Tanzania.

Nkrumah believes that society and ideology are generically related. Ideology arises from the social milieu. A revolutionist ideology, according to Nkrumah, does not merely express the wish that a present social order should be abolished; it also seeks to create and maintain a new order. Societal ideology thus expresses itself in political, moral, and social terms.

The substance of Nkrumah's professed ideology is consciencism, which he defines as a "philosophical standpoint" based upon the African conscience and indicating the ways that progress is forged out of "conflict in that conscience." Basic to philosophical consciencism is the concept that man is endowed with individual value, dignity, and integrity. He is a spiritual being without original sin. This African conception of man imposes "duties of a socialist kind." The individual, as Nkrumah sees him, has both idealistic and materialistic tendencies which are in tension rather than equilibrium. He believes that traditional African values of communal concern and cooperation will harmonize man's inner conflicts.

If socialism is true to its purpose, it will re-create the humanist, egalitarian, precolonial African past. It will prevent the spread of class privilege and destroy the remnants of "colonial mentality." Where individuals are treated as *ends* and not as *means*, according to philosophical consciencism, there occurs a transition to politics. Philosophical consciencism preserves the ethical principle of initial human value.

Nkrumah asserts that the humanist traditions embedded in African society should form the basis of any modern cultural synthesis. Communal elements must prevent excessive individualism in economic matters, and the community must exercise control over alien influences. The traditional African humanist and cultural base must be preserved. Thus, for Nkrumah, the chief vehicle for change is the birth of African individuals asserting their tradition in the twentieth-century milieu.

Nkrumah is authoritarian insofar as he believes in the necessity of a one-party state, insists on strict party discipline within the elite group, and outlaws opposition to party programs and policies once they have been instituted. From 1960 until his overthrow in 1966, Nkrumah fostered a cult around himself as a leader of a pan-African union which would dutifully follow the doctrines of Nkrumaism. His faith does not lie so much in the mass of the population and in popular democracy as it does in the "principles of communalism" in socialist planning and in the vanguard party which he believes can build a new African continental society.

Fanon, like Touré and Nyerere, has devoted much attention to the use of the political party in the process of revolution. However, Fanon is more critical of political parties than are his contemporaries. He sees them as possessing faults not only in methodology but also in ideology. In contrast, Fanon claims that most of the African nationalist parties do not try to give the country any specific objective. They merely hope that the movement will continue indefinitely, thus perpetuating their position. Nationalist parties make use of spontaneous rebellions and revolts, but they make no effort to lead or organize them. Though they wish their rebellions to continue, they do not openly support them, leaving their conduct to the spontaneous ebb and flow of mass passions.

Nationalist party politics are described by Fanon as a struggle between the wish to destroy colonialism and the wish to be in friendly agreement with it. Thus schisms which weaken the movement develop between intellectual and activist elements of the party.

Fanon clearly recognizes the problem of building a national consciousness and identifies several of the cleavages which make such an undertaking difficult. He asserts that the native bourgeoisie is split from the masses because of its identification with the European bourgeoisie colonial elements. This split often results in the destruction of the native middle class, a downfall which may be hastened by the ties with its Western mentor.

Fanon feels that since the African national bourgeoisie is incapable of matching the accomplishments of its European counterpart, namely, the creation of a large industrial proletariat, it is harmful to progress and should thus be abolished. He feels that questions as to whether the bourgeoisie phase of national development can be stopped should be answered not by rhetoric but by revolutionist action. He is disgusted with the rise of dictatorships in the transnational phases of national development. He believes that this will lead to a betrayal of the people. Democracy is a form of government which places power in the hands of a mass party, not of a single leader. A country which is genuinely interested in answering the questions that history puts to it, that intends to develop the minds of its citizens, as well as its cities, surely needs a "trustworthy" political party.

Only a decentralized party can bring life to all the regions of a state. The party must educate the masses politically, for it is only through education that the entire nation can be bound into a cohesive reality. A leader who provides nationalism alone fails in his mission. On the other hand, a blind demand to meet social and political needs without humanism is also destructive of national goals. To Fanon, the nation—the true nation—is one in which all the people participate through a mass party.

Political parties, therefore, must have their roots in the masses and must be direct expressions of the popular will. Fanon believes that for a party to be a true party, it must not be merely an administration transmitting governmental orders. His unbounded and unquestioned faith in the people is deeply rooted in a strong sense of mass democracy, a conviction that popular welfare should be the objective of government and party action and not its victim.

In contrast to other African leaders, Senghor, like Fanon, is not an advocate of one-party states. Rather, he feels that the dominant party concept, with a strong but not alienated opposition, is best suited to African political needs. The parties must be representative of the mass citizenry for they are the central focus of political activity which can provide the substance of either cohesion or factionalism. Parties must be national and strive toward nation building by socialization through planning and development. There is both the room and the need for differing plans and programs in order to make the democratic egalitarianism of Senghor's socialism work.

Violence is inherent in the proposals of Nkrumah and Touré. If Africa is to proceed from her present state to one of socialism, such a rapid transition demands violence. Perhaps the most unique analysis of the role of violence is provided by Fanon. He believes that the native never looks to violence as an absolute line of action, but rather sees it as a useful tool because it unifies diverse peoples. It is a cleansing force which frees the native from fear, inferiority, despair, and inaction. It restores native self-respect and dignity. Fanon points out that in every respect the great figures of colonized peoples have led national resistance movements against foreign domination. He attributes the breakdown of the colonial epoch to native resistence, either through violent popular revolution or through popular action and unrest which have acted as a brake on the excesses of colonialism. The native intellectual has been forced to accept certain essential Western values. Fanon observes that deep in every intellectual's mind one can find a "vigilant sentinel ready to defend the Graeco-Latin pedestal."[25] But during the struggle for independence, when the native intellectual comes into contact with his own peoples, all Mediterranean ideas of human rights, beauty, and clarity vanish. They become worthless to him because they are irrelevant to the struggle.

Fanon believes that self-criticism is a traditional African institution and is not typical of the West. In the villages of North and West Africa, public communal self-criticism is quite common. Thus, individualism is the first Western value to fall in the process of decolonization. According to Fanon, it has been hammered into the reluctant mind of the intellectual by the bourgeoisie. But after the revolution it

[25] Fanon, *op. cit.*, p. 37.

will be replaced by communalism. Henceforth, the interest of one will be the interest of all. In short, the individualist motto, "Look out for yourself," will be forbidden.

To Fanon, truth serves a pragmatic purpose in the national cause. To the native, truth is that which is bad for the settler. It is that which spurs the breakdown of the colonial era. It is that which creates the nation, protects the native, and destroys the settler.

Every native who takes up arms against the colonialists is, according to Fanon, a part of a nation which will spring to life as soon as the old regime is destroyed. Programs of violence, organized by the nationalist leaders and carried out by the people, make it possible for the masses to understand social truths. Without violence, without knowledge of the politics of action, there is nothing but "a fancy dress parade and the blare of trumpets." The result of nonviolent struggle is a waving of flags and a few reforms at best. The masses will remain at the bottom, unredeemed.

6
•••••••• PERCEPTION
OF
POLITICS

Domestically, revolutionists live in a state of ferment. In most cases their societies reflect the after-effects of division of the world by colonial powers, rather than spontaneous political growth. Their governments are authoritarian yet minimal in effect, with little or no visible symbols of national identity. Most of the revolutionist states have thus far failed to develop basic concepts and assumptions for ordering relations among citizens and groups in their respective societies.

Internationally, revolutionist states have heightened the threshold of world politics and simultaneously widened the gap of consensus. There is little agreement on issues considered vital in international politics, and revolutionists have been quick to seize upon this factor.

The systematic qualitative and quantitative changes brought about by advanced weapons systems and the increased number of states have added to the instability of the international system but have not transformed it. While revolutionists seek transformation of the present system, their attempts to project their own image on the system have met with frustration. The declarations of Bandung, Cairo, Algeria, and Havana have been betrayed by their spokesmen.

Contemporary revolutionist perception is visionary in nature. The literature of revolution is filled with programs and manifestos derived from theoretical constructs. Initially, at least, reality must conform to the ideology of revolution. The early stages of revolutionist behavior eschew the pragmatic approach. In later stages, especially in the consolidation period, behavior becomes more reflective of the exigencies of the prevailing situation. However, the concept of the revolutionist vision always remains since this was the *raison d'être* of the change.

Any general theory of the revolutionist vision must account for several variables. The rationale concerning the unsatisfactory nature of the past is combined with aspirations for the future in an attempt to excuse or explain away the necessity for the present revolution. Revolutionists are repelled by certain past elements and attracted by hopes for the future. In the case of the latter, it has been popular to refer to grievances to justify the reasons for change. These are normally stated in social, economic, or political terms. Since most men have grievances, it is necessary to determine when grievances become intolerable and what initially generates these grievances.

A society whose structures are irrelevant may become revolutionist. It is the societal structures which produce the grievances that are themselves merely manifestations of unsatisfactory social, political, and economic distribution. Grievances, by themselves, have little meaning if the systemic foundation is still believed to be pertinent. In the United States, for example, Appalachia and the blacks have many similar grievances. The fundamental difference between the two groups turns on their respective perceptions of the present relevance of the system. It is in this perception that the contemporary revolutionist experience discovers its genesis. Groups in Appalachia are politically docile while black activists have discovered various methods for its expression of their aspirations.

Image of Domestic Politics

Increased institutionalization of the nation-state, a result partially due to technology, has accentuated the traditional confrontation of the individual with the state in many Western countries. In the non-West, the emergence of the embryonic nation-state has caused explorations, and sometimes conflagrations, in the relationships between traditional groups and the state.

In the West, the myths which have tended to support the institutions and structures of the nation-state have lost much of their relevance. The increasing complexity and number of societies and the swollen size of governments and their programs, both designed to cope with a wider range of problems and issues, have placed man in a constantly narrower and more constrained situation. As a result, politically invisible groups have been challenging core assumptions of society. This is especially true with regard to the blacks in the United States. It is no less true in Europe, especially when one considers that the increasing middle class in nations of that continent is seeking class articulation of values and objectives.

In the United States, one perceives a small but articulate group that has little use for the "liberal ethos" which affords it protection. In England and France, rising middle classes have no use for the myths of empire, world leadership, or national grandeur. Aristocratic systems on the national level are subjected to challenge by these new classes, which have adopted a severe materialism as their *raison d'être*.

In the midst of these trends, the mythos of individual rights is repeatedly challenged by governmental intervention in those areas once deemed the domain of the individual. The preoccupation of Western leaders with stability, both domestically and internationally, has been the cause and the effect of their increasingly discernible tendency toward an ever greater reliance on authoritarianism.

Technology is closely related to this particular phenomenon. Deprived of the technology of the twentieth century, the power of governments would be limited. Technology has enabled many institutions of government to outstrip their human environment, thus menacing the relevance of the entire myth of Western liberalism. As evidenced in the behavior patterns of Western youth, the inheritance of the Enlightenment has little to contribute to new modes of existence. The life of the past generation is clearly not for them; they do not believe that what was once held is necessarily self-evident. We are now entering (or may well be into) a period when the individual is the sum total of those qualifications which can be objectified, while the soul has been cast aside to make way for the transition of the new state.

The newly emergent states of the non-West must cope with a different set of conditions. Conflict is not between the state and the individual, but rather between the state and traditional groups. The old myths which gave authority to leaders of these traditional groupings and their institutions are being challenged by the state. Yet only a certain segment of the people in any non-Western country live under the authority of the new state; most continue to live under the authority of traditional groups and are thus removed from that sector which is considered modern. The process of nation-building, however, has required the state to enter into competition with traditional authority. This in turn has prompted the attempt to inject new values, interests, and goals in an effort to supplant those currently held and accepted.

The main difficulty encountered has been that of articulation. In these new states, the government or modern sector rarely speaks the political idiom of the masses. In many cases the old has been destroyed, but the new has not yet appeared. The reasons are technical as well as ideological. The new states have no commonly accepted mythos, hence their new national structures are easily perishable; many of the citizens refuse to transfer their traditional allegiances to these structures. New institutions have outstripped the domestic environment; thus, the majority of these new states have enjoyed little or no political development.

One of the paradoxes complicating this situation is that the international political environment evidences a reverse situation from that which exists domestically. When these new countries have tried to project outwardly into the international system, they have been confronted by the realization that the gap between domestic environments has outstripped the mechanisms of international relations, a condition they themselves have helped to create.

Image of the International System

The present posture of revolutionists in the international system is a function of both their image and their judgment of contemporary international politics. Their attitude towards international politics comes from the search for a uniquely independent identity and role in the world. They are attempting to strengthen their individuality, and are thus almost inevitably cast into a position flanked by either superpower, yet subservient to neither.

Revolutionists conceive their function as one of setting the world straight. Whatever disagreement there might be over details, they have concurred that a unique responsibility for the peace and security of the entire world has been transmitted to them. Knitting together the disparate strands of their foreign policies, a set of intellectual and operational assumptions may be found. These a priori foundations of their decisions and actions have formed the framework of their respective national missions in recent years. They may be phrased as follows:

1. Neocolonialism poses the principal threat to their existence.
2. The East-West conflict is merely a struggle for power and domination of smaller states.
3. The bipolar international system is not reflective of their interests and objectives.
4. They are uniquely suited to ameliorate the conditions of the international system.

Their own experiences have led revolutionists to believe that colonialism as a world force is on the defensive, but they assert that it is merely the old forms of colonialism which are passing rapidly. In the concept of neocolonialism as espoused by Fidel Castro, Gamal Abdel Nasser, Sékou Touré, and others, revolutionists have found further justification for jealously guarding their national independence. Foreign domination may take many new and insidious forms which are just as dangerous as the old.

Western critics are quick to point out what they think is an unwarranted preoccupation with the outside danger of Western domination. At the same time, many Westerners insist that revolutionists are blinded by this preoccupation to the real threat of communism. Two factors are significant here. First, Western domination is a part of the immediate past of most of the revolutionist states and is connected to the highly emotional issue of racism and exploitation. Throughout the colonial period, they were pawns of the West, controlled by the West with comparatively little regard for legitimate native interests. Second, revolutionists are acutely conscious of the dangers of Soviet or Chinese domination, as is evidenced by their refusal to be controlled by either.

Revolutionists quite naturally seek a position in international politics which would assure continued freedom from the domination of any foreign power. Within the context of the cold war, this has been a genuine policy alternative; these states have had the opportunity to accept courtship by both camps while refusing marriage to either. The ability to do so obviously depends on the continuation of great-power rivalry and on the will of revolutionists themselves. Their successes make it obvious that their ability has been continuously underestimated by both East and West.

Revolutionists cannot see either ideology—communism or democratic liberalism—as a prime menace to their autonomy. Rather, what concerns them most is the continuation of international political tensions which may lead eventually to their physical destruction or their subjection to a new foreign domination. It is between these alternatives that they are trying to steer an independent course reflecting their own national interests.

Revolutionists recognize the possibilities of major war as directly threatening their continued existence. The climate of international political tensions into which they were suddenly injected is not the most auspicious for their security. Both sides in the global bipolar struggle are potential sources of infringement on their sovereignty, and a nuclear war would destroy all their hopes for development. They feel that they are able, by the very fact of their aloofness from any bloc, to contribute conclusively to the lessening of international tensions. Their reasoning is that if they were to divide along bloc lines, a highly volatile situation would result. The world would be split into a tight bipolar pattern; there would be no group of mediators between the two antithetical poles, and freedom of movement—political fluidity—would virtually disappear. Under such conditions, conflict would be institutionalized, détente would be much harder to achieve, and the possibilities for disaster would multiply. The fluidity of the system must be retained and increased. Revolutionists believe that the interplay of opinion, the expression of multiple interests, and the existence of mediating groups can have a definite effect on progress toward reduction of international tensions and, consequently, toward prevention of nuclear war.

They seem to have concluded that containment of the great-powers is necessary, both for the maintenance of their sovereignty and for an overall détente. To achieve this, they must work to exclude from their states political, economic, and military dominance by either bloc, thus creating an "off limits" area to the protagonists of the cold war. East and West must follow the revolutionists' dictates. This leads to a seesaw effect as revolutionists deal with both blocs, supporting first one and then the other; all the while receiving massive aid from both yet becoming subservient to neither.

Revolutionists sometimes characterize their policies as expressions of an international conscience, or as elements of rationality which help to temper the predominance of irrationality on the international scene. They see themselves as having a special international mission in enunciating the basic world desire for peace. They feel that through their positions as mediators, and because of their objective stance between the two blocs, they will be heard by all. They can assume this because they feel they have vested interests merely in peaceful cooperation and not in any bloc participation.

Espousing these basic attitudes, revolutionists place increasingly greater faith in international organizations. They feel that the United Nations can and should exert a very strong influence in settling international disputes, even among the great powers. International organizations, like nonalignment itself, become vehicles for increasing the political power and influence of what traditionally would have been insignificant states. Thus, revolutionists, by various means, are literally attempting to force the great powers to pay them heed.

Perceived Role in International Politics

Revolutionists reject the bipolar international system through their allegiance to nonalignment, with anticolonialism and third world solidarity as its corollaries. They transcend the split between the East and West by adopting a posture that is allegedly more relevant than the alternatives embodied by either great power.

Nonalignment

Nonalignment is permeated by themes of alienation and anomies. It embraces a variety of psycho-social sentiments including anxiety, futility, and moral and intellectual skepticism.

As translated from perception into practice, nonalignment is designed to serve specific functions. Reduced to their essence, these include:

1. Reconciliation between national sovereignty and the requirements of security.
2. Harmonization between political independence and economic dependence.
3. Maintenance and enhancement of national solidarity.
4. Maximization of foreign policy alternatives and power in international politics.
5. Establishment of an independent role and individuality in world politics.

Nonalignment must be distinguished from the traditional concept of neutrality, for there are striking differences. Neutrality is essentially a legal condition of a state's external relations which allows it to remain uninvolved in international disputes or wars surging back and forth around it. It is passiveness, abstention, and even indifference to what is happening. A neutral state does not have official opinions on international matters; it does not even attempt to decide, for its own benefit, who is right and who is wrong in a dispute. It takes no sides in any conflict, verbal or military, and maintains an officially equal attitude toward all belligerents. Neutral states are officially satisfied with whatever the status quo happens to be; they have no demands to make on any other countries or blocs. This is not to say that a neutral will not defend itself when attacked or when its vital interests are seen as being threatened.

Nonalignment presupposes an international situation characterized by power blocs. A nonaligned state is one that has no binding military, political, or economic ties to a power center outside its borders. It formulates its foreign and domestic policies, insofar as it can, in an independent manner free from any outside considerations of, and pressures from, allies or bloc leaders. It has no obligations other than to its own definition of its national interest, though it may carefully consider the effects of its actions on other states if it chooses to do so. It need never fear being pulled into a conflict where it might be forced to compromise its national interests, and it need never fear being regarded as an "enemy by association" by a state with which it has no quarrel.

From these distinctions it may be inferred that all neutral states, by definition, are nonaligned countries. The nonaligned states have the choice of remaining truly neutral or of participating in technically nonneutral activities while maintaining a nonaligned status. It is precisely this element of choice, this freedom of decision, which the nonaligned states view as essential.

The nonaligned states carry on active foreign policies, both in direct contact with members of the two major blocs and through international organizations such as the United Nations. They have opinions and express them freely. To the extent that they are able to do so, they exert pressures for and against parties to disputes. They have even gone so far as to form ad hoc blocs of their own for the joint pursuit of common objectives. Yet such states remain absolutely unaligned with either major power center. Their support may see-saw between the two as they take independent positions on issues and seek support from both sides or from other nonaligned states.

Among the nonaligned states, three main groups or types can be identified. There are those who look primarily to the West for their form of government, their ideological orientation, or aid for their development. Likewise, there are those states who look primarily to the Soviet Union or Communist China for ideological identification and economic assistance. And, finally, there are those which appear to be trying consistently to remain aloof from either bloc while actively seeking aid from both. This last position is very difficult to maintain, but it may be the most effective in terms of both domestic benefits and international influence acquired.

Since revolutionists have attached an absolute quality to their independence, they take intense pride in both domestic and international self-reliance. They are loath to commit themselves to policies before they examine them in terms of their own national interests and goals. They fear that alignment with either bloc would commit them to future courses of action over which they would have little or no control, and that future conditions could easily lead them into compromising their national interests.

Nonalignment has a snowballing effect—it has become the fashionable position for new states. Great prestige has accrued to leaders among the nonaligned states, and the international influence of otherwise weak states can be strengthened effectively through nonaligned policies.

Revolutionists are quick to point out that nonalignment is not synonomous with ethical fence-sitting. They view their position as the truest expression of an acute moral and idealistic sense; they can and do judge the policies and actions of both blocs and accept or condemn what they find to be objectionable.

They have fully assumed the traditional international ideal of the sovereign state as a vehicle for expressing their particular identities. Revolutionists, upon assuming power, began to act as sovereign leaders have acted traditionally. Militant nationalism was applied as an active defense and assertion of independence. Anticolonialist feelings were extended to include all types of foreign domination as these states became determined to define their own national destinies free of any outside pressures.

Their immediate goal is national development—in short, modernization. Revolutionists realize that this cannot be achieved alone, hence the necessity of aid from industrialized states. But they also recognize that economic dependence can lead to at least partial domination of their internal and external affairs by foreign powers. Revolutionists have long attempted to reconcile the basic dilemma that confronts them: on the one hand they are determined to avoid foreign controls and to maintain their sovereignty; yet, on the other hand they greatly desire vast amounts of aid from the great powers. They have constructed a partial solution by seeking aid from all available sources, but in doing so they have made it clear that their political allegiance is not for sale.

Inasmuch as both blocs view their aid programs as political weapons to halt the undue accretion of influence by the other, it has been possible for revolutionist states to exploit both sides in their ideological struggle. By thus trading on the anxieties of East and West, these states have been able to obtain the required aid to further their development, and yet have remained aloof from either bloc.

The practical and immediate benefits of nonalignment are perhaps the most important and the most appreciated by present revolutionists. Their states are in the enviable position of being able virtually to demand economic assistance from both sides in the American-Soviet competition. Through a sort of blackmail, they can insure the continuation of aid from both sides, so long as each side believes that its aid is diminishing the influence of the other over the nonaligned state. This calls for some occasional fancy footwork, but revolutionists have proven that experience makes for a nearly perfect performance. Some have been receiving aid continuously from the United States, the Soviet Union, and Communist China and have been alternately lauding and damning their benefactors.

Nonalignment plays yet another important role for these states a role that derives its form from domestic political considerations: to act as a rallying point, mobilizing widespread support behind governmental actions vis-à-vis the external world. Revolutionist leaders are caught in the middle of domestic factional struggles, among groups which are either closely identified with the values of the Western tradition, or are ultranationalist—whose response to the outside world may border on xenophobic racism—or who describe themselves as quasi-Marxist, neocolonialist, or socialist and are generally inclined toward emulation of the Soviet or Chinese regimes.

To preserve an already tenuous and strained national unity, to create a national consciousness, and to progress along the road to development which has been promised, the groups within the state require that the revolutionists pursue policies which will satisfy each of them. This must be done to avoid the dual disaster of civil war or domination through subservience to either bloc. Nonalignment seems to offer revolutionists just such a possibility. An assertive foreign policy and demonstrations of willingness to support, cooperate with, and receive aid from both blocs are attempts to satisfy the domestic power factions in the interest of unity. When revolutionist states combine these factors with the colonialist common enemy, they feel that they have arrived at a winning combination domestically at the same time that they are serving their interests abroad.

Since they are trying to pursue foreign policies that are in response to their own national identities, needs, and desires, revolutionists realize that to maintain the greatest possible range of policy alternatives they have to be free to side with any state as the situational conditions vary. Their foreign policies are eminently consistent when viewed not through the glasses of the United States or the Soviet Union, but through the glasses of the national interest of the states in question.

In terms of political strategy, nonalignment is one of the two choices open to these states, and either alternative is the result of their weakness in relation to the great powers. Some, realizing their very vulnerable positions, have opted for alignment with a bloc. But this is not to imply that the nonaligned revolutionists do not realize their vulnerability, as some Western critics would have us believe.

On the contrary, revolutionists, fully aware of their relative position to both blocs, have decided that nonalignment offers them the best possibility of maintaining and developing their national identities in the face of the global hostilities which surround them. Instead of choosing between the great powers, they have decided to try to improvise an alternative which will maximize their operational choices and give them the greatest opportunities for independent pursuit of their own national interests. For them, nonalignment is a means of gaining strength through weakness. They can exploit their economic and political positions. Their diplomatic voices can continually work to lessen the importance of military power in international politics; and, as the importance of force declines, their influence rises.

Revolutionists are constantly trying to justify their neutralist position to the rest of the world. Pressures from Moscow, Peking, and Washington are denounced. Charges of "expediency" are heatedly denied. They reiterate constantly that they are primarily concerned with their own interests and that nonalignment is the only course available to them.

They have concluded that it is in their national interest to act as a mediating force between the two antagonists. Their goal is the creation of an international political system which avows coexistence as a basic value, tolerates diverse ideologies, and fosters free development of a state along the lines it desires to follow.

Undoubtedly, idealistic concerns for world peace, for mediating East-West conflicts, and for eliminating the use of force in world politics play a part in determining the outlines of nonalignment. There is a feeling among revolutionists that the existence of a definite group of non-aligned countries, who do not have vested interests in the power of either major bloc, is the only hope for a truly objective solution to the problems caused by international tensions. They feel that both blocs will recognize their impartiality in disputes and will accept mediation efforts from them or from the United Nations. This feeling has led from time to time to calls for the formation of a "neutralist bloc" in the hope that such a concert would be able to bring effective pressure on parties involved in a dispute to agree to a mediated settlement.

Anticolonialism

Revolutionists are searching their societies for principles and values which could be wedded to their own anticolonialist impulse. While they were still colonial peoples, revolutionists had something specific, concrete, and immediately apparent on which they could blame virtually everything. The colonial regime was held responsible for disease, poverty, oppression, and illiteracy—all the ills of their societies. The nature of colonialism was portrayed as solely exploitative.

By concentrating their fire on the colonial powers, revolutionists were able to arouse the degree of public sentiment and support necessary for the political revolution that would put them in power. They rode into office on waves of passionate anticolonialism, but their promises of a bright future were not easily or quickly fulfilled.

The logic of anticolonialism promised that once independence was won, all barriers to justice, freedom, and progress would be demolished. The promised land would be readily at hand. When this did not prove to be the case, social cohesion began to break down almost immediately. The unity achieved in the face of the common enemy was threatened, and with it the very existence of the new states and their nationalist regimes.

Faced with problems, frustrations, and instability as the facade of unity began to disintegrate, revolutionists had to do something to preserve what they had sought for so long. Because many of them had been bred on Marxist-Leninist doctrines of imperialism, it was not unusual that they should seek the image of a new foe which could serve a unifying purpose similar to that of anticolonialism.

During the national liberation campaigns, colonialism was usually described by the nationalists as unjust economic domination and exploitation by European finance capital. Starting with the premise that capitalist interests controlled the colonial powers, nationalists charged that the capitalist interests continued in a post-independence attempt to exert de facto political control through economic means. Revolutionists thus created a new bogey man: neocolonialism. They claimed that the independence and progress of the new states were threatened by continued foreign economic domination. This form of covert control was denounced as the direct cause of the immediate failures of the post-independence period.

On the surface, anticolonialism is almost synonymous with anti-Westernism. But this is at least a partial misconception. At the same time that revolutionist states are passionately derogating the West, they are actively attempting to imitate Western achievements. Anticolonialism provides a convenient screen for their contradictory and intense attempts to achieve what they believe to be the hallmark of modern nationhood.

Third World Solidarity

Since the rise of territorial states out of the political vacuum that was medieval Europe, men have tried to go beyond the balance of power by enforcing systemic norms. Emerging victorious from World War II, Russia and the United States attempted to consolidate the states of the world into two rigid systems.

The cold war period was both pleasing and frustrating to the great powers. Direct interaction between them was limited to ideological rites, with neither side gaining more than occasional libidinal satisfaction.

The new states were politically, economically, and ideologically accosted by Moscow and Washington. Rather than succumb to the bipolarized configuration of power they opted for the development of a third force in the international system.

The idea of a third force was conceived by Nehru as a tactic arising from India's strategic needs. The concept rapidly gained acceptance in the capitals of new states around the globe. It became a rallying point for third world solidarity.

In 1955 the newly independent states of Africa and Asia met at Bandung under the tutelage of Nehru. They expressed a concerted opinion regarding the evils of colonialism and the desirability of nationalism and socialism. They extended friendship to their sister state, China. It appeared that the "spirit of Bandung" would transform these states into a unit of truly political action—a third force in world politics.

A series of Afro-Asian solidarity conferences of governments, peoples, parties, labor unions, and students followed during the next decade. Nasser in 1957, Nkrumah in 1958, Touré in 1960, Tito in 1961, Boumedienne in 1965, and Castro in 1962 and 1966 were among their articulate sponsors. The rhetoric of these meetings, the denunciations of colonialism and neocolonialism, and the expressed desires to mediate the cold war became increasingly divorced from the realities of world politics. The several decisions of the 1966 Tricontinental Conference of Havana, designed to set up a tricontinental solidarity organ and to strengthen the unity of Asia, Africa, and Latin America, have had little effect upon the course of international politics.

In Africa and Asia the emergence of many additional states from colonial status since 1955 destroyed the basis of the anticolonialist barrage; it also destroyed the myth of third world solidarity projected from Bandung. Whereas in 1955 there were less than thirty independent Afro-Asia states, in recent years the number has increased to more than seventy-five. As the Afro-Asian states achieved independence, they found they had diverse opinions and interests. In addition, China's invasion of India in 1963 demolished the pretense that the third world as a whole even adhered to the principle of coexistence. China's denunciation of the Nuclear Test Ban Treaty of 1963 further dispelled the image of the compromising and placid third world soul.

Furthermore, third world solidarity was relevant only as long as the bipolarization of international power was a fact. Evident today, however, is polycentrism in both Eastern and Western camps; China and Rumania, France and Pakistan, are the malcontents in the Russian and American blocs. This situation leaves the mediator without a function. Third world foreign ministers become lonelier as the great and lesser powers pursue their national interests without respect for bloc or ideological commitments.

The embarrassingly abrupt end of the Afro-Asian conference at Algiers in 1965 was symptomatic of the demise of the "third force." Yet it merely dramatized what most third world exponents had long suspected: that their solidarity, if ever a reality, had become an irrelevant myth, like that of the "free world" or the "communist bloc." Unlike these latter phenomena there was no great power to constrain fragmentation. At Algiers it was openly acknowledged that the alleged solidarity had not been subverted by neocolonial forces, but rather divided by the stresses of changing conditions and conflicting national interests. In the third world, as in the West, because of the absence of substantive systemic norms the realities of sovereign states burst into the myth of unity.

Third world solidarity is the logical result of acceptance by revolutionist leaders of the traditional doctrine of sovereignty and of attempts to apply it to contemporary international conditions. It flows from the doctrine of sovereign independence and from their own passionate attachment to an absolute aura or mystique of state freedom.

Image vs. Reality

Revolutionists are trying to cover a century in a decade; they are attempting to telescope the achievement of the Enlightenment and the Industrial Revolution in one generation. Their states are in marked discontinuity with the old. The family, the king, the tribe, and religion have outlived their usefulness as organizing principles.

The central structures of government in most revolutionist states are modern in form only, not in substance. Their societies display a lack of political integration, partly because they are characterized by ethnic, religious, social, and cultural pluralism, partly due to limited operation of the process of modernization. A general characteristic of most of these states is the wide gap in modernization between the masses and the elite.

Revolutionist states seem to react to the intrusion of traditional European values, and serve the same particularistic, value-maximizing function that was the *raison d'être* of all European nationalist movements. The immediate goal of the nationalist movements of nineteenth-century Europe was to replace alien dynasties with republican, locally oriented governments. The emerging bourgeoisie simultaneously pursued an internally pluralistic goal—the breakdown of rural-based control over the economy and polity. The bourgeoisie hoped to rationalize these dimensions of life according to middle-class standards.

In the recent experience of revolutionist states, particularly in the non-West, the democratization of society by means of increased commercial participation and secular education was accomplished by an elite hostile to traditional values. Thus, the emergence of these new states lies well within the generic framework of most modern revolutions. In the sense that revolutionists are attempting to consolidate their economies, educate the masses in national consciousness, and suppress irredentism, they are responding to the same revolution in thought that accelerated the development of modern Western civilization. Arbitrary boundaries, ethnic diversities, and fresh memories of colonialism make the modernization effort excessively parochial in approach, but essentially these states serve as a vehicle for the values of the revolutionist individuals.

In most of the states, the dichotomy between economic reality and idealistic aspiration is staggering. They aspire to goals which at this time seem almost unattainable. The populations of most of these states are growing far more rapidly than food supplies. There is poverty, hunger, disease, illiteracy, low productivity, and mass unemployment. These societies are predominantly agricultural, and the middle class is very small, lacking enough influence to stabilize the economy. The deficiency of many of these states in natural as well as human resources is considerable.

One of the major problems in developing technicians and managerial personnel is that those educated sufficiently for these positions no longer wish to engage in this type of work. The social status of such occupations does not offer the prestige rewards of such professions as medicine or law, thus the reluctance of talented people to enter these fields. There exists not only a shortage of leadership, but also a frequent distrust of innovation because of the nonmechanical orientation of the population.

Modernization in governmental structure has mainly occurred at the level of formal structure where there has developed a progressive trend toward the establishment of Western institutions. In most of these states the parliamentary and the presidential system have become the favorite models of imitation with American and French influence predominant. Most of the revolutionist states have had long experience with executive bureaucratic governments, either through traditional or colonial structures. The most distinctive innovations displayed in the formal structure of their political systems are two: central representative parliaments endowed with constitutional legislative power and a constitutionally secular and independent judiciary.

In practice these new innovations are not operational and remain mere exotic importations. Instead, the working form of most revolutionist political systems is characterized by two phenomena: a tendency toward unitary government with a heavy centralization of decision-making, and the continuing predominance of the executive-bureaucratic branch. The predominance of the executive branch is paramount in the revolutionist states; the legislative and judicial branches of government consistently occupy subordinate places. The participation by Parliament in the authoritative functions of rulemaking is severely restricted. The independence of the judiciary in rule adjudication is generally a myth, and courts are utterly dependent on the executive.

The patterns of recruitment into the political arena in revolutionist states operate in the context of narrow-based oligarchies with little breadth of political participation. Leaders are recruited in the urban centers from such elements as the professional and business groups, civil servants, and army officers. This situation explains the high degree of substitutability of role in the political processes. Accordingly, in many of these states, there is little consensus as to the legitimate ends and means of political action. The intensity and magnitude of political discussion have little relationship to political decision-making. The rate of recruitment and change of social categories from which political participation is drawn is becoming relatively more rapid.

Revolutionist states display many similarities in the manner in which interests are expressed and organized. Interest groups are limited in development; where they exist, they have not become an integral part of the political process. Hence, particular economic or occupational interests are generally latent and are not expressed by functionally specific associations. These conditions have brought into political focus the role of the military.

In many of these states, political groups have very narrow bases and serve essentially as vehicles for competition between different elements drawn from the modern sector of society. These political groups are generally organized around particularly strong revolutionist individuals. Hence the political process is characterized by a prevalence of cliques. This special character of political loyalty gives to the revolutionist individuals a high degree of freedom in determining matters of strategy and tactics. Opposition parties and political opponents can easily be presented as revisionist movements. One-party systems tend to predominate, ranging from comprehensive nationalist movements to dictatorial parties.

In many of these states, the political sphere of life can hardly be differentiated from the spheres of social and personal relations. The lack of a clearly differentiated political arena prejudices the clear formulation by political parties of distinct points of view. Political parties tend to take a world view and feel that they represent competing ways of life. Instead of engaging in internal reform programs, they concentrate almost exclusively on issues of foreign policy.

As revolutionists try to cope with issues of foreign policy, they confront further difficulties. The prime characteristic of the contemporary international system is that no state—not even a great-power—can act solely on the basis of its own narrowly interpreted interests. The few exceptions of naked unilateral intervention by states in the post-1945 period—such as the Russian crushing of the Hungarian and Czechoslovakian revolts or the American Bay of Pigs invasion—prove this rule. Absolute independence is now utterly out of the question. State action must result from a careful analysis of the effects it will produce on the other states and on the international system as a whole. Very real limits are placed on the scope and nature of state ends and means.

Yet, precisely at the time when sovereignty and independence of action are becoming anachronistic and when an assertion of such an absolute conception of sovereignty borders on irresponsibility, revolutionists have become intoxicated with these ideas. Their first objective since assuming power has been to preserve and assert their independence. It is jealously guarded and strongly argued; any attempt, real or imagined, by a foreign government to encroach on its absoluteness are met with near-violent reactions and bitter denunciations.

Claims of uniqueness from revolutionist states serve a vital internal function and project themselves outwards into the international system largely as a posture of convenience and profit. Claims of uniqueness can be traced back, possibly, to a deep sense of insecurity, but this very stressing of their uniqueness may serve only to slow down the process of modernization in their countries. Rejection of all things Western in favor of a real or imagined unique perception of things can only prove detrimental to present and future attempts at development. Their concern is more with the trappings of sovereignty and less with the practical and real problems associated with modernization.

The existence of competing blocs has helped make possible the revolutionists' juggling act. So far they have been able to exploit the anxieties of both East and West in such a way as to maximize the economic and political benefits and to minimize their loss of freedom.

In one sense, nonalignment is an elaborate rationale for a policy of exploitation. By "playing hard to get," revolutionist states are assured of short-term benefits. Their calculations seem to be based on the hope that by the time conditions have changed enough to negate the possibilities of such exploitation, either they will not need further aid for development, or else the aid will be naturally forthcoming, through institutionalized international cooperation.

Such an assumption is the direct result of two basic premises: (a) either cold war competition will continue in its classical post-1945 form enabling the exploitation of the split to continue, or (b) the major cold war issues will be settled, leading to a period of free international cooperation for development.

Revolutionists see their response of nonalignment as meeting whatever contingencies might result from either of the two above conditions. Nonalignment is a sort of insurance policy against the future which pays immediate dividends as well. By not committing themselves to either side, they can use both for their own purposes as long as possible. If, through some unforeseen course of events, one side gains a dominant position in the struggle, they will not be tainted by a "guilty" association with the loser.

Third world maneuvers in the United Nations and through other international organizations serve a similar purpose. They are designed to defend the argument that cooperative development and advancement are duties of the modern states; the wealthy states ought to help the poor ones to gain a similar position. Such efforts to institutionalize aid programs—national and international—are obvious.

However much revolutionists may be idealistically concerned with the peace of the world and with cooperation, their prime consideration is obviously directed to their own progress and development. Having decided that their goal is the creation of a modern, industrialized nation-state, they logically have asked themselves: What is the best way to get us from where we are to where we want to go? The years of bitter anticolonialist nationalism, plus their absolute ideas about sovereignty, precluded alignment with either bloc. Following the successful lead of India, Burma, and others, they chose nonalignment.

In spite of all its virtues for the revolutionists, ambitious nonalignment is potentially dangerous, for these states are essentially disjointed, faction-ridden, weak, and underdeveloped. By assuming unjustified and disproportionate political influence in relation to their actual capacities and strengths, they could easily be lured into a position of trying to use power and influence which they do not possess. An inflated sense of importance and power is very satisfying to peoples who are accustomed to being treated as inferiors, and it is very useful in domestic politics. But it could also prove explosive.

Yet, on the other hand, the more established nations must develop a greater sensitivity to the revolutionary temper of our time. The fact that communists have infiltrated some of the present-day revolutions should not obscure the truths of change. The smallness of the world brought about by communication has enlarged the existing level of perceptions relating to the relevant political socioeconomic gaps between various actors.

In such a fluid environment, reorderings will continue to occur, instability will be escalated, and political tensions will mount. A new wave of revolutionism is forming, and its crest threatens to reach total wave proportions. In the path of such an onrush, the present international system could be irreparably changed.

7
•••••••• DIRECTIONS OF REVOLUTIONISM

The early seventies may not contain the revolutionist content found in the fifties and sixties. There are no new revolutionist ideas, and revolutionist leadership is generally quite old and in many cases has been discredited. There is a conservative streak on the horizon in the international system. Only the rhetoric of revolution exists in many states formerly considered revolutionist. Man cannot live by revolution alone, as so many national leaders have discovered.

The significant theories of the past seventy years developed because those who wrote them did so without the burdens of state leadership. They planned and wrote from exile (Lenin), from a cave (Mao), and from prison (Gandhi). The next true generation of revolutionists might well be nurtured from the relative luxury of a similar situation of being outside the formal apparatus of a state.

The international system is experiencing a reaction to revolution and its imbalances. The next revolutionist wave may come a decade from now. For the U.S. to be prepared to respond to revolution in the future, now is not too soon to see the world as it is within the context of a constantly changing international order and to adopt a pragmatic attitude toward the existence of the phenomenon of revolutionism.

The international system is caught between two developmental phases, one dying and the other not yet born. Nations today must not only suffer the high-pitched tensions of an age of great danger and constant crisis, but must also wander through the apparently blind alleys intrinsic to an era of maximum transition. Environmental change has outstripped institutional structures; carried far enough, this trend could lead either to the collapse of the entire system, or to civilization-destroying upheavals.

The entire international system today is gripped by inhibitions and frustrations. The technological and political developments of the second half of the twentieth century have created a set of entirely new conditions of world politics. Statesmen, however, have not as yet succeeded in adjusting to this new political system. The assumptions of classic doctrines of statescraft have been largely invalidated; the old masters have so little to say to us today because the kind of a world they knew has vanished. The state that defines its ends in the old terms and seeks them by the old means must reconcile itself to living indefinitely with crisis.

The nature of the international order may be characterized as a crude form of international democracy that may be contrasted with the essentially hierarchical state system it is replacing. "Democracy" in this sense refers only to interstate relations rather than to any international political arrangements. States approach each other differently today. Whereas before they pursued their interests and resolved their conflicts within a rigid social system, now they function within a flexible and egalitarian one.[1]

The old order and its configurations of traditional forms of power have been unable to cope with the issues of the contemporary world. Stalemate has become the usual fate of any issue involving great-power relations. States, apparently unable to achieve their own objectives, still retain the ability to frustrate each other. Although everyone has been trapped in this dilemma, it has been the great-powers, deprived of their former dominance, who have found the situation most frustrating. Power relations have become futile and statesmanship unproductive.

The old international system is dying because of two mutually reinforcing historic developments. First, war as traditionally conceived is no longer a useful instrument of foreign policy and has thus con-

[1] The concept of international egalitarianism is elaborately developed in a brilliant unpublished essay by Charles O. Lerche, Jr., "Thoughts on the New Democracy in World Politics." The discussion here represents a summary of the essay.

tributed to the rapid decay in the position of former great powers. Second, a new concept is moving to take the dominant place once occupied by great-power military hegemony; the egalitarian and transforming urge of the new states who look on the old leaders as their natural enemies and who are frankly seeking a drastic reordering in the international system.

The range of alternatives of the great-power policy maker has been sharply circumscribed. He may persuade or compromise as freely as before, but his freedom of choice to coerce is severely limited. A state can and does go to war, but it has become fantastically difficult to create a situation in which war would be an expedient policy decision in terms of any rational cost-risk calculation. Military scholars have made an impressive intellectual effort to incorporate the new technology into the principles of warfare, but no one has yet solved the basic issue: How is the conduct of a thermonuclear war to be fruitfully related to rationally conceived foreign-policy ends?

The new and small states no longer fear the military preeminence of larger ones. Stripped of its ability to coerce "peacefully" its smaller counterpart, the large state faces a cruel dilemma in a conflict situation. Threat does little good, and time continues to dull its effect. The great-power has only two alternatives open to it: it may risk the use of force, or it may instead abandon any attempt at dictation. The first choice has not been popular; today neither the Western bloc nor the Communists contemplate a resort to war, either against each other or in their dealings with lesser powers. On the other hand, large-state dictation to smaller members of the system has become increasingly costly.

The glaring fact of present-day world politics is that an era has ended. The old great-powers can no longer control what goes on in the world; the traditional great-power club has become something of the past. The only workable instrument for the ratification of interstate decisions in the contemporary world must proceed from a consensual base of governments and peoples.

It is true that no eulogies have marked the passing of an age. Historical change always proceeds spasmodically; not everyone is equally sensitive to the dawn of a new era. There are the fools who insist that no new change has taken place and that eventually, after the disruptions are eliminated, everything will again settle down in its original mold. There are those who, while recognizing the evidence of their senses, lack the courage of their convictions.

The United States of America

If only because the prospects for open rebellion are minimal in the United States, revolutionism is different. As in other areas where violence is a norm, there has been a shift to violence. But in the United States, the real question turns on whether revolutionists will be able to achieve their goals in a revolutionist manner, or whether they will be co-opted by the system to become what they so passionately detest.

The black revolution in the U.S. is dependent on the following question: Can the consensus which endows the American myth with life survive the revolution with which it must now contend? Or will American political life in the future be plagued by the exclusivism, factionalism, and violence which characterize most political systems?

Were the balkanization of their political world to occur, Americans might become racists by default. They relied as a nation on the liberal-democratic myth; therefore, they failed to cultivate the ideological and class commitments which became the bases of the European party systems after the French Revolution. America is faced with the possibility that political activity may become the wholly devaluated assertion of objective identities and biological passions—attributes of man which had been relegated to the socio-economic spheres of life—which had been submerged politically during the heyday of the American myth. A variation of the Marxian dictum would explain American politics if objective, biological man and political man found an organic synthesis.

Like the blacks, the members of the New Left would like to radicalize the system, but they have tended to work within the existing system, a process which is basically unsatisfactory to them. As their attacks increase, the system naturally tightens its resistance to the change they promote. Their assault, for example, on the liberal ethos has tended to make the system more authoritarian and less responsive to their demands. This has added to the frustration and anger of the New Left, which in turn has reinforced their emotional outbursts against societal elements that offend them.

This initial desire to work within the system was evidenced by the support the New Left gave to Senator Eugene McCarthy in 1968. McCarthy was closely identified with a phenomenon described as the New Politics. Few of his supporters, and perhaps not even McCarthy himself, knew exactly what this term encompassed. Its meaning became highly individualistic and its proponents defined it viscerally rather than intellectually. It appeared to be related to mass politics rather than to special-interest politics and was contingent upon a highly audible, participatory democracy. While the New Politics may or may not be a dead issue on the national level, the candidacy of McCarthy is now history. Without him, the New Left has lost all present hope of influencing the system by electoral means. One suspects that in the future the trend of its efforts will be directed more to radical change of the system than to trying to work within it, as evidenced by recent bombings.

Any attempt to analyze the influence of the New Left must start at the level of the political community. Partially because of the increased effort of mass communications and partially because it has struck some exposed nerves in the populace, the New Left has polarized political emotions and reactions. Although its origins are middle-class, it attacks the latter's values without respite. By revealing existing dissatisfaction, it has caused value gaps among the population which, over a period of time, might well become irreparable.

The primary target of the New Left's influence has been youth— particularly those on the campuses. It is among this segment of the population that the effect of the New Left has been felt the most. Part of this influence can be attributed to the issues spawned by poverty, Vietnam, and the environment. The larger portion, however, has been related to the attempt to condemn middle-class values as the root source of the perceived evils in the society.

Many of the New Left's ideas, and especially those of its more radical element, rest on the conviction that violence represents the only means to influence the society. Since middle-class life is based on "rules of the game," the radical New Left's reliance on violence, both as a vehicle for social change and as a means of protest, is directly antithetical to this. Laws, it would affirm, are to be disobeyed not merely for protest value but also because the individual conscience is obligated to disregard what it cannot accept. In this respect, the New Left has tended to legitimize individualism to the brink of anarchy and has not hesitated to condemn systematically those of differing opinions.

Conventional wisdom would have it that the student activists have been influenced by the New Left. Up to a point this is true. However, the radical student element is a reaction against the conventional liberalism that dominates most of the New Left. The intangible facets of the student activists' program have not illuminated the practical, political goals of the movement. As mentioned before, the students have been most reticent, perhaps incapable, to delineate alternative proposals of action. Thus the assignation of such goals is left to the observer.

If viewed within the context of other utopias—and the student movement can be considered utopian-oriented—it could be inferred that the movement not only wants to reform the system but the human condition as well. Indeed, if the goal is truly the total reconstruction of society and its foundations, the movement becomes more religious than political.

This concept of action is another principle expounded by the student protesters. They refrain from the traditional requirement that the construction of a philosophical base is mandatory before any action can be initiated, but adhere instead to the conviction that action itself provides its own rationale. A new independent philosophic principle may ultimately be produced through the pursuit and implementation of direct, strident action. Unequipped, and probably therefore unencumbered, by this customary ideological baggage formerly deemed necessary for revolutionary success, student protest moves, nevertheless, to present its challenge to the system, to effect that system's amelioration, and, perhaps, to acquire its own secular philosophical perspective in the process.

However, student groups such as the Weatherman faction of the SDS are becoming increasingly committed to violent solutions. This unique perception of politics necessarily results in the rejection of the old forms of ideology, discipline, and conventional political methods. Student protest is an attempt to rectify the inequities of an antiquated system through new and innovative means.

Like the ecological crisis, which has only recently assumed the proportions of a crisis in the public mind, women have been economically oppressed for decades. The movement toward the liberation of women—often discussed over tea by fatigued suburban matrons—is an appendage of the breakup of the politics of consensus that has highlighted the sixties. The statistics of discrimination are, of course, glaringly in favor of an indictment of American males—and assuredly, the egalitarian instinct that has guided America since the rustic days of Andrew Jackson will yield results. More women will enter medical schools, law schools, and other areas of elite specialization. The dilemma of the overeducated, functionless woman will increase—as more women graduate from colleges and find little in society to fulfill their quest for satisfaction beyond the confines of the home and the husband.

Yet one wonders how many braless campus coeds will seek happiness in the industrial order that they supposedly despise anyway. The women who work the eight-hour day cannot help but become an extension of it. But in a culture which has long since abandoned a philosophical ideal of its women, it is evident that feminism will not meet concerted resistance. Instead, our increased demands for production and consumption will make available to women more and more spiritless jobs. Although the liberation movement will probably become just another chapter in the feminist annals of the twentieth century, the demands of women for equal roles in society will continue to haunt a society already dangerously close to abandoning its most traditional institutions—and the retention of the family unit has an undeniable value in a society which is certainly experiencing a crisis of profound purpose.

China and Asia

Revolutionists in Asia appear to be proceeding faster than in other areas. While this may be an illusion, perhaps there is more to be done—certainly the problem has a vastness not shared elsewhere. China, of course, defied comparison to other revolutionist states whose resources belong on a lower scale. Mao and Asian revolutionism are inseparable, and, correctly or not, aspects of Maoism have influenced revolutionism in all other areas of the world.

The awakening of Asian masses has been accomplished by Asian revolutionists. The politicization of rural masses is far from complete, but this effort is slowly shifting to urban areas as they become more important. Successor revolutionists to the old guard are poised to replace them. However, the revolution in Asia will continue to be dominated by the old-line revolutionists.

In spite of events in Vietnam, Chinese revolutionism is the phenomenon upon which attention should be focused. In this respect, there are a host of unanswered and unanswerable questions about the future in Asia. Revolution in word has been at variance with revolution in deed. And while the Chinese have spoken irrationally at times, they have thus far not behaved in such a manner internationally.

It would be difficult to assess the past and discuss the future in Asia without some consideration of the interaction of the U.S. and the

U.S.S.R. there. Both the United States and the Soviet Union are the principal protagonists of this category. Their contemporary approaches include similar aspects and interests. China looms as the primary problem for both. Although their aid to India during the Sino-Indian conflict was not cooperative, their desire to see a viable, counterbalancing India produced a potent mutuality of interests.

More significant, however, is the desire on the part of both states to maintain the status quo in Asia. There is a school of thought which would say that the Soviet Union and the United States—when in Asia—*act as Asians*. And the primary concern of the Soviet Union is, of course, its territory in Asia, since these disputed frontiers represent a great source of antagonism with China. The bulk of Soviet land is contiguous to China, and the latter has coveted what it feels to be traditionally Chinese territory. In the case of the United States, the most significant quarrel between itself and China turns on the U.S.'s recognition of Nationalist China as well as on the United States presence in Asia. As long as a U.S. presence remains on the continent, China can never be predominant and any resurgence of the concept of "Middle Kingdom" becomes meaningless.

As long as the Soviet Union maintains the northern frontiers and the United States supports various nations in the southern periphery, China will find itself encircled. Its ambitions for cultural as well as territorial supremacy thus thwarted, China's frustrations will increase; its image of other nations will reflect this frustration. China has raised the issue of who the "paper tiger" is in Asia on numerous occasions. Although this issue is more relevant to influence than political-military power, it is nevertheless salient to the nature of revolutionist phenomena in Asia. This involves the rejection of Western influence (for our purposes here, the U.S.S.R. is considered a Western nation) and the status quo which it represents.

The complexity of international relations in Asia is due in part to the diversity of interests and peoples found in the region and also to the constantly evolving international relationships in Asia. At the present time, the Soviet Union, the United States, Japan, India, and China must be considered the dominant powers in the region. China must be viewed as the pivotal regional power because the interests of the other states are always energized by the former's military-diplomatic maneuvers. China is the only Asian power which seeks political and cultural influence over the entire region, and the other major powers have tended to consolidate their interests to prevent its success. It is one thing to consolidate interests; however, it is a completely different proposition to prevent Chinese success.

Because China is a revolutionist state, its behavior has caused concern among other Asian countries, partially because its actions have been unpredictable and partially because they have been hostile and internationally antisocial. One of the unspoken Western rules of interaction requires states to signal which moves have intrinsic and deep meaning for them and which ones are for public consumption. In an age when the nuclear sword of Damocles hangs over our heads, such a requirement is undoubtedly necessary; yet, China has not adhered to this rule and never has had to do so. China was incapable of doing so during the Cultural Revolution. The evidence increasingly points in the direction of spiritual rather than pragmatic ideology as the driving force of Chinese policy.

At a time when other Asian states, including North Vietnam, are pragmatic in their policies, we view Chinese policy as essentially spiritually motivated. By themselves, the romanticized utterances of the Chinese leadership do not indicate irrationality, but the danger of irrational behavior seems greater in the China of today than in the 1950s. Although irrational behavior is hardly novel among states, the possession of advanced weapons has in the past assumed the rationality of their possessors. The uneasiness with which other actors view China stems from the fact that no such assumption has been made with respect to that country.

The unique feature of this situation is that China is the first non-Western power to possess such weapons, and the unpredictability of its actions has increased the apprehension of both the U.S.S.R. and the U.S. It is assumed by some that for the Chinese leadership the development of nuclear power is designed to make that country more relevant in its initial quest for regional domination. From a historical standpoint this would be the reestablishment of the "Middle Kingdom" around which all other nations revolve in orbit.

On the other hand, there is the view that Chinese nuclear weapons are primarily for self-defense. This view is supported by those who see Chinese action as essentially reaction to states China perceives as hostile.

The broad objectives of Chinese foreign policy are the securing of influence in Asia, in the socialist camp, and in the international system as a whole. This behavior is quite normal. As Chinese power is relative as well as subjective, it is not acquired for its own ends but for the reestablishment of the perception of traditional Chinese power at the lowest possible cost to itself. Mao has attempted this, but it remains a matter of interpretation whether this should be viewed as essentially an offensive or defensive orientation.

Because there are in Asia so many facts to be digested, so much information to be incorporated and accounted for, the mind is easily overwhelmed by the amorphous plethora which is the end result. To explore by analogy, as some scholars have, the resemblances and the differences between the U.S.S.R. of Stalin and the China of the Cultural Revolution is interesting but not very useful. Events proceed with a terrifying rapidity today, but their significance is digested rather slowly. Circumstances in the world at large have affected the thrust of events not only in China but in Asia as a whole.

Insofar as the Cultural Revolution is concerned, it should be viewed as an internal phenomenon which has been little influenced by external events. To the extent that day-to-day developments in the world at large have hardly influenced the course of internal events over the past two and one-half years, the China experts are probably correct. Its complexity is multileveled, but its rationale should not be viewed solely as a power struggle. Its implications appear far more extensive than most scholars have divined. On the subliminal level, the attempt to make reality conform to Mao's philosophy was the basis of the transformation attempted by the Cultural Revolution, which was an ultrarevolution within a continuing revolution. The unanswered question in this regard is: Has the Cultural Revolution succeeded to the extent that Mao or his successors can now address themselves to other matters?

If the Chinese have been politicized to the extent that the ideas of Mao constitute an adequate explanation of events, China will be on the threshold of a new age domestically and internationally. This prospect is not particularly attractive to the other major states in Asia—the United States and the Soviet Union included.

The implications of the Cultural Revolution and its meaning for the international system and Asia in particular must be assessed. To do this, several observations are necessary. During the period of the Cultural Revolution, the most significant overseas enterprise of the Chinese regime was rendered ineffective (the PKI in Indonesia); while Chinese influence increased in Latin America and parts of East Africa, substantial numbers of U.S. forces established themselves in Vietnam on the Asian rimlands, and all other external Chinese activities were reduced. The Chinese leadership seemed to lose interest in the outside world because of its presumed preoccupation with domestic events.

This internal preoccupation should not have come as a surprise because Lin Piao in his manifesto of 1965, entitled "Long Live the Victory of the People's War," informed the faithful of other nations that if revolution were to be made, it would have to be done without significant Chinese assistance. This was not a departure in policy because the Chinese have never actively exported their revolution in any form other than rhetoric and advice. China did not turn its back on subversion or revolutionist activities—it merely announced what had already been a fact of life.

There are two reasons that the Chinese have backed off from trying to export revolution. The first turns on capability broadly conceived, and the second is related to effectiveness. Both were viewed in the context of their contributions toward Chinese goals. While it has been a relatively popular assumption that "wars of national liberation" are low in cost, the cost of Chinese sponsorship has been rather high when consideration is given to the lack of efficacy of these revolutionist programs. No Chinese-abetted revolution has in fact succeeded. The Chinese leadership has also discovered that its revolutionist experience is not as exportable as once assumed.

While China has not completely abandoned the desire for world revolution, it has increasingly wider options from which to choose courses of effective action. The advent of advanced weapons and the potential to develop equally advanced delivery systems will make China determined to secure the influence it perceives as its due once its ICBMs become operational.

There is no evidence that Mao has any desire to incorporate China into the present Western international system. It would seem that the China of the not-too-distant future will, with new capabilities, seek a new system in which it will feel relevant. Mao has written, "Marxist philosophy holds that the most important problem does not lie in understanding the laws of the objective world and thus being able to explain it, but in applying the knowledge of these laws actively to change the world."[2] As an operational assumption, this passage elucidates how the "East Wind" will attempt to destroy the old and establish a new system with which it will be satisfied. Only then will the revolutionist process be completed. At this time, there is no ideological middle ground. China will continue to advance with only an occasional tactical retreat. However, Mao will not live forever and the important question

[2] Mao Tse-tung, *On Practice* (July, 1937), *Selected Works*, Vol. I, p. 304.

concerns the destiny of a China without Mao. Although Lin Piao is most likely to succeed Mao, one cannot rule out the possibility that political power may be diffused on a regional basis after Mao's death. As a matter of fact, there is some evidence that regional authorities are becoming increasingly more important in China, since approximately half of the Central Committee of the Ninth Party Congress have regional bases of power or are members of provincial revolutionary committees. Their commitment to the revolutionary ideals of Mao is less certain than that of Lin Piao.

Latin America

Similar to that of the Arab world and Africa, Latin American revolutionism has been co-opted by the military, who have derevolutionized the process. Perhaps Nasser serves as a model to the military socialists in Latin America. Both in Peru and Panama, military authorities have opted for a socialistic ultranationalistic approach. As a consequence, a deep sense of frustration has set in among revolutionists, who seemingly have to set their hopes back another generation.

Latin America today possesses many of the conditions that have tended to make some men revolutionists in other times and places. But revolutionists cannot make a revolution unless the historical moment is ripe and unless certain objective conditions are present. Fervor, compassion, and even fanaticism unallied with significant revolutionist potential sometimes not only fail to produce a revolution, but can even set back the cause of revolution and of human welfare and freedom. There are revolutionists and revolutionist movements in Latin America today; the question remains: What are the possibilities for revolution, and, if a revolution is possible, what kind of revolution will it be?

It could be argued, but not demonstrated in scientific specifics, that Latin America "turned a corner" in its history sometime between 1963 and 1968. World War II was a time in which some Latin Americans were awakened to the possibilities of modernization and development, and the post-war period was the beginning of a period of hope for the future. The Universal Declaration of Human Rights, the fall of the dictators, the promises of apparently rapid industrialization, a certain widespread naïveté about the possibilities of creating a solid, middle-class society—all these mental sets—led Latin America to assume that its future was to be relatively better than its past. The fairly easy overthrow of the dictators who had endured World War II heightened the sense of expectation. But frustration began to replace its mother, hope, as Latin America observed the speedy recovery of Western Europe and Japan and the emergence of the Soviet Union as a mighty industrial power, while its own development was fitful and uneven. This frustration gave vent to the "Nixon riots," but soon hopes were restored by the Alliance for Progress.

But, recently, these hopes have given way not only to frustration (and, in some cases, despair) but also to a general fear of change, even among those who had been exponents of reform. Fidel Castro, who appeared first as a comeuppance to Batista, but then became a spectre that still haunts the very groups who should be expected to lead reform efforts, may be seen as a tragic epitome of Latin American revolutionist hopes. That is, tragic in the sense that the revolution has not only been contained but also has begotten a powerful counter-revolutionist "backlash," which has submerged the possibilities of real revolution in Latin America for at least the next few years.

The "Castro complex" affected not only the Latin American middle class but also the government and people of the United States. At first there was an attempt to react positively through the reformist programs called for in the Alliance for Progress. But the enunciation of the so-called "Mann Doctrine" (never an official statement of policy, but evidently a "new mood" among the U.S. government officials of the time) signalled the real end of this period of hopeful reformism as far as the United States was concerned. That is, as of January, 1964, the United States essentially gave up trying to "embrace democratic governments and gave a handshake only to dictatorships," and withdrew in exasperation from its benevolent attempts to engineer the development and the democratization of Latin America through aid programs.

But far beyond the change of attitude among government officials occasioned by their frustration, the military forces of Latin America had decided that hemispheric security depended upon the capacity of the armed forces to contain agitation and subversion, and that development was not possible without stability (implying a top-to-bottom reformist process, instead of a process led by a dissident elite, or a bottom-to-top restructuring).

With the emergence of Castro, both U.S. and Latin military strategists decided that the United States armed forces must assume the role of "shield of the hemisphere" from external threat, while the Latin American military establishments assumed the role of protecting the "internal security" of these nations from internal subversion inspired by "foreign" revolutionists ideas and efforts of Cuba and other countries of the socialist bloc. Thus did the Latin American military establishments grow in armament and competence even as the civilian politicians and government officials were increasingly frustrated in their (usually feeble) attempts to initiate significant reforms. As a result, in common with the majority of nations of the rest of the third world, Latin American nations have tended of late to fall increasingly under the overt or covert influence, if not dominance, of the military forces. The process of the militarization not only of international diplomacy but also of internal politics that began with the cold war is not finished yet.

The United States exercises a massive and pervading influence in Latin America, whatever the official policy may be and whatever the attention given to the rest of the hemisphere by the government in Washington. A lack of interest in Latin America by the U.S. government does not necessarily mean that the impact of U.S. pressure will be much less, but only that it will be exercised more exclusively by groups not responsible to the process of public debate and political decision-making that characterizes official policy.

But what in effect has happened is that official policy also tends to reflect the discouragement of frustration with the enthusiastic but minimal and naïve programs of reform aid characterized by the Alliance. Thus, the U.S. presence must be characterized as either nonrevolutionist in its public policy or counter-revolutionist in its military posture and programs and the majority of its banking and business interests. And this means that until the political balance shifts decisively in the world, or until there is a significant new approach and a decided move to the left in the United States itself, the U.S. presence, allied with the residual traditional groups, the new social engineers and technocrats, and the military of Latin America, will be able to keep revolutionist activity well below the danger level, even though there will be occasional calls of "wolf" (communism or "chaos") for purposes of strengthening political support from the frightened North and Latin American middle classes.

Twenty years of hope and frustration have given way to an indeterminate period of retrenchment of the somewhat modified but essentially unshaken status quo. The leadership of the defenders of the status quo has passed from the great landowners and bankers, and the politicians linked to them, to the military officers, at least in most countries. It is true that these military officers are often anti-American, nationalistic, and even interested in nation-building, conceived of as a process of maximization of national self-sufficiency in basic industry. But, as a group, they are not inclined to allow any significant modification of the social structure; they insist that progress can only come from the top down.

The revolutionists are dismayed. The leadership of the opposition is increasingly shared with "old liberals" who are themselves dismayed at the loss of the civil liberties they had once assumed were inevitably to spread over the whole society in time. The opposition to the "mili-technocrats" is still an uneasy alliance, united by its opposition but split over its program between revolutionists and reformists, radicals and liberals. In this process, the traditional communist parties have declined precipitously both in intellectual and organizational vigor and in popular appeal. Instead, the leadership of the opposition, and in some cases the "vanguard of the revolution," has passed to the hands of nondogmatic national Marxists and to liberal and/or radical Catholic bishops, priests, and laity. Even as some North Americans during the 1950s were convinced that the hope of Latin America would be fulfilled in the "democratic left," so today these romantic spirits see in the belated birth of compassion and identification with the Latin American poor by Roman Catholicism a cause for great hope in the future. Unfortunately, the novelty of seeing bishops lead marches of peasants and of an occasional priest taking up arms has deluded some into seeing what there probably is not: a massive, popular understanding and support that can be effectively organized for political and/or revolutionist purposes. Sadly, part of the Church will probably be (quietly or dramatically—it depends on the case) intimidated into silence, and another part of it will be persecuted into impotence.

Some still believe that the university students of Latin America, with their long history of involvement in protest and political movements, will again reignite the flame of effective opposition to the military caretakers increasingly dominant in Latin America. But although this may happen in a few years, it appears as if the present student movements have either been broken or been intimidated into quasi-silence.

The Arab World

The appearance of Palestinian liberation movements (Fedayeen) such as al-Fatah and the Popular Front for the Liberation of Palestine is not new to the Arab world. While their commitment to revolution in the areas is uncertain, they could well become a revolutionizing force in the area. Since these movements are transnational in character, they do not bear political comparison to other revolutionist groups elsewhere. But like Latin and African revolutionists', the Arabs' deep sense of frustration stems from their dissatisfaction with the way things are and the lack of their ability to alter circumstances. More than in other areas, the Arab revolutionist must be a prophet who can articulate the message; unfortunately, none currently exists.

Arab revolutionists, in the aftermath of the ebbing of the euphoria of independence, projected upon the state not only norms and values but organization and aspirations as well. Lacking the intricate dialectic components of the communist ideology, they developed goals of social and economic change but failed to find the internal resources—human and physical—to approximate such goals. Radical pronouncements of policy and showpiece projects have been used to gain popular support and sacrifice in regard to agrarian reform, industrialization, and resettlement.

The resulting revolutionist ideology in the national context relies on an eclectic, pragmatic borrowing. The Leninist-disciplined organization, the long-range economic plan, token agrarian reform, superficial Western liberalism and fascism, all form this amalgam adapted to perceived local needs. It is cloaked in terms of basic questions of social hierarchy and human purpose without providing solutions to the problems these questions raise. In a decade and milieu in which the inherited institutions and customary relationships no longer appear natural, inevitable, or immutable, that which is borrowed assumes an indigenous character for lack of alternatives.

In the search of those revolutionists for new institutions and refashioned relationships, hierarchy and control remain as vital as they have been in the past. The complex coordination of human effort required to meet the promissory notes of the revolutionist leadership is attempted in an economic-demographic set of conditions that foretells an inherently pessimistic result.

These conditions make it plausible for the few to defy these principles during the democratic socialist experiment. The few must manage, plan, and foresee developments. The majority must obey, sacrifice, and endure, impotent to change or validate the direction of the society.

Bound together by their repudiation of the traditional political and social structures, revolutionists find themselves even more frustrated in the social aspect of the revolution. At least in the realm of rhetoric, revolutionism in the early sixties shifted the focus of ideological attention of these regimes to the class structure and economic organization of the state. To the extent that parliamentary democracy was frustrated for the lack of a middle class, revolutionist Arab socialism emerged under army control without the firm base of a working class. Its intellectual sources are to be found in the example of the Leninist organization.

The quality and quantity of social and economic change in Arab states will inevitably be the result of the direction and effort placed in various development programs and the extent to which the masses identify with the goals of the leadership in radical reform. Such development, it would seem, will not be prejudiced greatly by an ideological conception of the ideal society, no matter how revolutionist. When, however, progress is realized in any given area, it will be clothed in such guise, more for external benefit than for anything else. The further these ideals are separated from reality, the more frustrated and potentially explosive will become the political situation in societies which must run to stand still.

The manifestations of military regimes in the Arab states reveal that revolutions occur mainly for military and political considerations and rarely for economic and social causes. The legitimacy of these regimes is derived from their predecessors' inability to make good on their political and military promises. The inability to fulfill promises results from a serious and recurring imbalance in the means-ends relationship of these regimes, military or civilian. This recurring imbalance is mainly due not to the unavailability of means, but rather to Arab inability to deal effectively with operational modifiers influencing the flexibility of their means and the priority of their objectives.

After two decades of unsuccessful outpouring of energies toward the one and only irreducible factor in Arab politics—"a just and equitable solution to the Palestine problem"—responsible Arabs are still indifferent to the fact that they have to deal with two simultaneous revolutions—an internal revolution against centuries of social demoralization and an external revolution aiming for a higher degree of Arab freedom of action in foreign policies. Only a successful prosecution of these two revolutions makes possible any attainment of that objective.

The general atmosphere prevailing over the area for the past fifty years has been one of calling for radical change from traditional means and methods for solving internal problems. The creation of the state of

Israel was perhaps the foreign input that most affected an internal issue anywhere in the world. On the one hand, it has stimulated internal reforms and developments; on the other, the military imperatives of the Arab-Israeli conflict have constrained the Arabs to allocate increasingly large resources to nonproductive sectors.

The intensity of the nature of disequilibrium brought about in the Arab world can in part be explained by the fact that Western ideas—such as parliamentary democracy, nationalism, and socialism—clashed with the conditions of the Arab social environment. The call to independence in the Arab world was overtaken by the call for Arab unity. The survival of one preempted the other, and the Arab revolutionist experience has yet to come to grips with the internal contradictions of Arab society, turning power vacuum into power base.

In the Arab world the revolutionist takeover of power has always preceded any objective understanding and articulation of the revolutionist processes and goals. Their defeat in the June, 1967, war brought the Arabs face to face with reality. There could be no excuses—and none was accepted as readily as the excuses given in 1948 and 1956. The prestige of Arab governments, as sources of leadership, reached a new low in the Arab world. The problem now is not just the liberation of Palestine—a then distant goal to which all Arab governments paid lip service—but also the liberation of the so-called revolutionary as well as the reactionary regimes, along with the best methods with which to achieve it. Clearly the traditional approach had failed, and a more radical alternative was needed. This may explain the infatuation of the Arab masses with the Palestinian liberation movements, which in themselves are expressions that mass participation is the road to action and goal fulfillment.

Aware of this new climate in the Arab world, and taking advantage of the general weakness of the Arab regimes and their inability to restore their rights in Palestine, the Palestinians have moved on their own. For the first time since 1949, the Palestinians found themselves free and willing to act with militancy, independently of their hosts. The ability of the Palestinians to achieve their goal will depend on whether they can unite into a single revolutionist vanguard, link up with the restive Arab masses, and elicit their participation. They must also consider the problem of overcoming the restraints imposed by the Arab regimes and, in some cases, the open hostility of those regimes.

Although the unity of the Palestine liberation movement is not yet a reality, a hegemonic group is emerging and is beginning to look to the next stage—that of linking up with the Arab intelligentsia. Both al-Fatah and the Popular Front for the Liberation of Palestine realize their success will depend on their ability to spread the revolution to non-Palestinian Arabs. It is in this stage that they will encounter their greatest challenge. Linking up with other Arabs will require an ideology and the creation of what may be called "parallel organizations."

Although ideologically uncommitted, al-Fatah has so far rejected the Marxist–Leninist approach of the Popular Front on the grounds that it is part of the traditional revolutionary approach, and thus fails to overcome the impasse in which the Ba'th and other Arab revolutionist movements have floundered. It has thus far relied on a nationalist and anti-imperialist (Israel) approach. Greater emphasis must be accorded, at this stage, to structures and organization. If al-Fatah or the Popular Front fails to develop these structures, they will lose control over the non-Palestinian Arabs, and the whole movement may suffer from "war-lordism." On the other hand, the Arab governments will view with alarm the development of an organized mass movement that can only threaten their continued existence, and will thus not countenance the development of these "parallel organizations."

In its Palestinian context, al-Fatah represents the willingness of the Palestinian Arabs to seize the initiative in securing what they believe to be their rights in Palestine. In its greater Arab context, it represents a reevaluation, if not outright rejection, of Arab governments. It is in this context that student and associational groups' unrest in the UAR (without precedent in the regime of President Nasser), in Lebanon, and in Jordan, must be viewed.

The approach of al-Fatah so far, has been along the lines suggested by Regis Debray, namely: that guerrilla action will lead to political action and political structures and that the former is not dependent upon the latter for success. Thus it is only now that al-Fatah is beginning to come to grips with the cultural inputs to what may become its ideological orientation and platform, and two trends appear. One trend calls for a reconciliation of Islamic tradition with the requirements of the day through the reform of Islam—reopening the doors to Ijtihad (religious interpretation and jurisprudence)—while the other trend suggests a completely secular left-of-center approach.

The prospect of a peaceful settlement may hasten these developments and bring about a major confrontation. There may be an attempt by the Palestinians to take a short-cut approach: a direct bid to the masses without the benefit of parallel organizations. In such a situation they may find themselves stalemated, emotionally supported by the masses who, lacking organization, will not be a match for the organized, repressive force at the disposal of their governments.

This overall preoccupation with the Palestinian cause as the hard nut to crack, may serve as the vehicle for a Pan-Arab movement of liberation. The cause of Palestine, many involved Arabs feel, can be served correctly only through a Pan-Arab Union. This has resulted in a state of affairs where liberation from without is pushing the agenda for liberation from within—from rulers reluctant to gamble over sectional, particularistic interests.

The Arabs may have a revolutionary experience coming, one that will rank among and parallel those of France in 1789, Italy in 1871, or Russia in 1917.

Africa

The search for identity has dominated the thought and actions of both U.S. and African revolutionists. Both are preoccupied by this idea for entirely different reasons. In the U.S., revolutionists are rejecting their identity for something new, while Africans are trying to develop both a personality and an identity. This sets Africa apart from other areas; and the immediate African future, like the past, will be dominated by this preoccupation. When Africans can achieve this goal, African revolutionism will be removed from its tedious confines.

The direction of African revolutionism is determined by responses of Africans to internal needs within their respective states, external conditions within the international system, and requirements of liberation from remnants of foreign sovereignties. The dominant African response to the internal challenge of change assumes the form of nationalism–socialism. In dealing with each other and the international system at large, African states assume postures of Pan-Africanism and nonalignment. To cope with the issues of liberation, Africans are utilizing guerrilla, political, and psychological tactics.

During the independence period, African revolutionists employed nationalism as a propaganda tactic to rally mass support against colonialism. In recent years, African nationalism has hit a different note. It is used increasingly not only as an ex post facto justification for the revolutionist movement, but also as a means and an end in maintaining cohesiveness in a fragmented society in order to maintain a viable nation-state.

Concepts of nationalism and socialism stimulate much of the activities of African revolutionists. Nationalism is designed to safeguard the state from fragmenting into geographic or tribal units while socialism is utilized to effect development, yet the application of these concepts in an environment characterized by a scarcity of viable myths to support national consciousness is fraught with difficulties. In the African context, the dichotomies between individual freedom versus political order, group allegiance versus national loyalty, and vested versus the common interest compromise the integrity of the political system. As the manifestations of military subcultures become dominant, the seceding of tribal, ethnic, or religious subcultures and the clashing of class interests will increase and continue to characterize the African political landscape in the immediate future.

In the meantime, these political patterns will continue to compromise African socialist effort in the realm of development. Socialism has not as yet provided an effective expression to the principles which underlie African communalism. Traditional communalism remains disorganized and has not been channelled through the machinery of African states. In fact, class cleavages will continue to rise and magnify economic inequalities and political factionalism.

While these conditions will most probably prevail in the immediate future, it is not unlikely that within five to ten years, the present-day African revolutionist and military elites will face the hostile opposition of a wave of young revolutionists whose perceptions of the military and present revolutionists reveals their inner antirevolutionary character.

In the realm of Pan-Africanism, there has not developed a commonality of means. While African revolutionists agree that the Africa which emerges from the revolutionist setting must unite to create an African identity and personality predicated on the principles of the uniqueness of the African revolutionist temper, disagreement upon methods continues to prevail. The political viability of Africans lies in the fragmentation of the African system of states, while their economic viability necessitates integration. Caught in this dichotomy, Pan-Africanism has not yet experienced itself in its originally perceived form. The struggle for freedom crystallized desires for unity; the acquisition of independence magnified the will to retain national sovereignty.

The myth of Pan-Africanism of the early sixties has not become a basis for consensus. It is not unlikely, however, that common experiences in the forseeable future will narrow the area of differences in approaches to solutions of national problems. Regional organizations could materialize in various parts of the African continent.

Part of the revolutionist temper of Africa has focused upon the emergence of Africa into the international system in a period of intense East-West conflict. During the heyday of the cold war, the United States and the Soviet Union, both powers, sought to gain the political upper hand in Africa. Rather than succumb to the domination of either great-power, Africa chose to pursue a nonaligned course of action in foreign affairs.

From a position of nonalignment, Africans have attempted to achieve their own domestic goals supported by economic and technical assistances from both great-powers, Communist China, and other states. While African revolutionist states refuse to become firmly entrenched in one camp or the other, in general, Russia, Communist China, and Eastern European states seem to enjoy a greater appeal.

The ideas of nonalignment are linked to that of Pan-Africanism. However, African states pursue nonalignment independently; the idea that a united Africa can pose a threat to the super-powers—to bringing its pressures to bear on key issues in which this support is crucial —has been ambushed by the breakdown of the monolith of communism and the erosion of the tight bipolarization of the early sixties.

The late arrival of independence to Africa, together with the preoccupation with the search for identity, will continue to slow the pace of revolution in the continent for the immediate future. However, during the next five to ten years, the momentum gained by the various African liberation movements may prove to be greater than the burden of these tedious confines. The white regimes of Africa are heading into an impasse because an outmoded colonial tradition and a precarious police state are all that keep them in power.

In the case of the Portuguese territories—Mozambique, Angola, and Guinea—the myth of the policy of *assimilado*, depicting Portugal as a civilizing agent maintaining peace while defending Western Christian culture from communism, is rapidly losing its credibility. In Guinea, the African Party for the Independence of Guinea and the Cape Verde (PAIGC) has frustrated Portuguese efforts to maintain authority. It is only a matter of time before Guinea secures its independence.

In Angola, nationalists have been involved in guerrilla activities since the early sixties. The Revolutionary Government of Angola in Exile (GRAE) received recognition by the Organization of African Unity in the early sixties. The activities of the National Liberation Front of Angola (FLNA), the Union of the People of Angola (UPA), and the Popular Movement for the Liberation of Angola (MPLA), though not well-coordinated, cannot help but effect a reordering of Portuguese-Angolan relationships in the near future.

In Mozambique, as early as 1960, nationalists left to neighboring countries to form political movements. Several political parties were formed: UDENAMO in Rhodesia, UNAMI in Malawi, and MANU in Tanzania and Kenya.

In 1962, these movements gained in the establishment of the Mozambiquan Liberation Front, FRELIMO. The founding leader, Dr. E. Mondlane, drew up a plan of operation encompassing the following principles: consolidation and mobilization, preparation for war, education, and diplomacy. Since then, FRELIMO guerrillas have received Algerian training, weapons from the Soviet Union, Communist China, and East European states and financial assistance from the OAU. It is not unreasonable to assume that FRELIMO activities will continue to spread in Mozambique in the near future.

The present leaders of FRELIMO, Marcelino dos Santos and Samera Machuel, continue to emphasize their independence and their refusal to pattern their movements after the Soviet or Communist Chinese models. FRELIMO ideology seems to resemble the brands of nationalism and socialism that have evolved in the independent African states.

In Rhodesia, the unilateral Declaration of Independence in 1965 stimulated the emergence of guerrilla activities. Since then, Rhodesian nationalists have been crossing the border to neighboring countries for pamphleteering and military training. The neighboring states of Zambia and Tanzania offered sanctuaries for training Rhodesian guerrillas. As in the case of the Portuguese territories, the Rhodesian nationalist groups, the Zimbabwee African Peoples Union (ZAPU), and the Zimbabwee National Union (ZANU) receive training and financial assistance from other African states and communist powers.

In South Africa, the issues of apartheid and Southwest Africa will continue to command attention from revolutionists. As the insensitivities of the South African government persist, Africans—depicted in the African National Congress (ANC)—and the Pan-African Congress (PAC), are coming to feel that all constructive channels for action have been closed, thus leaving only one alternative—violence. It is this feeling of hopelessness and mistrust that characterizes the mood of the African majority in South Africa.

The Odendaal report of 1964, proposing greater administrative ties between South Africa and Southwest Africa, has served to deepen the hostility of Southwest Africans. Although still sporadic, the Southwest African Peoples Organization (SWAPO) and the Southwest African National Union (SWANU) are waging guerrilla activities.

The social and racial inequities existing in the white regimes of Africa summon socialistic ideological solidarity while the conditions of waning authority in the larger setting of African liberation are opening new possibilities for Chinese and Soviet influences. The United States finds itself in a quandry since the nationalists are being radicalized as they come to identify the United States as an ally of European colonialism. Because many of the black African leaders seek assistance from either Peking or Moscow and inspiration from the socialist ideology, the United States finds itself encumbered by certain lingering vestiges of cold war interactions.

American insensitivity toward the plight of black majorities dominated by white minorities has caused many Africans to question even the validity of American liberal pretentions. The Marxian analysis, demonstrating how economic interests undermine diplomatic intentions, is growing in its appeal to black Africans who see economic investment and trade completely neutralizing such Western values as self-determination, majority rule, and political equality.

The U.S. Response to Revolutionism in the Future

For twenty years following World War II, the United States tended to view revolution in two frameworks which were not always conceived as mutually exclusive. There was the nationalist context associated with Algeria and several African and Asian states, and there was the revolution in the operation arena of the cold war such as China, Indochina, and Cuba. The United States perceived revolution to be closely associated with, if not the handmaiden of, communism. Regardless of changed circumstances and perception, the United States tended to be skeptical of revolution to the extent that the U.S. became identified as a conservative state in the eyes of world opinion.

During this period, Americans attempted to project their concept of order on the international system to compensate for their own fear of disorder and insecurity that was being manifested in the United States. As a consequence, stability qua stability became a value for its own sake and a justification for actions. The attitudes fostered by this stance lacked flexibility and did not discern between the various categories of revolution. In a more succinct sense, there was a near-paranoid feeling toward the consequences of revolution.

With the increased commitment in Vietnam, the American perception began to change because revolution, or at least its framework, had started to make its appearance in the U.S. The level of credibility in the system dropped considerably as more citizens lost faith in the myths. Thus, the U.S. experienced some of the manifestations of revolutionism without undergoing revolution.

In addition to perceiving revolution as an outgrowth or by-product of the cold war, the U.S. viewed revolution more as a product of its manifestations than it viewed its manifestations as a product of the revolutionist spirit. This, of course, should be altered. For, above all, revolution is a political and social phenomenon that may take on other trappings. In order to understand the nature of revolution, our vision should not be obscured by its more sensational physical characteristics.

Revolution is neither good nor bad; it is irreversible in certain places at certain times and anticipated by the perception of man's dislocation. It must be recognized that change takes place. Revolutionist change has no fixed value in itself. The U.S. should treat it as neither good nor evil until its direction and values conflict with those of the U.S. In this connection, the values of conserving the status quo should be selective to allow far greater flexibility in policy formulation. More discernment should be exercised with respect to the revolutionist experiences of the future.

This will be difficult for U.S. policy-makers because stability has been built into societal values for so long. Because of domestic unrest, the desire to project this value into the international system could become an irresistible temptation in spite of the fact that these policies were effective in the past.

The primary conditioning element toward revolution will be the domestic rather than international environment. There are three fundamental reasons for this: 1) the United States is in a stage of development substantially different from that of the rest of the world; 2) the problems associated with this stage of development have not been previously experienced in the context of this stage of development; 3) the third reason is an outgrowth of the preceding two and turns on their conditioning the U.S.'s perception of revolution in the international context.

Regardless of what values the U.S. may or may not hold regarding revolution, its ability to influence world revolutionist trends has been and will be limited. There are three major reasons for this. First, American power in international politics has not been particularly relevant or useful in dealing with revolution because it has focused on the manifestations rather than on its nature; secondly, if revolution is to be influenced, a great deal of effort and energy is required which may make the cure unduly prohibitive or even counter-productive; and, thirdly, the domestic sources of support for the U.S. involvement and intervention in revolutionist situations is limited now and will be even more limited in the foreseeable future.

From this analysis, it is in the interest of the United States to adopt a pragmatic posture toward revolution in general. In order to do this, a mental attitude stressing a realistic rather than an ideological approach should be used. The U.S. policy-maker should look at revolution as a socio-political phenomenon over which his influence is limited. From this viewpoint, we are suggesting that change—whether revolutionist or other—be accepted and left alone unless a concrete threat indicates otherwise. For in evaluating the criteria for U.S. support for revolution, we must not invert the ideological zenophobia of the fifties and narrowly embrace the revisionist dogma that has poured from disgruntled academics during the sixties.

Rather than suggesting that we happily commit ourselves to all revolutions—regardless of origin or purpose, and thus act as dogmatically as the proponents of orthodox anticommunism—we must evaluate the role of morality that has heretofore been regarded as a phenomenon that political scientists, certainly since the waning days of the Great Debate, hardly take seriously. As the nineteenth-century expounders of American foreign policy have stated, America is still a moral exemplar to the world. Our actions in the domestic sphere influence the worldwide reception accorded to our foreign policy ventures. The Vietnam war, for instance, encouraged many critics to indict its moral cruelties rather than debate its strategic implications.

The U.S. political response to revolution should be discriminating.

In some cases, short-term instability can lead to long-term stability. At some time in the future, the U.S. may well support preventive revolution in opposition to weak regimes whose repressive measures often cause violent swings of power. This is not to say that the U.S. should seek out alternatives for revolution in these countries, but should always be ready to act in its own interest. Consider, for a moment, the benefits of having had revolutions that supported the aspirations of the people in the hands of other than Castro in Cuba and Mao in China. The regimes that they replaced were no longer relevant, but the U.S. supported them. In future situations, the U.S. may choose to aid no side, but it certainly should not support a faction which cannot gain support from its own population.

But economically we must take more dramatic measures to alter our economic perception of the world in order that we might preempt hostile domestic public opinion to the imminent nationalization of American investments abroad. It will become the duty of the statesman and the policy maker to prepare American public opinion to receive these changes. This can be accomplished with a minimum of McCarthyite hostility if we begin to do so now.

If the United States can remain politically distant from those processes of change over which we have no control, it is relatively inconceivable that American security interests will demand military intervention in Latin America, Africa, Asia, or the Middle East.

However, the prevailing danger, and possibly the most significant threat to American relations with the third world, is that an unprepared public opinion will interpret the seizure of American economic interests in a political context, thus encouraging another series of roguish misadventures. Economic issues will emerge as the most visible U.S. preoccupations in these regions. They must be identified and isolated as such.

A factor that compels another "agonizing reappraisal" in our current foreign policy is the suggestion—distant and penetrating—that our nation might not be able to alter its outlook toward worldwide revolution without a far-reaching alteration of our domestic milieu. The questions that rebound in radical caucuses on American campuses ask whether capitalist, quasi-democratic America can evolve a foreign policy that essentially violates its most revered domestic values. If we accept the dominance of American industry with a shrug that the "business of America is business," then it will certainly be difficult for us to understand, accept, and support the nationalization of industry abroad—or to welcome state-controlled industralization. It is this provincial adolescence that America has experienced which prohibits us from adopting a policy that even begins to approximate the realities of the world condition.

The present and future revolutionary temper turns on the expectations of man. Stability will be difficult to achieve if these expectations are suppressed. When this has occurred in the past, the result has always produced a more undesirable change from the standpoint of the international system. Where there is a desire for change, there are reasons which must be explored. Stability bought at the expense of change results in a greater evil.

We must not forget that every era is an age of transition. Although the specific nature of the historic challenge may vary, the need for adequate response remains constant. Failure to measure up to the challenges of one's age invites tragedy; success contributes to growth.

Although ecologists have abounded in gloomy predictions in recent years, political scientists also must take note of the darkening prospects that confront our nation. We are faced with the dilemma that our expectant subcultures—the poor, the black, the young—might become so articulate that a Constitution designed for an essentially homogeneous society undergirded by an aura of consensus, might become unworkable. Or else, the politics of positive polarization might bear some negative results—and our society could very well become unprecedentedly suppressive—enforcing a homogeneity that has faded with the disruptions of revolutionism. The political scientist, then, must be arduous in his search for new ways to meet the politics of maximum transition. Reliance on political parties, regional and national studies, as exclusive tools for analysis, must not be the sole preoccupation of the seventies. Political scientists, until now, mere theoreticians of a revolutionary world, must now become the vanguard of devising rational alternatives for a world in danger of being overtaken by a polarization of tragic proportions. A great danger that political scientists must find frightening is that protagonists of change have no vision or model for the future. The traditional critiques of the recent past—the American liberal ethos, the Marxist–Leninist–Maoist models—seem unduly influential in contemporary thought and expectation.

When we forget that yesterday's ideas might not conform with today's perceptions, we shall be constantly surprised by historical dislocation tomorrow.

Bibliography

General Works on Revolution

Adams, Brooks. *The Theory of Social Revolutions*. New York: Macmillan Co., 1913.

Ali, Tariq (ed.). *The New Revolutionaries*. New York: William Morrow, 1969.

Andrews, William G., and Uri Ra'anan (eds.). *The Politics of the Coup d'Etat*. New York: Van Nostrand-Reinhold Books, 1959.

Apter, David E. (ed.). *Ideology and Discontent*. New York: Free Press, 1964.

Arendt, Hannah. *On Revolution*. New York: Viking Press, 1963.

———. *On Violence*. New York: Harcourt, Brace & World, 1970.

Barnet, Richard. *Intervention and Revolution: America's Confrontation with Insurgent Movements Around the World*. New York: Meridian Books, World Publishing Co., 1968.

Barnett, H. G. *Innovation: The Basis of Cultural Change*. New York: McGraw-Hill, 1953.

Black, Cyril E., and Thomas P. Thornton (eds.). *Communism and Revolution: The Strategic Uses of Political Violence*. Princeton: Princeton University Press, 1964.

Brinton, Crane. *The Anatomy of Revolution*. New York: Vintage Books, 1957.

———. *The Jacobins: An Essay in the New History*. New York: Macmillan Co., 1930.

Brogan, Dennis W. *The Price of Revolution*. New York: Harper & Row, 1952.

Burns, C. D. *The Principles of Revolution: A Study in Ideals*. London: Allen & Unwin, Ltd., 1920.

Califano, Joseph A. *The Student Revolution: A Global Confrontation*. New York: W. W. Norton & Co., 1970.

Camus, Albert. *The Rebel*. New York: Alfred A. Knopf, Inc., 1954.

Carr, E. H. *Studies in Revolution*. New York: Grosset & Dunlap, Inc., 1964.

Cohn, Norman. *The Pursuit of the Millennium*. Fairlawn, N.J.: Essential Books, Inc., 1957.

Coser, Lewis A. *The Functions of Social Conflict.* New York: Free Press, 1956.

Crozier, Brian. *The Rebels: A Study of Post-War Insurrections.* London: Chatto & Windus, Ltd., 1960.

Dahrendorf, R. *Class and Class Conflict in Industrial Society.* Stanford: Stanford University Press, 1959.

Debray, Regis. *Revolution in the Revolution?* New York: Monthly Review Press, 1967.

Durkheim, Emile. *Suicide.* Translated by John A. Spaulding and George Simpson. Glencoe, Illinois: Free Press, 1951.

Foster, George M. *Traditional Cultures and the Impact of Technological Change.* New York: Harper & Row, 1962.

Guevara, Ernesto Ché. *Guerrilla Warfare.* New York: Monthly Review Press, 1961.

Gurr, Ted Robert. *Why Men Rebel.* Princeton, N.J.: Princeton University Press, 1970.

Haas, Ernest B. *Beyond the Nation-State, Functionalism and International Organization.* Stanford: Stanford University Press, 1964.

Harris, Richard. *Independence and After: Revolution in Underdeveloped Countries.* London: Oxford University Press, 1962.

Hobsbawm, E. J. *The Age of Revolution: 1789–1848.* Cleveland, Ohio: World Publishing Co., 1962.

———. *Primitive Rebels: Studies in Archaic Forms of Social Movement in the 19th and 20th Centuries.* New York: Praeger, 1963.

Hoffer, Eric. *The True Believer: Thoughts on the Nature of Mass Movements.* New York: New American Library, 1958.

———. *The Ordeal of Change.* New York: Harper Colophon Books, 1964.

Janos, Andrew C. *The Seizure of Power: A Study of Force and Popular Consent.* Princeton: Center of International Studies, 1964.

Johnson, Chalmers. *Revolutionary Change.* Boston: Little, Brown & Co., 1966.

Kautsky, John H. (ed.). *Political Change in Underdeveloped Countries: Nationalism and Communism.* New York: John Wiley & Sons, 1962.

Lasswell, Harold D., and Daniel Lerner (eds.). *World Revolutionary Elites: Studies in Coercive Ideological Movements.* Cambridge, Mass.: The M.I.T. Press, 1965.

Mao Tse-tung. *On Guerilla Warfare.* New York: Praeger, 1961.

Marcuse, Herbert. *An Essay on Liberation.* Boston: Beacon Press, 1969.

————. *Eros and Civilization*. Boston: Beacon Press, 1955.

————. *One Dimensional Man*. Boston: Beacon Press, 1964.

Marek, Franz. *Philosophy of World Revolution*. New York: International Publishers, 1969.

Mead, Margaret. *Culture and Commitment*. Garden City, N.Y.: Doubleday and Co., 1970.

Meisel, James H. *Counterrevolution: How Revolutions Die*. New York: Atherton Press, 1966.

Moore, Barrington. *The Social Origins of Dictatorship and Democracy*. Boston: Beacon Press, 1966.

Nomad, Max. *Apostles of Revolution*. Boston: Little, Brown & Co., 1939.

Ortega y Gasset, José. *The Revolt of the Masses*. New York: W. W. Norton & Co., 1932.

Parsons, Talcott, and Edward A. Shils. *Toward a General Theory of Action: Theoretical Foundation for the Social Sciences*. New York: Harper Torch Books, 1962.

Pomeroy, William J. (ed.). *Guerrilla Warfare and Marxism*. New York: International Publishers, 1968.

Schmitt, Karl M., and Carl Leiden (eds.). *The Politics of Violence in the Modern World*. Englewood Cliffs, N.J.: Prentice-Hall, Inc., 1968.

Talmon, J. L. *The Origins of Totalitarian Democracy*. New York: Praeger, 1960.

Weber, Max. *The Theory of Social and Economic Organization*. Translated by A. M. Henderson and Talcott Parsons. New York: Free Press, 1965.

The United States of America

Abrahamsen, David. *Our Violent Society*. New York: Funk & Wagnalls, 1970.

Boorstin, Daniel J. *The Decline of Radicalism: Reflections On America Today*. New York: Random House, 1969.

Broderick, Francis L., and August Meier (eds.). *Negro Protest Thought in the Twentieth Century*. Indianapolis: Bobbs-Merrill, 1965.

Carmichael, Stokely, and Charles V. Hamilton. *Black Power*. New York: Random House, 1967.

Cleaver, Eldridge. *Soul on Ice*. New York: McGraw-Hill, 1968.

Cobbs, Price M., and William H. Grier. *Black Rage*. New York: Basic Books Inc., 1968.

Cohen, Mitchell, and Dennis Hale (eds.). *The New Student Left: An Anthology*. Boston: Beacon Press, 1966.

Draper, Hal. *Berkeley: The New Student Revolt*. New York: Grove Press, Inc., 1965.

Erikson, Erik. *Identity: Youth and Crisis*. New York: W. W. Norton and Company, Inc., 1968.

Feuer, Lewis S. *The Conflict of Generations*. New York: Basic Books Inc., 1969.

Goodman, Paul. *Growing Up Absurd: Problems of Youth in the Organized System*. New York: Random House, Inc., 1960.

Gregory, Dick, *The Shadow That Scares Me*. Garden City, N.Y.: Doubleday and Co., 1968.

Harrington, Michael. *The Other America: Poverty in the United States*. Baltimore: Penguin Books, 1963.

Hook, Sidney. *Academic Freedom and Academic Anarchy*. New York: Cowles Book Company Inc., 1970.

Howe, Irving. *Decline of the New*. New York: Harcourt, Brace & World, 1970.

————, (ed.). *Student Activism*. Indianapolis: Bobbs-Merrill Company, Inc., 1967.

Keniston, Kenneth. *Young Radicals: Notes on Committed Youth*. New York: Harcourt, Brace and World, Inc., 1968.

King, Martin Luther. *Where Do We Go From Here?: Chaos or Community?* Boston: Beacon Press, 1968.

Kunen, James S. *The Strawberry Statement: Notes of a College Revolutionary*. New York: Random House, Inc., 1969.

Lipset, Seymour M. (ed.). *Student Politics*. New York: Basic Books, 1967.

————, and Philip G. Altbach (eds.). *Students in Revolt*. Boston: Houghton Mifflin Co., 1969.

Lomax, Louis E. *The Negro Revolt*. New York: NAL, 1963.

Luce, Philip Abbott. *The New Left*. New York: David McKay Co., Inc., 1966.

Malcolm X. *The Autobiography of Malcolm X*. New York: Grove Press, 1966.

Masotti, Louis H., and Jerome R. Corsi. *Shoot Out in Cleveland: Black Militants and the Police: July 23, 1968*. A report to the National Commission on the Causes and Prevention of Violence. Washington, D.C.: U.S. Government Printing Office, May 1969.

McCabe, John (ed.). *Dialogue on Youth*. Indianapolis: Bobbs-Merrill Company. Inc., 1967.

McKissick, Floyd. *Three-Fifths of a Man*. New York: Macmillan, 1969.

Newfield, Jack. *A Prophetic Minority*. New York: The New American Library, 1966.

Rader, Dotson. *I Ain't Marchin' Anymore!* New York: David McKay Co. Inc., 1969.

Ridgeway, James. *The Closed Corporation: American Universities in Crisis*. New York: Random House, 1968.

Riesman, David, and Christopher Jencks. *The Academic Revolution*. Garden City, N.Y.: Doubleday and Co., Inc., 1968.

Rose, Thomas (ed.). *Violence in America: A Historical and Contemporary Reader*. New York: Random House, 1970.

Rubenstein, Richard E. *Rebels in Eden: Mass Political Violence in the United States*. Boston: Little, Brown & Co., 1970.

Walker, Daniel. *Rights in Conflict*. New York: E. P. Dutton and Co., Inc., 1968.

Wills, Gary. *The Second Civil War: Arming for Armageddon*. New York: Signet Books, 1968.

Wolff, Robert Paul. *The Poverty of Liberalism*. Boston: Beacon Press, 1968.

Young, Alfred F. (ed.). *Dissent: Explorations in the History of American Radicalism*. DeKalb, Ill.: Northern Illinois University Press, 1968.

China and Asia

Bendix, Reinhard. "Reflections on Charismatic Leadership." *Asian Survey* (June, 1967), pp. 341–352.

Chinh, Truong. *The Resistance Will Win*. New York: Praeger, 1963.

————. *Primer for Revolt*. New York: Praeger, 1963.

Cross, James E. *Conflict in the Shadows: The Nature and Politics of Guerilla War*. Garden City, N.Y.: Doubleday and Company, 1963.

Eckstein, Harry (ed.). *Internal War: Problems and Approaches*. New York: Free Press, 1964.

Elliott-Bateman, Michael. *Defeat in the East: The Mark of Mao Tse-tung on War*. London: Oxford University Press, 1967.

Fairbairn, Geoffrey. *Revolutionary Warfare and Communist Strategy: The Threat to South East Asia*. London: Faber, 1968.

Fall, Bernard B. (ed.). *Ho Chi Minh on Revolution*. New York: Praeger, 1967.

Galula, David. *Counterinsurgency Warfare: Theory and Practice.* New York: Praeger, 1964.

Gasster, Michael. *Chinese Intellectuals and the Revolution of 1911.* Seattle: University of Washington Press, 1969.

Giap, Vo Nguyen. *People's War, People's Army.* New York: Praeger, 1962.

Hoang, Van Chi. *From Colonialism to Communism.* New York: Praeger, 1964.

Le Duan. *On the Socialist Revolution in Vietnam.* Hanoi: (Govt. Publication) 1965.

Lifton, Robert J. *Revolutionary Immortality: Mao Tse-tung and the Chinese Cultural Revolution.* New York: Vintage Books, 1968.

Lin Piao. *Long Live the Victory of People's War.* Peking: Foreign Language Press, 1965.

Liu, Shao-ch'i. *How to Be a Good Communist.* Lectures. Boulder, Colorado: Panther Publication, 1967.

Mao Tse-tung. *Selected Works,* 5 Volumes. New York: International Publishers, 1954–62.

McCall, Robert W. "A Political Geography of Revolution: China, Vietnam, and Thailand." *Journal of Conflict Resolution,* 11 (June, 1967), pp. 153–167.

Meisner, Maurice J. *Li Ta-chao and the Origins of Chinese Marxism.* Cambridge: Harvard University Press, 1967.

Methuin, Eugene. "Ideology and Organization in Counterinsurgency," *Orbis,* VIII (Spring, 1964), pp. 106–124.

Oksenberg, Michel, *et al., The Cultural Revolution in Review.* Michigan Papers in Chinese Studies, No. 2. Ann Arbor, Michigan: Center for Chinese Studies, University of Michigan Press, 1968.

Pike, Douglas. *The Viet Cong.* Cambridge: M.I.T. Press, 1966.

———. *War, Peace and the Viet Cong.* Cambridge: M.I.T. Press, 1969.

Purcell, Victor. *The Revolution in Southeast Asia.* London: Thames and Hudson, 1962.

Pustay, John S. *Counterinsurgency Warfare.* New York: The Free Press, 1965.

Rejai, M. (ed.). *Mao Tse-tung on Revolution and War.* Garden City, N.Y.: Doubleday & Co., 1969.

Scalapino, Robert A. (ed.). *The Communist Revolution in Asia.* Englewood Cliffs, N.J.: Prentice-Hall, 1965.

Schram, Stuart R. *Mao Tse-tung*. New York: Simon and Schuster, 1967.

Schwartz, Benjamin. *Chinese Communism and the Rise of Mao Tse-tung*. Cambridge: Harvard University Press, 1951.

Thompson, Sir Robert. *No Exit from Vietnam*. New York: McKay, 1969.

Weatherbee, Donald E. *Ideology in Indonesia: Sukarno's Indonesian Revolution.* New Haven: Yale University Press, 1966.

Latin America

Adams, Richard N. *The Second Sowing: Power and Secondary Development in Latin America*. San Francisco: Chandler Publishing Company, 1967.

————*et al. Social Change in Latin America Today: Its Implications for United States Policy*. New York: Harper and Row, 1960.

Aguilar, Luis E. (ed.). *Marxism in Latin America*. New York: Alfred A. Knopf, 1968.

Alexander, Robert J. *The Bolivian National Revolution*. New Brunswick: Rutgers University Press, 1958.

Anderson, Charles W. *Politics and Economic Change in Latin America*. Princeton: Van Nostrand, 1967.

Blasier, Cole (ed.). *Constructive Change in Latin America*. Pittsburgh: University of Pittsburgh Press, 1968.

Cumberland, Charles C. *Mexico, The Struggle for Modernity*. New York: Oxford University Press, 1968.

Debray, Regis. *Revolution in the Revolution?* New York: Monthly Review Press, 1967.

Draper, Theodore. *Castro's Revolution: Myths and Realities*. New York: Praeger, 1962.

Fagen, Richard A. *The Transformation of Political Culture in Cuba*. Stanford, Calif.: Stanford University Press, 1970.

Guevara, Ernesto Ché. *Guerrilla Warfare*. New York: Monthly Review Press, 1961.

Horowitz, Irving L., Josué de Castro, *et al. Latin American Radicalism*. New York: Vintage Books, 1969.

Jackson, D. Bruce. *Castro, the Kremlin, and Communism in Latin America*. Baltimore: Johns Hopkins Press, 1969.

Johnson, John J. (ed.). *Continuity and Change in Latin America*. Stanford, Calif.: Stanford University Press, 1964.

————. *The Military and Society in Latin America*. Stanford, Calif.: Stanford University Press, 1964.

Lieuwen, Edwin. *Arms and Politics in Latin America* (rev. ed.). New York: Praeger, 1961.

————. *Generals vs. Presidents, Neomilitarism in Latin America*. New York: Praeger, 1964.

Lipset, Seymour, and Aldo Solari (eds.). *Elites in Latin America*. New York: Oxford University Press, 1967.

O'Connor, James. *The Origins of Socialism in Cuba*. Ithaca: Cornell University Press, 1970.

Payne, James L. *Labor and Politics in Peru*. New Haven: Yale University Press, 1965.

Petras, James, and Maurice Zeitlin (eds.). *Latin America: Reform or Revolution?* Greenwich, Conn.: Fawcett, 1968.

Pike, Frederick B. (ed.). *Freedom and Reform in Latin America*. South Bend, Ind.: University of Notre Dame Press, 1959.

————, (ed.). *Latin American History: Select Problems: Identity, Integration, and Nationhood*. New York: Harcourt, Brace and World, 1969.

Powelson, John P. *Latin America: Today's Economic and Social Revolution*. New York: McGraw-Hill, 1964.

Ross, Stanley R. (ed.). *Is the Mexican Revolution Dead?* New York: Alfred A. Knopf, 1966.

Silvert, Kalman H. *Reaction and Revolution in Latin America: The Conflict Society*. New Orleans: Hauser Press, 1961.

Skidmore, Thomas E. *Politics in Brazil, 1930–1964, An Experiment in Democracy*. New York: Oxford University Press, 1967.

Suarez, Andres. *Cuba: Castroism and Communism, 1959–1966*. Cambridge, Mass.: M.I.T. Press, 1967.

Taber, Robert. *The War of the Flea: A Study of Guerrilla Warfare, Theory and Practice*. New York: Lyle Stuart, 1965.

Vega, Luis Mercier. *Roads to Power in Latin America*. New York: Praeger, 1968.

Veliz, Claudio (ed.). *Obstacles to Change in Latin America*. New York: Oxford University Press, 1965.

————, (ed.). *The Politics of Conformity in Latin America*. New York: Oxford University Press, 1967.

The Arab World

Abu-Jaber, Kamel S. *The Arab Ba'th Socialist Party: History, Ideology, and Organization.* Syracuse: Syracuse University Press, 1966.

Antonius, George. *The Arab Awakening.* New York: Capricorn Books, 1965.

Berger, Morroe. *The Arab World Today.* Garden City, N.Y.: Doubleday & Co., 1962.

Binder, Leonard. *The Ideological Revolution in the Middle East.* New York: J. Wiley & Sons, 1964.

Brown, Leon C. (ed.). *State and Society in Independent North Africa.* Washington, D.C.: Middle East Institute, 1966.

Cooley, John K. *Baal, Christ and Mohammed: Religion and Revolution in North Africa.* New York: Holt, Rinehart & Winston, 1965.

Fanon, Frantz. *A Dying Colonialism.* New York: Grove Press, 1967.

Haim, Sylvia G. (ed.). *Arab Nationalism: An Anthology.* Berkeley and Los Angeles: University of California Press, 1962.

Halpern, Manfred. *The Politics of Social Change in the Middle East and North Africa.* Princeton: Princeton University Press, 1963.

Hourani, Albert. *Arabic Thought in the Liberal Age 1798–1939.* London: Oxford University Press, 1962.

Humbaraci, Arslan. *Algeria: A Revolution that Failed.* New York: Praeger, 1966.

Hurewitz, J. C. *Middle East Politics: The Military Dimension.* New York: Praeger, 1969.

al-Husri, Khaldun S. *Three Reformers: A Study in Modern Arab Political Thought.* Beirut: Khayats, 1966.

Karpat, Kemal H. (ed.). *Political and Social Thought in the Contemporary Middle East.* New York: Praeger, 1968.

Keddie, Nikki R. *An Islamic Response to Imperialism.* Berkeley and Los Angeles: University of California Press, 1968.

Kedourie, Elie. *Afghani and Abduh: Essay on Religious Unbelief and Political Activism in Modern Islam.* London: Frank Cass and Co., 1966.

Kerr, Malcolm. *The Arab Cold War: 1958–1967: A Study of Ideology in Politics,* second edition. London: Oxford University Press, 1967.

————. *Islamic Reform: The Political and Legal Theories of Muhammad 'Abduh and Rashid Rida.* Berkeley and Los Angeles: University of California Press, 1966.

Laqueur, Walter Z. *Communism and Nationalism in the Middle East.* London: Rutledge and Kegan Paul, 1956.

Lerner, Daniel. *The Passing of Traditional Society: Modernizing the Middle East*. Glencoe, Illinois: Free Press, 1958.

Moore, C. H. *Tunisia since Independence: The Dynamics of One-Party Government*. Berkeley: University of California Press, 1965.

Nasser, Gamal Abdel. *Egypt's Liberation: The Philosophy of the Revolution*. Washington, D.C.: Public Affairs Press, 1955.

Nuseibeh, Hazem Zaki. *The Ideas of Arab Nationalism*. Ithaca: Cornell University Press, 1956.

Quandt, William B. *Revolution and Political Leadership: Algeria 1954-1968*. Cambridge, M.I.T. Press, 1969.

Rivlin, Benjamin, and Joseph S. Szyliowicz (eds.). *The Contemporary Middle East: Tradition and Innovation*. New York: Random House, 1965.

Rosenthal, E. I. J. *Islam in the Modern National State*. Cambridge, England: Cambridge University Press, 1965.

Sharabi, Hisham B. *Nationalism and Revolution in the Arab World*. Princeton: Van Nostrand, 1966.

Zeine, Zeine N. *The Emergence of Arab Nationalism*. Beirut: Khayats, 1966.

Zurayk, Constantine K. *The Meaning of the Disaster*. (Translated from the Arabic by Bayly Winder.) Beirut: Khayats, 1956.

Africa

Abraham, Willie E. *The Mind of Africa*. Chicago: University of Chicago Press, 1962.

Bretton, Henry L. *The Rise and Fall of Kwame Nkrumah*. New York: Praeger, 1966.

Brockway, Fenner. *African Socialism*. London: Bodley Head, Ltd., 1963.

Cameron, James. *The African Revolution*. New York: Random House, 1961.

Emerson, Rupert, and Martin Kilson (eds.). *The Political Awakening of Africa*. Englewood Cliffs, N.J.: Prentice-Hall, Inc., 1965.

Fanon, Frantz. *Black Skin, White Masks*. New York: Grove Press, 1967.

———. *Pour la Révolution Africaine*. Paris: Francois Maspero, 1964.

———. *The Wretched of the Earth*. New York: Grove Press, 1963.

Ferkiss, Victor. *Africa's Search for Identity*. New York: George Braziller, 1966.

Fortes, M., and E. E. Evans-Pritchard (eds.). *African Political Systems*. London: Oxford University Press, 1940.

Friedland, William H., and Carl J. Rosberg, Jr. *African Socialism*. Stanford, Calif.: Stanford University Press, 1964.

Green, Reginald H., and Ann Seidman. *Unity or Poverty? The Economics of Pan-Africanism.* Baltimore: Penguin Books, 1968.

Hooker, James R. *Black Revolutionary: George Padmore's Path from Communism to Pan Africanism.* New York: Praeger, 1967.

Kenyatta, Jomo. *Facing Mount Kenya.* London: Secker and Warburg, 1938.

Lloyd, P. C. *Africa in Social Change: Changing Traditional Societies in the Modern World.* Baltimore: Penguin Books, 1967.

Lystad, Robert A. (ed.). *The African World: A Survey of Social Research.* New York: Praeger, 1965.

Mazrui, Ali A. *Towards a Pax Africana: A Study of Ideology and Ambition.* Chicago: University of Chicago Press, 1967.

Mboya, Tom. *Freedom and After.* Boston: Little, Brown and Co., 1963.

Mezu, S. O. (ed.). *The Philosophy of Pan-Africanism.* Washington, D.C.: Georgetown University Press, 1965.

Nkrumah, Kwame. *Africa Must Unite.* New York: Praeger, 1963.

————. *Consciencism.* New York: Monthly Review Press, 1965.

————. *Handbook of Revolutionary Warfare.* New York: International Publishers, 1969.

————. *I Speak of Freedom.* New York: Praeger, 1961.

————. *Neo-Colonialism: The Last Stage of Imperialism.* New York: International Publishers, 1965.

Odinga, Oginga. *Not Yet Uhuru.* New York: Hill and Wang, 1967.

Onuoha, B. *The Elements of African Socialism.* London: Deutsch, 1965.

Quaison-Sackey, Alex. *Africa Unbound.* New York: Praeger, 1963.

Robson, Peter. *Economic Integration In Africa.* London: Allen & Unwin Publishers, 1968.

Rosberg, Carl G., and John Nottingham. *The Myth of Mau Mau: Nationalism in Kenya.* New York: Praeger, 1966.

Senghor, Leopold. *African Socialism.* New York: American Society of African Culture, 1959.

————. *On African Socialism.* New York: Praeger, 1964.

Sheppard, George W. *The Politics of African Nationalism.* New York: Praeger, 1962.

Segal, Ronald. *African Profiles,* Baltimore: Penguin Books, 1963.

Thiam, Doudou. *The Foreign Policy of African States; Ideological Bases, Present Realities, Future Prospects.* New York: Praeger, 1965.

Touré, Ahmed Sékou. *L'Afrique et le Révolution.* Paris: Présence Africaine, 1967.

Index